BLESSINGS OF FREEDOM: CHAPTERS IN AMERICAN JEWISH HISTORY

Edited by
Michael Feldberg

KTAV Publishing House, Inc.
in association with
The American Jewish Historical Society

The American Jewish Historical Society thanks Lief D. Rosenblatt for making possible the publication of this collection of essays in loving memory of

Franklin D. Rosenblatt

A man proud of the enormous contributions made by Jewish Americans to the advancement of our great nation

Library of Congress Cataloging-in-Publication Data

Feldberg, Michael.
    Blessings of Freedom: chapters in American Jewish history / Michael Feldberg.
        p. cm.
    Includes bibliographical references (p.)
    ISBN 0-88125-755-9 - ISBN 0-88125-756-7 (pbk.)
    1 Jews--United States--Biography. 2. Jews--United States--History. 3. Jewish
soldiers--United States-Biography. 4. Jewish women--United States-Biography. 5.
Jewish athletes--United States--Biography 6. Jewish business people--United
States-Biography. 7. Jews in public life-United States--Biography. 8. Zionists--United
States-Biography. 9. United States--Biography. I. Title.

El 84.37 .F47 2001
973'.04924--dc21

                                                            2001029986

Distributed by
Ktav Publishing House, Inc.
900 Jefferson Street
Hoboken, NJ 07030
201-963-9524 FAX 201-963-0102
Website: www.ktav.com
Email: orders@ktav.com

Contents

Introduction

Since January 1997, the American Jewish Historical Society has published a weekly column entitled "Chapters in American Jewish History" in the English-language edition of the *Forward* and, subsequently, in other American Jewish newspapers. Over the years, the column has appeared in Hebrew, Russian, and Yiddish as well as English. There have been more than 170 installments. *Blessings of Freedom: Chapters in American Jewish History*, contains 120 of the best.

This book is not a complete history of American Jewry but a collection of vignettes and episodes that, taken together, limn the overriding directions and tendencies of the much larger tapestry that comprises the American Jewish experience. The weekly "chapters" are nontechnical 800-word windows through which the reader is given an interesting and illuminating glimpse at important and often colorful aspects of the American Jewish story. In the bibliography at the back of the book are references to more complete treatments of the field.

Rather than reprint the 120 chapters in their original order, we have chosen to group them by subject or time period. The first three parts of the book, with the exception of one chapter, focus on the era before the Civil War, when American Jewry was demanding and obtaining its political, religious and civil rights, demonstrating its patriotism and its willingness to sacrifice on behalf of the nation, and just beginning the struggle—one that continues virtually unchanged—to balance the desire to maintain a unique Jewish identity with participation as a full partner in the blessings and freedom, the promise of American life.

Part IV focuses more tightly on Jews in politics and on the impact of non-Jewish political leaders on the Jewish community. Part V deals with the varieties of American Judaism, the rise of Reform and the responses of Modern Orthodoxy, and the evolution of Jewish observance in the context of American religious values. Part VI traces the varieties of anti-Semitism in the United States and the efforts of American Jewry to fight this scourge at home and abroad.

Parts VII through IX comprise the "American Jewish Pride" section of the book. Unlike the chapters on anti-Semitism, they recount tales of accomplishment and triumph in sports, in the war against disease, in building industries and labor unions, and in helping to create a new nation in the State of Israel.

Blessings of Freedom: Chapters in American Jewish History exists because Justin L. Wyner, former president of the American Jewish Historical Society, persisted in getting me to write the individual "Chapters in American Jewish History" that appeared in the *Forward*, America's most influential national Jewish newspaper. Justin's model was the Mobil Corporation ads on the op-ed page of the *New York Times;* he insisted that we get the same position on the *Forward*'s op-ed page. His personal experience as a high school student had convinced Justin that a solid grounding in the long, distinguished history of the American Jewish people could be a source of pride and affiliation for American Jews of all ages, and that the Society was the right organization to provide this grounding.

For almost two years, Justin urged me to write such a weekly column, but I demurred, claiming I was too busy with my administrative duties at the Society. As Justin was the Society's president, I eventually relented. I drafted a test column (which appears here as "Beyond Seltzer: Rabbi Geffen and the Kashering of Coca-Cola") and sent it off to Seth Lipsky, then editor of the English-language *Forward.* During a visit to New York for Thanksgiving 1996, I met with Lipsky to see what he thought of the idea. He told me that the *Forward* was willing to run the feature on the op-ed page. Still reluctant to commit to a weekly column, I told him we would begin "sometime after the first of the year." Lipsky replied, "Let's start next week!" Lipsky volunteered the *Forward*'s talented Adam Brodsky to copyedit the columns, and we experimented with the format for a couple of weeks until we got it right. The first installment of "Chapters in American Jewish History" appeared on January 10, 1997, and the columns have continued every week since then.

The responsibility has kept me scrambling. My background does not include formal training or research in American Jewish history. Each week, I have had to read (quickly and intensively) articles and books by specialists in the field, searching for an appropriate anecdote, a biography, an incident, or a moment in American Jewish history that I could translate into the form we had adopted.

It is said that scholarship stands on the shoulders of those who came before. In no case is this truer than for this book. To produce a chapter every week, a writer needs two things: good source material and generous friends and colleagues willing to edit, correct and improve what he writes. The most frequently used source for these chapters has been the American Jewish Historical Society's own scholarly journal. For 108 years, the Society has published *American Jewish History.* I am grateful to the many authors whose articles have appeared in its pages and to its distinguished editors over more than a century for keeping the enterprise alive.

Literally dozens of editors, critics, friends, family members, and colleagues—not to mention careful readers of the *Forward* and other newspapers and magazines—contributed to improving "Chapters" and saving me from error and infelicity. It would be impossible to name them all. Among those to whom I owe the greatest thanks are Rachel Chodorov, Gabriel Feldberg, Libby Finkelstein, Elaine Greenfield, Kathryn Allamong Jacobs, Andrea Karlan, Blair Kramer, Kenneth Libo, Charles Liebling, Rafael Medoff, Laura Peimer, Stanley Remsberg, Michelle Sampson, Abigail Schoolman, Lyn Slome, Ellen Smith, Bette Rothe Young and Sheldon Mike Young. The late Edward Schilder provided enthusiastic assistance and research support. Despite their best efforts to prevent mistakes, every error of fact or interpretation found in these pages is mine and mine alone.

Several individuals and families provided financial support for the series when it first appeared in the *Forward*: Bruce and

Francesca Slovin, Norman and Gerry Sue Arnold, Frenkel and Company, Harold and Frances Rosenbluth, Sherman and Jill Starr, Efrem and Kelly Weinreb, Justin and Genevieve Wyner, and Kenneth J. and Ann Bialkin. Ricky Greenfield, publisher of the *Connecticut Jewish Ledger*, has regularly published "Chapters" in that paper as a service to his readers.

After all the thanks are given, the important credit for this work goes to Genevieve Wyner, who read and improved many of the columns in draft; Justin L. Wyner, to whom I owe more than I can ever express and to whom this book is dedicated; and my wife, Ruth Feldberg, who has sustained me through the rigors of producing a column a week and, as steadfast as her biblical namesake, has stood by me through the past twenty-four years.

Part I

JEWISH RIGHTS IN EARLY AMERICA

1

Joachim Gaunse:
The Jew with Sir Walter Raleigh

In 1584, Sir Walter Raleigh, a favorite of Queen Elizabeth I, received a royal patent to explore the Virginia territory and found a permanent settlement. The queen hoped that the colonists would discover copper, silver, and gold, or at least find a passage to the Orient. Sir Walter recruited Joachim Gaunse, a Bohemian (Czech) Jewish metallurgist and mining engineer, to join the Virginia expedition. Gaunse thus became the first recorded Jew to set foot on English soil in North America.

Invited to England by the Royal Mining Company in 1581, Gaunse had completely revamped English methods for smelting copper. In 1584, England was preparing for war with Spain and desperately needed copper, a critical element in the production of bronze, from which the English manufactured the accurate cannons that gave their warships an advantage over the Spaniards' inferior cast-iron cannons. The superior firepower provided by bronze cannonry proved crucial in the English navy's victory in 1588 over the much larger Spanish Armada.

Gaunse's contributions to English bronze manufacturing were monumental. Before his innovations, English smelters required a minimum of sixteen weeks to purify a batch of copper ore. Gaunse's

process reduced the time to just four days. As an added bonus, he found a way to use the impurities removed from the ore to dye textiles. In an age when many still believed in alchemy (the "science" of turning base metals into gold), Gaunse pioneered modern scientific methods. Francis Bacon, lord chancellor of England and advocate of scientific research to advance English supremacy, probably used Gaunse as the model for the heroic Jewish scientist Joabim, a character in his utopian novel *The New Atlantis* (published in 1627).

Because of his renown, Sir Walter Raleigh asked Gaunse to serve as metallurgist and mining supervisor to the Roanoke expedition. Lumps of smelted copper and a goldsmith's crucible discovered by archaeologists in the ruins of the Roanoke site are thought to have been Gaunse's.

Despite the discovery of copper, the Roanoke colony did not endure. Worn out, ill, homesick, fearful of conflicts with the Indians and discouraged by the failure of the Royal Mining Company to send additional supplies, the Roanoke colonists accepted an offer from Sir Francis Drake, whose fleet was passing nearby, to carry them back to England. Joachim Gaunse and his comrades left the New World.

Soon after, Sir Walter Raleigh fell

into Elizabeth's disfavor, in part at least because many believed that he did not accept the divinity of Jesus. As a member of Raleigh's circle, Gaunse attracted unfavorable attention. Having moved to the town of Bristol, Gaunse gave Hebrew lessons to English gentlemen who wanted to read the Bible in its original language. In 1589, Reverend Richard Curteys visited Gaunse and, learning that he was a Jew, asked him, "Do you deny Jesus Christ to be the Son of God?" Gaunse replied, "What needeth the almighty God to have a son, is he not almighty?"

Having spoken "blasphemy," Gaunse was brought before the mayor and aldermen of Bristol. Had he been a Christian, he might have been burned as a heretic. As the archival record indicates, however, Gaunse "affirmeth and sayeth that he was circumcised and hath been always instructed and brought up in the Talmud of the Jews and was never baptised." Thus, he could not be a heretic, but simply an infidel, a nonbeliever, much like a Muslim or a Confucian. Edward I in 1290 had expelled the Jewish population of England, but by the time of Elizabeth's reign, enforcement of the expulsion decree was greatly relaxed. Rather than deal with this Jew who was connected to the Royal Mining Company, Bristol's town fathers referred his case to the queen's Privy Council, which included some of the mining company's major investors. Gaunse was transported to London for judgment.

Frustratingly, at this point the historical record simply ends. Historians speculate that Gaunse was protected by his friends on the Privy Council, for whom his metallurgical innovations had reaped rewards. He may have remained quietly in England, or perhaps he returned to Bohemia. In any case, there is no record that Gaunse was punished further, and his name drops from the public record.

Joachim Gaunse's experience foreshadowed that of many American colonial Jews: he was simultaneously an insider and an outsider, useful as a scientist but denied full rights in a Christian society. Recruited to America by Raleigh for his expertise, protected by the Privy Council for the money he earned its members, Gaunse was apparently accepted by the settlers of Roanoke but not by establishment Christians. Gaunse revolutionized English metallurgy and helped England defeat the Spanish Armada, but a year later he was charged with blasphemy and disappeared from both public view and the historical record. Despite his contributions to English and American history, as a Jew Gaunse remained on the margins of society.

Sponsored by Drs. Judith and Arthur Obermayer

2

Isaac de Castro:
A Martyr to His Faith

Born in 1625 in Amsterdam, Isaac de Castro was a *converso*, a Jew of Portuguese descent whose family, in 1498, had converted to Catholicism to avoid expulsion. Like many *conversos*, however, the family continued secretly to practice Judaism. In 1647, the Inquisition in Brazil compelled de Castro to choose between his faith in Judaism and being burned alive. He chose Judaism and martyrdom.

The tale of Isaac de Castro's martyrdom begins in northeastern Brazil, conquered by the Dutch from Portugal in 1630. From then until the Portuguese reconquered the area in 1654, several hundred European Jewish families settled there, founding a vibrant community centered in the town of Recife. The Dutch were tolerant of Judaism, and Recife attracted both Jews who had been living freely in Amsterdam and Jews from elsewhere who had been forced to practice their religion in secret while pretending to live as Catholics. The community they built was the first significant Jewish settlement in the Americas.

In 1641, at age sixteen, Isaac de Castro migrated from Amsterdam to Recife. Three years later, for unknown reasons, he left the relative safety of Recife and went to Bahia, the capital of Portuguese Brazil, where he came under the scrutiny of the Inquisition. Historian Arnold Wiznitzer

speculates that the Amsterdam Jewish community sent de Castro to Bahia as an emissary to encourage *converso* families living there as Catholics to continue observing Jewish rituals. If Wiznitzer is right, de Castro's mission to these secret Jews cost him his life.

Soon after his arrival, someone denounced Isaac de Castro to Dom Pedro da Silva, the bishop of Bahia and head of the Inquisition in Brazil. The bishop's informant said that while in Recife he had seen de Castro visiting the synagogue. Contrary to popular belief, the Inquisition did not execute professing Jews who refused to convert. It only had jurisdiction over Catholics, and its targets were Jews who were officially Catholic, having accepted baptism, but continued to maintain or promote Jewish practices. For this reason, de Castro did not deny the charge when brought before the bishop in December 1644, but instead claimed that he was a Jew, not a Catholic. He swore that he was really José de Liz, a circumcised Jew born in France, and not Isaac de Castro, whose family had converted to Catholicism. He testified that he had developed doubts about Judaism while studying at a French university and had come to Bahia to learn more about Catholicism.

The bishop did not believe his story, especially when de Castro's Catholic Bible and tefillin were introduced as evidence that he had been leading a double life. He sent de Castro to Portugal for formal adjudication. At his ecclesiastical trial in Lisbon in June 1645, de Castro finally admitted his identity. He was indeed the son of Portuguese *conversos* and had lived outwardly as a Catholic when the family moved to France, but he claimed that his mother had substituted another baby at his baptism and thus he was free to practice Judaism without running afoul of the Inquisition. When the de Castro family moved to Amsterdam, Isaac, his brothers and his father had undergone circumcision and openly reclaimed their Jewish identity. De Castro said that he had migrated to Recife and then Bahia to avoid a murder charge pending in Amsterdam. Witnesses testified, to the contrary, that he had been sent to Bahia by the Jewish community to teach Judaism to the province's secret Jews.

The tribunal believed the witnesses and found Isaac de Castro, who in their judgment had been properly baptized a Catholic, guilty of secretly practicing and proselytizing for Judaism. He was offered two choices: continue to deny Catholicism and be burned at the stake, or confess his errors, return to the church, and serve a prison term not likely to exceed five years. According to Wiznitzer, de Castro understood that "he was expected to abjure Judaism and profess Catholicism as the vast majority of imprisoned apostates had done under similar circumstances." To his credit, de Castro "decided that such a price for saving his life was too high and preferred to perish . . . for the sanctification of God's name."

The trial transcript records that upon hearing his sentence, de Castro confessed that he prayed to God seven times each day, observed the Jewish holidays and fast days, observed the laws of kashrut, and complied as best he could with the 613 mitzvot prescribed by the sages—all this while presenting the outward appearance of a Christian. For two years, priests attempted to persuade de Castro that Christ was the Messiah and that he should accept him as his savior. Frustrated by de Castro's steadfast refusal, they finally informed the court that he was incorrigible.

On December 15, 1647, de Castro was retried in criminal court and sentenced to death. Offered another chance to convert, he refused. Taken to the square of the Royal Palace for public execution, de Castro was offered a final chance to embrace Catholicism so that he could be "mercifully" strangled before being burned. He refused once again. Eyewitness accounts indicate that as the flames rose, de Castro intoned the Shema and then called out his final words, *Ely, Adonai, Sabahot,* My God Lord of Hosts.

Sponsored by The Kislak Family Fund in honor of David R. Pokross

3

Asser Levy:
America's First Crusader for Jewish Rights

Religious freedom was not always a feature of early colonial life. The Puritan colonies in New England vigorously expelled Quakers, Lutherans, Catholics and Jews. Until 1759, Jews and Protestants were barred from New France. Throughout New Spain, the Inquisition actively persecuted (and even executed) *conversos,* Jews who professed Catholicism but were suspected of secretly continuing to practice Judaism and influencing others to convert.

Initially, even the generally tolerant Dutch tried to exclude all but members of the Dutch Reformed Church from their colony, New Netherlands. The first Jews who settled in the capital, New Amsterdam, had much to do with changing this intolerant policy. Asser Levy led the assault on anti-Semitic discrimination.

Asser Levy was one of a group of twenty-three men, women, and children who fled from the former Dutch colony of Recife, Brazil, in 1654. The Dutch had captured Brazil from the Portuguese in 1630, and Jews from Amsterdam had settled in the new colony, where they openly practiced their religion. When Portugal recaptured Brazil in 1654, it expelled the Jews. The twenty-three who landed in New Amsterdam had set out for Amsterdam on a vessel called the *Ste. Catherine.* En route, after stops in Jamaica and Cuba, the *Ste.*

Catherine was captured by a Spanish privateer and the passengers were stripped of their valuables.

A return to Europe was now out of the question. The refugees struck a deal with the ship's captain, Jacques de la Mothe, to take them to New Amsterdam, which they thought would be a hospitable destination. De la Mothe agreed to divert his ship for a fee of 2,500 guilders.

This was a one-sided bargain, struck in distress. When the *Ste. Catherine* landed in New Amsterdam, Captain de la Mothe sued his propertyless passengers for failure to pay the balance of their passage. Peter Stuyvesant (1592–1672), the Dutch colonial governor, seized the Jews' meager remaining possessions and ordered them sold at auction to meet their debts. When the auction failed to raise sufficient funds to pay Captain de la Mothe, Stuyvesant jailed two of the refugees and wrote to the Dutch West India Company in Amsterdam asking permission to expel the entire group. Noting that the Jews' indigence might make them a burden to the community, Stuyvesant "deemed it useful to require them in a friendly way to depart."

The Jewish community in Amsterdam petitioned the company on behalf of their fellow Jews in New Amsterdam, noting that Jews were allowed to reside in Holland, even to invest in the company, and thus should be allowed to reside in New Amsterdam. In April 1665, the company granted Jews permission to live in New Amsterdam "so long as they do not become a burden to the Company or the community."

Stuyvesant now tried another tack. He persuaded the colonial council to bar Jews from serving in the volunteer home guard and impose a special tax on them to pay others to serve in their place. On November 5, 1655, Asser Levy and Joseph Barsimson filed a petition with the colonial court asking that they either be allowed to stand watch on the same terms as other citizens or be relieved of the tax. After an initial rejection and a two-year legal battle, Levy won the right to stand watch.

In December 1655, Stuyvesant's troops captured the Swedish territory along the Delaware River, adding it to the Dutch possessions in New Netherlands. Stuyvesant refused to issue trade permits to Jewish settlers in the new territory. Levy and others wrote to their associates in Holland protesting this discrimination and the company again disciplined Stuyvesant for his anti-Jewish actions. The company specified that from then on, Jews in the colony were allowed to trade and own real estate but not to hold public office, open a retail shop, or establish a synagogue.

In 1656, Levy received one of the first trading permits granted to a Jew. However, he chose to fight the ban on Jewish participation in retailing. In 1657, he was denied the right to open a butcher shop, but petitioned this injustice and won. When he received his butcher's license in 1661, it explicitly exempted him from having to slaughter pigs.

When the English captured New Amsterdam in 1664 and renamed it New York, Levy swore an oath to support the British crown, doubtlessly feeling, after his ill treatment, that he owed no allegiance to the Dutch. All the rights he had fought for and won despite Stuyvesant's hostility were confirmed by the English. In 1671, Levy became the first Jew to serve on an English jury in North America. Ironically, one of the defendants tried before him was Peter Stuyvesant, who stood accused of misuse of office.

Asser Levy lies buried in an unknown grave somewhere in lower Manhattan. In tribute, a public school and park in Brooklyn and a street in lower Manhattan bear his name. From his humble beginnings as a penniless refugee from Recife who was almost expelled from America, Asser Levy became a successful businessman, crusader for religious equality and defender of Jewish rights.

Sponsored by Betsy and Donald Landis in honor of Edgar J. Nathan III

4

Jacob Lumbrozo's Blasphemy

In the textbook version of history, we are told that the first English settlers—the Puritans of Massachusetts Bay Colony, the followers of Anne Hutchinson in Connecticut—came to America in search of religious freedom. The full story is more complex. While the colonists who settled in the New World were indeed seeking religious freedom, it was only their own freedom that concerned them. What the textbooks usually omit was that equal freedom was often denied to others, particularly Catholics and Jews. One of the first persons charged with blasphemy (anti-Christian speech) in the English colonies was a Jew: Jacob Lumbrozo of Maryland.

Established in 1634 by Cecilius Calvert, Lord Baltimore, under a grant from King Charles I of England, Maryland was intended as a refuge for Calvert's Catholic co-religionists. At this time, Catholics were more persecuted in England than atheists, Muslims or Jews. Appreciative of being allowed to create a Catholic haven in the colonies, Calvert gave his appointed governor in Maryland careful instructions not to offend the surrounding Protestant majority. Catholic mass was to be held in private. Further, the governor was to "treat the Protestants with as much mildness and favor as Justice will permit." Calvert was silent on the question of Jews.

Calvert encouraged Puritans from neighboring Virginia, themselves an unpopular minority, to settle in Maryland, which they did in unexpected numbers, soon becoming the majority. In 1649, to keep the Puritans from persecuting Catholics, the Maryland General Assembly adopted an "Act Concerning Religion," the primary provision of which required toleration of all believers in Jesus Christ, regardless of which church they attended. No form of Christianity was to be exalted over any other.

While placing Catholics on an equal footing with Protestants, the act also took aim at all, including Jews, who denied the divinity of Christ. The act provided that those who "blaspheme God . . . or deny our Saviour Jesus Christ to be the sonne of God, or shall deny the Holy Trinity . . . shall be punished with death and confiscation or forfeiture of all his or her lands and goods to the Lord Proprietary and his heires."

Maryland's Puritans resented the act because it forced them to tolerate Catholics. In an armed uprising in 1654, they removed Calvert's governor after the so-called Battle of the Severn, renounced Calvert's rule and expelled all Catholics from the General Assembly. For two years, Catholics could not worship in Maryland and members of the Jesuit order were expelled. Curiously, the punishment for blasphemy was reduced from death to mere admonishment.

In 1656, Calvert persuaded Oliver Cromwell, ruler of England, to restore his title. Upon resuming control, Calvert ordered the 1649 act reinstated, including its provision that blasphemy be punished by death.

Ironically, one of the first persons tried under the blasphemy provision was a Jewish physician, Jacob Lumbrozo, whom historian Abram V. Goodman describes as a 1656 immigrant to Maryland from Lisbon, Portugal. In Europe, Lumbrozo had lived as a Christian, but in the New World he had reverted to Judaism. While Maryland's Puritans and Catholics fought each other, they mostly ignored the few Jews who lived there. Jews could not vote or hold public office, but they were treated more as a curiosity than a threat. In this atmosphere of indifference, Lumbrozo miscalculated how openly he could proclaim his beliefs.

In 1658, Lumbrozo met a proselytizing Quaker named Josiah Coale. In the hearing of witnesses, Coale asked Lumbrozo a number of theological questions. Lumbrozo answered honestly, according to his faith. A short time later, he was accused of blasphemy and called to a hearing. Witnesses testified that to Coale's question, "Did the Jews believe in a messiah?" Lumbrozo answered in the affirmative. Coale asked who had been crucified at Jerusalem. Lumbrozo answered, "A man." And how did he perform his miracles? "By the art of magic." And the resurrection? Lumbrozo speculated that disciples had probably stolen the corpse. Another witness present accused Lumbrozo of calling Jesus a necromancer. The court transcript notes, "To which said Lumbrozo answered nothing but laughed."

Having sufficient probable cause, the court required that Lumbrozo post bail. Before the trial could resume, however, the governor of Maryland, celebrating the accession of Richard Cromwell, Oliver Cromwell's son, as lord protector of England, issued a pardon to all who "stood indicted, convicted or Condemned to dye." Lumbrozo's case was dropped.

Five years later, in 1663, Lumbrozo again appears on the historical record. He served on a jury and obtained denization papers, which granted him all the rights of an English citizen. Soon after, he was allowed to represent his two indentured servants in a court case. One can conclude from these facts that Lumbrozo's principles did not cause him ongoing trouble with the law. Fortunately, no other Jews were charged with blasphemy after Lumbrozo and no Marylander of any religion was ever put to death for the crime. However, it took another 160 years for Maryland's Jews to gain full relief from the discriminatory aspects of the state's laws (see page 110).

Sponsored by Anne and Milton C. Borenstein

5

Jewish Rights in Early Connecticut

The Pilgrims who landed at Plymouth Rock in 1620 and the Puritans who founded Boston in 1630 saw themselves as authentic successors to the ancient Hebrews. New England was to be their New Jerusalem, a society based on the covenant between God and Abraham. Just as Moses had led the Jews out of Egypt, through the wilderness and into the promised land of Canaan, John Winthrop had led the Puritans out of a corrupt church in England to the wilderness of New England, where a pure church and polity could be established. By the Puritans' own account, the Jews of the Bible were the inspiration for their vision and aspirations.

Yet New England's Puritans were less than hospitable to the Jews they actually found among them. The Connecticut colony offers a clear example of the contradiction between their high regard for biblical Jews and their reluctance to have real-life Jews as neighbors.

According to historians David Dalin and Jonathan Rosenbaum, the Puritans' goal in colonizing Connecticut was largely spiritual: "The opportunity to establish a 'city on a hill' in which the values of the Puritan community would remain forever enshrined provided the central appeal [to build new towns] for all the heirs of the *Mayflower*." The Connecticut colony's 1662 royal charter declared that "the Christian faith is the only and principal end of this plantation." The Puritan or Congregational Church became the official, or "established," form of worship. In 1708, the Puritan-dominated legislature granted limited toleration to Anglicans, Quakers, and Baptists and, in 1727, as a concession to the English crown, Anglicans were permitted to build their own churches and hold services openly.

As Dalin and Rosenbaum note, however, Jews were lumped "with heretics, Catholics [and others] to whom it was illegal to give food or lodging under the early legal codes of Hartford and New Haven." The royal charter explicitly denied Jews the right to build synagogues, worship as an assembled group, purchase land for a cemetery and vote or hold public office. It is no surprise, then, that only a handful of Jews resided in Connecticut during the years of Puritan domination. The first reference to a Jew in Connecticut is to one "David the Jew," who was arrested and fined by a Hartford court in 1659 for illegal peddling. A more telling case is that of Jacob Lucena, identified as "Jacob the Jew" in court records, who in 1670 was charged, in a manner reminiscent of twentieth-century Southern lynch mobs, with the crime of being "notorious in his lascivious dalliance and wanton carriage and proffers to several women."

Lucena was found guilty of the charge and fined 20 pounds sterling, an astounding sum for those times. Two days later, the court reconsidered and, in its mercy, reduced the sum to 10 pounds. Still unable to pay, Lucena asked Asser Levy of New Amsterdam, one of the original twenty-three Jews who had landed there in 1654, to come to Connecticut to plead his case. "As a token of respect for sayd Asser Levy," the court once again halved the fine. Lucena paid it and quickly fled Connecticut.

Despite the ban on an organized Jewish community, a handful of Jews continued to migrate to Connecticut. By the time of the American Revolution, the east end of Hartford's State Street was referred to as "Jew Street," indicating that a hearty band of Jewish residents lived and worked together in the colony's capital. Jews also resided in Branford, Woodstock, Stamford, Norwalk and New Haven. In 1818, a state convention adopted a new constitution for Connecticut that disestablished Congregationalism as the state's official church and allowed Jews the right to vote and hold public office. The freedom to form congregations and worship publicly, however, was still limited to Protestants.

By the 1840s, conditions finally were ripe for change. Given their First Amendment rights, the middle-class, German-speaking Jewish immigrants in Hartford and New Haven refused to accept their second-class status. In May 1843, a petition was introduced in the General Assembly on behalf of the Jews of Hartford and New Haven asking for an amendment to the state constitution so that they could form synagogues and worship openly. The Assembly's Judicial Committee turned down the request but recommended legislation, rather than a constitutional amendment, to grant Jews religious rights. In June, the legislature enacted a bill providing "that Jews who may desire to unite and form religious societies, shall have the same right, powers and privileges which are given to Christians of every denomination." By the fall of 1843, a minyan was meeting in various private Hartford homes. In 1856, using a bequest from Judah Touro of New Orleans, the congregation, which took the name Congregation Beth Israel, built the first synagogue in Connecticut. After 220 years, Puritan resistance to Jewish life in Connecticut was laid to rest.

Sponsored by the children and grandchildren of Emil and Lillian Cohen

6

Aaron Lopez's Struggle for Citizenship

In 1782, Aaron Lopez, a Jewish merchant and philanthropist from Newport, Rhode Island, died in a carriage accident. On hearing of this sad event, Ezra Stiles, the president of Yale College, wrote in his diary that Lopez had been an "amiable, benevolent, most hospitable & very respectable gentleman . . . without a single Enemy & and the most universally beloved by an extensive Acquaintance of any man I ever knew." Despite the widespread esteem in which Lopez was held, however, only twenty-one years earlier he had not been allowed to become a naturalized citizen of Rhode Island.

The Lopez family left Portugal for New York in 1740. They had been living as *conversos* in Portugal. Once in America, the Lopezes reclaimed their Jewish identity. The family moved to Newport in the 1750s and

became active in shipping, whaling and the manufacture of candles. After living in Newport for nine years, Aaron Lopez applied to become a naturalized citizen.

There is no official record of why the Rhode Island Superior Court turned down the naturalization applications of Aaron Lopez and his fellow Jew Isaac Elizer, but the two men did not accept rejection. They appealed to the lower house of the Rhode Island legislature for redress. The house granted their request—but only grudgingly, and in part. The legislature voted to approve the naturalization applications if the two men returned to Superior Court and took an oath of allegiance. The legislature went on to say, however:

> Inasmuch as the said Aaron Lopez hath declared himself by religion a Jew, this Assembly doth not admit himself nor any

other of that religion to the full freedom of this Colony. So that the said Aaron Lopez nor any other of said religion is not liable to be chosen into any office in this colony nor allowed to give vote as a free man in choosing others.

Even worse, when Lopez and Elizer's appeal of the Superior Court's actions reached the upper house of the Rhode Island legislature, that august body voted to return the case to the court. The upper chamber explained that the English Parliament had given the courts jurisdiction over naturalization and therefore the legislature had no business interfering.

The case was reheard in Superior Court on March 11, 1762. Ezra Stiles recorded the day's events. First, the court pronounced a sentence of hanging on a notorious thief; then it sentenced an arsonist to the same fate. A perjurer was then sentenced to the pillory. Finally, according to Stiles, "The Jews were called to hear their almost equally mortifying sentence and Judgment: which dismissed their Petition for Naturalization." Stiles mused, "Whether this [the sequence of the cases] was designedly, or accidental in proceeding upon the business of the Court I dont learn."

The court reasoned that Parliament had authorized naturalization in the colonies to increase their population; since Rhode Island had become so crowded by 1762, the act no longer applied there. Furthermore:

by the charter granted to this colony, it appears that the free and quiet enjoyment of the Christian religion and a desire of propagating the same were the principal views with which this colony was settled, and by a law made and passed in the year 1663, no person who does not profess the Christian religion can be admitted free [i.e., as a voter or office holder] to this colony.

The court's verdict led Stiles, an assiduous student of Jewish history, to reflect, "I remark that Providence seems to make every Thing to work for Mortification to the Jews, & to prevent their incorporating into any Nation; that thus they may continue a distinct people."

At this point, Isaac Elizer dropped his quest to become a naturalized citizen of Rhode Island and an English subject. Aaron Lopez, however, persisted. Eighteen days after the Rhode Island Superior Court handed down its verdict, Lopez's agent began inquiries in Massachusetts to determine what was required for Lopez to be naturalized in that colony. The agent determined that Lopez needed only to produce proof that he had resided honorably in Rhode Island for seven years and to establish a few months' residency in Massachusetts.

In April of 1762, the Lopez family moved temporarily across the border to a home in Swansea, Massachusetts. In October, Aaron Lopez appeared in Taunton, Massachusetts, with a certificate from the deputy governor of Rhode Island that he had "deported [himself] as a good and loyal subject of his Britannic Majesty." The court granted Lopez his naturalization, after which the family returned to Rhode Island.

When British troops captured Newport during the Revolutionary War, Lopez fled to Leicester, Massachusetts, where he joined other displaced Newport patriots. On his way back to Newport when the Revolution ended, Lopez met his untimely end in the carriage accident for which he received the posthumous appreciation of Reverend Stiles and his fellow patriots.

Sponsored by Joseph F. Cullman 3rd in honor of Frances N. Jacobs

Part II

VARIETIES OF AMERICAN JEWISH IDENTITY

1

Judah Monis:
America's First Hebrew Professor

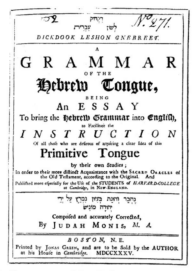

Judah Monis. *A Grammar of the Hebrew Tongue*. 1735. Title page.

Judah Monis, North America's first Hebrew instructor, taught students at Harvard College from 1722 to 1760. His career teaches us about the challenges of maintaining a Jewish life in early America.

Monis was born in Italy in 1683 into a family of Portuguese conversos. Educated at Jewish academies in Italy, Holland and Scotland, he emigrated to New York City around 1715, where he established a small store and taught the Hebrew language to Christians and Jews. By 1720, he had moved to Cambridge, Massachusetts, home of Harvard and an area in which few Jews resided.

At that time, all Harvard undergraduates except freshmen were required to study Hebrew, on the principle that a Christian gentleman was not truly educated unless he could read the Bible in its original tongue. Encouraged by friends who considered him "a great master of the Hebrew language," Monis presented his personal, handwritten manual of Hebrew grammar to the Harvard Corporation in 1720 for its "Judicious perusall." Two years later, the corporation voted "That Mr. Judah Monis be approved as an instructor of the Hebrew Language in that College," making him the first full-time instructor in Hebrew at Harvard—but not as a Jew, as its faculty members were required to be professing Christians.

Monis had been corresponding with

Protestant ministers on issues of kabbalah, the trinity and Christian doctrine and began studying Christianity with local ministers in Cambridge. One month before assuming his post at Harvard, Monis became a Christian.

Some Christian clergymen questioned his sincerity. They could not help wondering whether Monis had complied with Harvard's requirement in order to be appointed to the faculty. Jews in Europe, on the other hand, were outraged and dismayed. Monis defended his conversion in three books published in 1722. He argued that he had left Judaism out of religious conviction, not opportunism. To prove the point, he married a Christian woman and joined the First Church in Cambridge.

Monis's mode of teaching was based on the handwritten text he submitted to the Harvard Corporation in 1720. His students every year had to copy the entire text by hand, a painstaking task that could take up to a month. (A rare surviving handwritten version of Monis's text, copied by one of his students, resides in the archives of the American Jewish Historical Society). In 1724, Monis petitioned the Harvard Corporation to publish the work and the Corporation agreed. Hebrew type was shipped from London and set on a Cambridge press. In 1735, a thousand copies of Judah Monis's *A Grammar of the Hebrew Tongue* were published—the first Hebrew textbook published in North America.

Hebrew was never a popular course at Harvard in Monis's time. Students complained that the exercises and grammar were boring. College records show that his students frequently hazed Monis and attendance in his classes was a constant problem.

While in 1723 the college recorded itself "greatly satisfied with his assiduity and faithfulness in his instruction," in 1724 the teaching of Hebrew to undergraduates was turned over to tutors. Monis remained responsible only for teaching graduate students and the tutors.

Harvard employed Monis until 1760. By then, his responsibilities had dwindled to one weekly class with graduate students. His health declining and student interest flagging, he retired. Monis died in 1764 and is buried in a church cemetery in Northboro, Massachusetts.

Monis's life presents one case—if an extreme one—of how a Jew made a place for himself in colonial America. He chose to enter Harvard as a Christian. Having voluntarily left a mature Jewish community in New York City, Monis went to Cambridge, which had no Jewish institutions, to teach the Hebrew language to Christian students.

However, the Christian community apparently never ceased to view him with skepticism. The Cambridge First Church and the records of Harvard College often refer to Monis as "the converted Jew." Church records indicate concern that Monis might have continued observing the Sabbath on Saturday. The headstone of his grave bears witness to the ambiguous double identity by which Monis lived in Massachusetts. Using the Christian image of a grafted tree for conversion, the inscription reads in part:

> A native branch of Jacob see.
> Which once from off its olive brook,
> Regrafted, from the living tree.

Sponsored by Nancy and Morris Offit

2

Abigail Levy Franks and Jewish Continuity in Early America

In recent years, American Jewry has expressed concern about the rising rate of intermarriage between Jews and non-Jews. However, intermarriage is by no means a recent phenomenon. Maintaining Jewish communal life in America's highly absorptive, essentially secular culture has been a challenge since the earliest settlements in the New World. The story of the Levy Franks family, Jews immersed in the Protestant milieu of early eighteenth-century New York, is particularly illustrative.

The matriarch of the Franks family, (Bilhah) Abigail Levy Franks, was born in New York in 1696, one year after her parents, Moses and Rachel Levy, arrived there

from London. Abigail's husband-to-be, Jacob Franks, also came from London. He lived for a while as a boarder in the Levy household and married sixteen-year-old Abigail in 1712. Together, they had nine children, six of whom survived infancy.

The Levy and Franks families became leaders of New York's tiny Jewish community, which numbered fewer than fifty families. Jacob Franks served as *parnas* (president) of Shearith Israel, the oldest Jewish congregation in North America. Yet the Levys and Frankses included among their closest friends some of New York's elite Protestant families: the Livingstons, Bayards, DeLanceys, and Van Cortlands. Moses Levy and Jacob Franks were among the eleven Jews who contributed funds to complete the steeple of Trinity Church, which served both as a religious symbol and a beacon to guide ships into New York harbor.

At a time when women were meant to devote themselves to home and children, Abigail Levy's parents provided her with a classical education. She read the contemporary novels of Fielding and Smollett and the works of Dryden, Montesquieu and Alexander Pope (her favorite author) and encouraged her daughters to do the same. Her hopes for her children are known to us today primarily from the letters she wrote to her son Naphtali, who had gone to seek his fortune in London. Abigail's remarkable correspondence now resides in the archives of the American Jewish Historical Society, which published it in 1968.

Abigail prided herself on her strict observance of the Sabbath, holy days and dietary laws, as well as her regular attendance at Shearith Israel. Suspicious of the dietary observances even of close relatives, she repeatedly sent kosher food to son Naphtali in London and warned him not to eat anything at the home of his English uncle (her brother-in-law) "unless it be bread and butter . . . nor anywhere else where there is the least doubt of things not done after our strict Judaical method."

While observing kashrut in colonial New York was manageable, finding suitable Jewish mates for her children in the city's tiny Jewish community posed more of a problem. With so few local Jewish suitors, Abigail worried that her daughters would have to live, in her words, as "nuns." She encouraged Naphtali to marry his Jewish cousin in London, advice he followed.

Paradoxically, in at least one instance, the appearance of a rare Jewish suitor for one of her daughters did not please Abigail. She opposed the courtship of her daughter Richa by a member of the Sephardic Gomez family because she considered the prospective bridegroom a "stupid wretch." Richa later rejected the proposal of a Christian suitor to avoid adding to her mother's unhappiness. She finally married a Jew in England.

Abigail was profoundly dismayed when, in 1743, her daughter Phila eloped with Oliver DeLancey, the son of a wealthy and politically powerful Christian family. Although Jacob Franks soon reconciled himself to Phila's marriage because it allied the clan with the well-connected DeLanceys, Abigail refused to speak to Phila or let Oliver in her home. Mother and daughter never reconciled and Jacob died heartbroken.

The story of the Franks family marriages—and marriagelessness—illustrates the dilemma young Jewish men and women faced when seeking spouses in colonial America. Abigail Franks's New York, while a large Jewish community by American standards, was home to only a few hundred co-religionists. To compound matters, New York's Christian elite considered the city's Jews eligible marriage partners, which meant that Jews were not forced to marry only one another.

While the number of Jews in New York and America has increased exponentially since the 1730's, acceptance has grown even more. The question of how to maintain Jewish in-marriage in America's socially tolerant environment remains as challenging today as in the age of Abigail Franks.

Sponsored by Marilyn and Marshall Butler

3

Solomon Hays's Battle of the Balcony

In October of 1756, the *hazzan* of Congregation Shearith Israel in New York City read a proclamation from the pulpit declaring that no member of the congregation should have "Conversation Correspondance or Commasty" with Solomon Hays. Thenceforward, Hays, his wife and his children were excommunicated from Shearith Israel—officially cut off from religious interaction with members of the New York Jewish community. What had Hays done to merit this punishment? The hazzan explained that Hays was being expelled "because he has Candallise [scandalized] us among the Christens [*sic*]." In Yiddish, he had caused one of America's first recorded *shande far di goyim.*

The dread affair, which has come to be known as the Battle of the Balcony, began at Kol Nidre services on September 14, 1755. Historians Sheldon and Judith Godfrey describe that evening as "unseasonably hot and muggy and the weather unstable." Solomon Hays's wife, Gitlah, joined the other women of the congregation in the upstairs gallery, sitting in her assigned seat next to an open window. The window sash had been taken from its hinges to allow what little circulation of air was possible on such a stifling evening. According to the Godfreys, "Suddenly a violent storm arose. The rain poured in the open window drench-

ing Mrs. Hays. . . . When she arrived home after the service, she reported the incident to her husband."

Solomon Hays went to the synagogue the next morning, searched out the window sash and replaced it on its hinges so that his wife, when she resumed her place, would not receive another dousing. The morning, however, continued "hot and muggy," and the other women consigned to the gallery wished to open the window in order to allow a breath—any breath—of fresh air. Mrs. Hays closed the window. Her neighbors opened it. She closed it. They opened it again. She closed it again. And so on.

The other women complained to some members of the *junto*, or board of elders, about Mrs. Hays's intransigence. Moses Gomez, one of the elders, went up to the gallery and removed the window from its sash. According to the Godfreys, "Solomon Hays saw Moses Gomez taking the window outside and confronted him in the synagogue yard. Words passed between them while others came outside to lend their support." Ultimately, Solomon Hays was "forcibly evicted from the yard" by several of the elders, including Moses Gomez's father, Daniel.

Later that month, the board of elders fined Hays 20 shillings for causing a disturbance. In response—or retaliation—Hays brought charges in criminal court against the entire board of elders, accusing them of assault and battery against his person. Here, then, was the excommunicable offense: Hays had used the courts as an arena in which to wash the synagogue's dirty laundry publicly.

The court case went to trial in October of 1756, thirteen months after the original incident and the same month that the *hazzan* announced Hays's excommunication. After nineteenth days of hearings at which nine witnesses testified, the elders were acquitted on all counts. Adding insult to injury, the court ordered Hays to pay the defendants' legal costs.

There had been several conflicts between Solomon Hays and members of the New York Jewish community before the Battle of the Balcony. According to the Godfreys, Hays had once accused Daniel Gomez publicly of "charging a usurious rate of interest on a loan" Gomez had given him. In early 1755, Hays also testified that two immigrant Jews who claimed to have been born in Plymouth, England, and thus entitled to conduct business in English New York, had actually been born in Holland. For this apparently truthful testimony, the congregation accused Hays of being a "traitor" to his people. Soon after, the Battle of the Balcony

and Hays's dragging the *junto* into court exhausted the community's patience.

It was several years before Hays, his wife and children were readmitted to the congregation, and even then the bickering continued. Hays and his sons were accused of non-specific violations of the congregation's rules and defiance of the parnas (president) and other members of the *junto*.

The historical record is too skimpy for us to know the merits of Hays's charges that he was criminally manhandled by the *junto*. We can speculate that Hays had a personality that led him regularly into conflicts that, when contained within the Jewish community, were tolerated as "family business." When Hays took his case to court—when he made it a matter of public record *outside* the Jewish community—he exhausted the community's patience.

As early as 1755, it seems, American Jewry was trying its best to downplay any notorious public behavior by an individual Jew for fear of bringing opprobrium on the group as a whole. As we have grown more at home in the United States in our own times, it appears that most American Jews no longer worry that the actions of a co-religionist will taint the reputation of all.

Sponsored by Joseph F. Cullman 3rd in honor of Frances N. Jacob

4

Moses Michael Hays:
"A Most Valuable Citizen"

While some colonial Jews found it difficult to live both as Jews and Americans, Boston's Moses Michael Hays had a different experience. Boston's most prominent eighteenth-century Jewish citizen, Hays set a high standard of civic leadership and charity. Without the companionship and support of an organized Jewish community and without legal guarantees of religious freedom, Hays thrived in the "first circles" of Boston society while publicly practicing Judaism.

Moses Michael Hays was born in New York City in 1739 to Dutch immigrants Judah and Rebecca Michaels Hays. Judah Hays took his son into his shipping and retail business and, upon his death in 1764, left him the business.

Judah Hays left Moses Michael Hays something else as well: a firm grounding in his Jewish faith and responsibilities. Moses served New York's Congregation Shearith Israel as second *parnas* (vice-president) in 1766 and *parnas* in 1767. Even after moving to Boston, Moses retained an attachment to Shearith Israel, appearing on its donor list throughout his life.

In 1766, Moses married Rachel Myers, younger sister of famed New York silversmith Myer Myers. In 1769, the couple moved to Newport, Rhode Island, where Hays continued his shipping business. Business reverses landed him in debtors' prison, but under a 1771 reform law he liquidated his assets, gave them to his creditors and was set free. He immediately reestablished himself in the transatlantic trade in Newport.

The American Revolution brought Hays a new challenge as a Jew. In 1775, seventy-six men in Newport were asked to sign a declaration of loyalty to the American colonies that included the phrase "upon the true faith of a Christian." Hays publicly objected to the phrase and refused to sign, instead offering a letter affirming his belief that the Revolution was a just cause. After much wrangling, the Christian portion of the oath was omitted and Hays affixed his name.

In 1776, Hays and his family left Newport for Boston ahead of the British occupation. He opened a shipping office there and underwrote shipbuilding, trade, and insurance to newly opened Far Eastern markets. In 1784, Hays became a founder and the first depositor of the Massachusetts Bank, still doing business today as Fleet Bank Corporation. With his close friend Paul Revere and fourteen other Boston businessmen, Hays formed several insurance companies and helped establish the New England Masonic movement. When Hays was accepted into the Massachusetts Lodge in November 1782, he became its first Jewish member. In 1792, the lodge members elected Hays their grand master. Paul Revere served as his deputy.

The Hays family filled a large brick fifteen-room home on Boston's fashionable Middle (now Hanover) Street. The Hayses had seven children, and when Moses's widowed sister Reyna Touro died in 1787, Moses and Rachel raised his young nephews and niece. Samuel May, Louisa May Alcott's grandfather, was a close childhood friend of the Hays and Touro children and recalled "Uncle and Aunt Hays" for their pride in Judaism.

> If the children of my day were taught among other foolish things to dread, if not despise Jews, a very different lesson was impressed upon my young heart. . . . [The Hays] house . . . was the abode of hospitality. . . . He and his truly good wife were hospitable, not to the rich alone, but also to the poor. . . . I witnessed their religious exercise, their fastings and their prayers. . . . [As a result] I grew up without prejudice against Jews—or any other religionists.

As Boston lacked a synagogue, Moses Michael Hays conducted regular worship services at home. The household library contained dozens of Hebrew books. The Jewish commandment to give charity directed much of what the Hays family did for Boston and its citizens. Moses Michael Hays provided financial support to beautify Boston Common, establish theaters and endow Harvard College. His children and nephews went on to distinguished and charitable lives. Son Judah Hays was the first professing Jew elected to public office in Boston. Hays descendants helped found the Boston Athenaeum and the Massachusetts General Hospital. Nephew Judah went on to become America's first great national philanthropist.

Moses Michael Hays died in 1805. His obituaries in the secular press remembered him as "a most valuable citizen . . . now secure in the bosom of his Father and our Father, of his God and our God." Hays lived his life successfully as an American and a Jew, accepted by the Boston community with respect as both.

Sponsored by the Wyner/Stokes Foundation in honor of Genevieve G. and Justin L. Wyner

5

Gershom Mendes Seixas:
The First American–born "Rabbi"

In 1768, Congregation Shearith Israel, the Spanish and Portuguese synagogue in New York City, appointed 23-year-old Gershom Mendes Seixas as its *hazzan*, or reader. Seixas was one of six children of Isaac Mendes Seixas, a Portuguese *converso* whose family fled to London after Isaac's father was accused, in 1725, of secretly practicing his ancient faith. In 1730, Isaac emigrated to New York, where in 1741 he married Rachel Levy, an Ashkenazic Jew. Gershom was the product of this "mixed" Sephardic-Ashkenazic marriage.

New York City in the 1760s had fewer than 300 Jews and one Hebrew congregation: Shearith Israel. The congregation was a *kehillah,* a synagogue community, the center of communal life for this small outpost of American Jewry whose members struggled to retain their Jewish uniqueness in a society that offered them many opportunities to blend into the broader culture. They gathered at Shearith Israel to celebrate holi-

days and life events together: to marry, mark births and deaths, give thanks for the blessings of religious toleration in America and to pray for the coming of the Messiah. Despite the fact that a majority was of Ashkenazic, or northern European, origins, the congregation stuck to the ancient Sephardic minhag, or rituals. As *hazzan* of the congregation, Gershom Mendes Seixas was at the center of the community's effort to retain its Judaism while living in America's tolerant, absorptive atmosphere.

We note that Seixas was the *hazzan* of Shearith Israel, not its rabbi. It was not until the mid-19th century that America had its first *ordained* rabbi, that is, a religious leader and teacher formally trained and certified by ordained, senior rabbis in Europe. Before the 1850s, scholarly-trained European rabbis preferred not to live permanently in North America, without learned colleagues and among congregants who – with few exceptions – had fallen away from strict Orthodox practices and who possessed little formal learning in Jewish law. Accordingly, it was left to Seixas to do more than lead services in Shearith Israel. Although not a formally trained rabbi, he served as spiritual leader, interpreter of religious law, supervisor of kashrut, performer of marriages and funerals and all the other duties we now associate with ordained rabbis.

Gershom Mendes Seixas received his Jewish education primarily from his father. Not a college graduate, Gershom educated himself in Talmud and read widely in secular literature, including Christian texts. New York's Jewish community was simply too small to live in isolation from its non-Jewish neighbors and, like most of his congregants, Seixas had many friends and associates amongst the New York Christian commercial and social elite. One sign of the respect in which Seixas was held was his appointment, in 1784, to the board of trustees of Columbia College, now Columbia University.

Perhaps nothing better accounts for the source of Seixas' esteem in the New York community than his pro-independence actions during the American Revolution. Despite the fact that his congregants were split on the issue, in 1775 Seixas persuaded a majority that Shearith Israel should close its doors rather than operate during a British occupation of New York. Three weeks later, his wife Elkaleh had a miscarriage. With a heavy heart at leaving some of his flock behind, Seixas packed the congregation's sacred scrolls and texts and removed them, with his family, to his father-in-law's home in Stratford, Connecticut. In 1780, the Seixas's moved to Philadelphia, where Gershom became *hazzan* of congregation Mickve Israel. Despite personally abhorring war, in his sermons Seixas regularly called on God to bless the Revolution, the Congress and George Washington. Seixas considered the American cause, with its emphasis on individual liberty, a just war – one that represented the interests of American Jewry in freedom.

At war's end in 1784, Congregation Shearith Israel invited Seixas to reassume his pulpit. At the time, Elkaleh was ill and Gershom was content in his Philadelphia post, but Shearith Israel ultimately convinced him to return to New York, where he served as hazzan, or "minister" until his death in 1816. In 1787, when George Washington was inaugurated as the first president of he United States, Seixas was one of three clergymen who participated – a sign of respect for Seixas and the role that Jews had played in the founding of the new nation.

Seixas devoted much of his time and prestige to encouraging charity toward the poor. Contrary to the reigning Protestant doctrine of the time, Seixas preached that riches were no sign of grace, and poverty no sign of disgrace. Each status was a challenge that God gave humankind: for the poor to endure and overcome hardship; for the wealthy to grow virtuous by acts of charity. Seixas believed that the very purpose of a fortunate person's life was to help others, even if such virtue received no overt reward on earth.

When Seixas died, the trustees of Columbia College commissioned a medal with his likeness. His friend Dr. Jacob de la Motta noted that, during the last seven years of his life, Seixas's "sufferings were beyond the ken of human conception." Yet, Seixas served his congregation until near the very end. The first American-born *hazzan* still serves as a model for the contemporary American rabbinate.

Sponsored by Frederic Nathan and Edgar J. Nathan III

6

Mordecai's Female Academy: 1809

In 1809, having failed in business and needing to support his large family, Jacob Mordecai opened a private liberal arts high school for girls in Warrenton, North Carolina. In so doing, he revolutionized female education in the South. Jacob Mordecai was the first teacher of Southern belles to offer a classical, as opposed to merely domestic, education. He made it respectable for Southern girls to study the same subjects as their male counterparts.

The son of Moses and Esther Mordecai, observant Jews who in 1760 emigrated from Germany to Philadelphia, Jacob was born in 1762. He attended private schools and received a classical education. At age thirteen, he served as a rifleman when the Continental Congress was resident in Philadelphia, and later he helped supply the Continental Army as a clerk to David Franks, the Jewish quartermaster to General George Washington. After the war, Jacob Mordecai moved to New York and married Judith Myers. In 1792, the two moved to Warrenton, a small town well situated on the roads linking Richmond, Charleston, and Savannah. In Warrenton, Jacob first made his mark as a tobacco merchant.

Jacob and Judith had six children, four boys and two girls. Judith died soon after the birth of the youngest, and her sister Rebecca came to Warrenton to care for the children. Jacob and Rebecca married two years later, and she gave birth to seven additional children. The couple provided all thirteen children with an education that included philosophy, history, literature and Jewish religion.

According to historian Sheldon Hanft, Jacob Mordecai "broke new ground when he provided his daughters as well as his sons with the kind of public school education that was ordinarily reserved for the males of socially prominent families." Most Southerners, Hanft asserts, did not consider it "prudent to provide [girls] with an education that would equip them for public life," opting instead to teach them domestic skills such as sewing.

Although the only Jewish family in a small town, the Mordecais kept the Sabbath and observed *kashrut*. According to Hanft, the Mordecais never had any problems with their Christian neighbors. Their piety was respected, and in 1797 Jacob was elected master of the Warrenton Masonic Lodge.

Trouble came, however, in the form of business reverses. Jacob experienced heavy losses in tobacco investments in 1806 and was forced to sell his business and the family home to clear his debts. Fortunately, a male boarding academy opened in Warrenton and hired him as a teacher. Since the terms of employment included residence at the school, the Mordecais moved into cramped but homey quarters on the grounds. In 1808, local parents asked Jacob to leave the academy and establish a separate school for girls. They agreed to his condition that the school's curriculum would be as rigorous as that at the male institution.

Jacob bought back his house and converted it into a girls' academy. The school was truly a family project. Initially, Jacob and Rebecca taught all the classes, but they were soon joined in the classroom by their daughter Rachael and in later years by two of their sons (see page 50). The younger Mordecai children helped with the cooking and in cleaning the dormitories. Only the music teacher was not a member of the family.

The school's curriculum focused on academics but also stressed proper manners and demeanor. Jacob insisted on personal discipline and a highly structured day in which the students were kept constantly busy. They were required to wash their own utensils, scrub their hands and faces and brush their hair and teeth daily, even on the coldest mornings. The school's reputation blossomed so quickly that Mordecai, who began with thirty students in 1809, concluded by 1814 that he would have to cap the enrollment at 110.

Jacob Mordecai stressed that piety in any religious tradition was an important part of character development. The Mordecais included observance of Jewish holidays in the school's educational program. All of the Mordecai children, male and female, attend-ed and worked in the school, as did several cousins, so there was always a critical mass of Jewish students to observe holidays. Jacob equally encouraged the Christian students to observe their own holidays and attend church services. It mattered little what religious practices his students observed so long as they were respectful of the religious preferences of others. The curriculum included philosophical texts that raised moral and ethical issues his students could discuss together regardless of their religious differences.

In 1819, at age fifty-six, ten years after opening his Female Academy, Jacob Mordecai sold the highly successful enterprise and moved his family to Richmond, Virginia. He purchased a farm and became an active member of Richmond's Jewish community, serving as president of its congregation, K. K. Beth Shalome. Jacob died in 1838.

Driven into the educational profession by the failure of the family's tobacco business, Jacob and Rebecca Mordecai and their children became pioneers of equal education for women. As Jews in an overwhelmingly Christian setting, they earned acceptance of their religious views, just as they taught religious toleration to their students. Ahead of their time in the early 1800s, their educational and religious views have become the American norm.

Sponsored by Louise P. and Gabriel Rosenfeld in memory of Miriam and Maxwell W. Passerman

7

The "Pioneer" Jews of Martha's Vineyard

For small-town and rural Jews in the early twentieth century, one of the greatest challenges was maintaining their Jewish identity in a sea of non-Jewish neighbors. The Jews who settled on Martha's Vineyard, a tiny island off the coast of Massachusetts, faced this challenge and, in their own way, maintained a distinctly Jewish way of life despite their isolation from the mainstream.

Historian Kenneth Libo speculates that the first settlers of Jewish origin on Martha's Vineyard may have been Cape Verdean descendants of Spanish and Portuguese Sephardim who generations earlier had converted to Catholicism. The first definitively identified Jewish settler on Martha's Vineyard was Sam Cronig, who arrived there in 1905. Cronig was born in rural Lithuania, the oldest son of a Yiddish-speaking family who expected him to become a rabbi. At age fifteen, according to Libo, "after an encounter with a Cossack's whip, he left the yeshiva his parents had sent him to in Minsk and became a baker's apprentice." It took Cronig two years to save the $200 to purchase his passage to America.

At age seventeen, Sam Cronig landed in New York. Finding the atmosphere on the Lower East Side unhealthful, he visited relatives in New Bedford, Massachusetts, who found him a job as a farm worker on Martha's Vineyard. There he labored for a retired mariner, Captain Daggett, and his wife. The Daggetts took Cronig under their wing, teaching him English. At one point, they fantasized about adopting him, but Sam never forgot his family in Lithuania. Working on the Daggett farm and as a grocery delivery boy, he was able to save enough by 1917 to bring his three brothers, a sister, and, eventually, his future wife, Libby, from Minsk to Martha's Vineyard.

In 1917, despite having no previous entrepreneurial experience, Sam Cronig and two of his brothers opened a meat and grocery market on Main Street in Vineyard Haven. On the recommendation of a Christian islander whose daughter had gone to high school with Sam, a purveyor in New Bedford staked the Cronigs to a stock of merchandise. Today, Cronig's grocery store remains a mainstay of Martha's Vineyard commerce.

In 1913, a second Jewish family planted roots on Martha's Vineyard. Yudel Brickman, a cobbler, brought his wife and children from Lithuania that year. In 1914, the family of Mrs. Brickman's brother, Israel Isaakson, joined the Brickmans and the Cronigs to form the heart of the "pioneer" Jewish community on Martha's Vineyard. Israel Isaakson and Yudel Brickman pursued skills they had developed in the "old country": Isaakson became a tailor and dry cleaner; Brickman borrowed a few hundred unsecured dollars from the Martha's Vineyard National Bank and went into the retail shoe business.

These pioneer families did their best to perpetuate Jewish traditions and practices despite their sparse numbers. They held religious services in the Cronig's living room and imported kosher meat from New Bedford and Boston. According to his daughter, Israel Isaakson persuaded an island undertaker to visit a Jewish funeral home in Boston to learn Jewish funeral practices because if, "God forbid, something should happen, we're stuck." Prophetically, when Israel Isaacson died, a storm kept the New Bedford rabbi from reaching the Vineyard and the local Methodist minister conducted the service, reading a Psalm of David.

Before there were sufficient numbers for a *minyan* on the Vineyard, mainland New Bedford provided the setting for the island's organized religious life. The Cronig, Isaakson, and Brickman boys were sent to New Bedford for six weeks to make final preparations for their bar mitzvahs. For the High Holy Days, the families would worship in a New Bedford synagogue or gather at a hotel in Onset, on Cape Cod. For Passover, the pioneer Jewish families would gather at the Cronigs' home. A Cronig daughter recalled that each family would bring its own food and prepare it in the Cronigs' kitchen. Sawhorses and planks provided the Pesach table, which stretched from the dining room to the living room. Each family sat as a separate group, but in a sense they formed a single extended family.

Sabbath observance was more varied. While Sam Cronig's wife lit Shabbos candles, Sam felt obliged to tend his grocery store on Friday, which was the island's traditional payday, and Saturday, when many non-Jewish families had their only chance to shop. Regardless of their level of religious observance, the pioneer families kept Yiddishkeit alive, speaking the mother tongue at home, cooking such foods as *kneidlach* and stuffed cabbage, and encouraging their children to marry Jewish partners. In 1937, when ten Jewish households were permanently established on the island, they established the Martha's Vineyard Jewish Center.

Dorothy Brickman recalled that there were places on the Vineyard, such as Edgartown, where Jews were not welcome to purchase homes, and it was rare to be invited socially to the home of a non-Jewish family. By the measure of participation in organizations like the Lions and the Masons, however, or appointment to such posts as health commissioner or the board of the Martha's Vineyard National Bank, the island's pioneer Jewish families were accepted members of the broader community.

Historian Libo describes small-town settlers as "Jewish ambassadors to American society." Balancing Jewish identity with life among the non-Jewish majority, the pioneer Jews of Martha's Vineyard, like the Jewish residents of countless other small towns and rural areas, paved the way for later generations of Jews.

Sponsored by Elizabeth and Melvin Mark in memory of Sarah G. and Rudolf H. Wyner

1

Haym Salomon:
Revolutionary Broker

In the pantheon of American Jewish heroes, Haym Salomon (1740–1785) has attained legendary status. His life was brief and tumultuous, but his impact on the American imagination was great. The U.S. Postal Service issued a stamp hailing Salomon as a "Financial Hero of the American Revolution." The city of Chicago erected a monument jointly honoring Salomon, George Washington and Robert Morris, and Beverly Hills, California, is home to an organization called the American Jewish Patriots and Friends of Haym Salomon. No early American Jew is better known than Salomon.

However, Salomon's life was not all triumph. A successful financier in the early 1780s, he died bankrupt in 1785, leaving a wife and four young children. When his son petitioned Congress to recover funds he claimed his father was owed by the government, various committees refused to recognize the family's claims. In 1936, Congress voted to erect a monument to Salomon in the District of Columbia, but funds for the actual construction were never appropriated. Haym Salomon still awaits his national monument.

Born in Lissa (now Leszno), Poland, in 1740, Salomon spent several years moving around Western Europe and England. He developed fluency in several languages that served him well for the remainder of his life. Reaching New York City in 1772, he swiftly established himself as a successful merchant and dealer in foreign securities. Striking up an acquaintance with Alexander MacDougall, leader of the New York Sons of

Liberty, Salomon became active in the patriot cause. When war broke out in 1776, Salomon got a contract to supply the troops in central New York. In 1777, he married Rachel Franks, whose brother Isaac was a lieutenant colonel on George Washington's staff. The Salomon's *ketubbah*, or marriage certificate, resides at the American Jewish Historical Society.

In the wake of a fire that destroyed much of New York City, the British occupation forces arrested and imprisoned Salomon. He gained release because the British hoped to use his language skills to communicate with their German mercenaries. Instead, Salomon covertly encouraged the Hessians to desert. The British arrested him again in early 1778 for espionage and sabotage and confiscated his property. A court-martial sentenced Salomon to hang but he escaped—probably with the help of other Sons of Liberty—and fled penniless to Philadelphia. His wife and child joined him there soon afterward.

In Philadelphia, Salomon resumed his brokerage business. The French diplomatic representative appointed him paymaster-general of the French forces fighting for the American cause. The Dutch and Spanish governments also engaged him to sell the securities that supported their loans to the Continental Congress. In 1781, Congress established the Office of Finance to save the United States from fiscal ruin. Salomon allied himself with Superintendent of Finance Robert Morris and became one of the most effective brokers of bills of exchange to meet federal government expenses. Salomon also personally advanced funds to members of the Continental Congress and other officials, charging interest and commissions well below market rates. James Madison wrote to an acquaintance, "I have for some time . . .

been a pensioner on the favor of Haym Salomon, a Jew broker."

While supporting the national cause, Salomon also played a prominent role in Philadelphia and national Jewish communal affairs. He served as a member of the governing council of Philadelphia's Congregation Mikveh Israel, was treasurer of Philadelphia's society for indigent travelers and participated in the nation's first known rabbinic court of arbitration. Moreover, he helped lead the successful fight to repeal the test oath that barred Jews and other non-Christians from holding public office in Pennsylvania.

Salomon operated in a society and an age that assumed most Jews were Shylocks and moneygrubbers. In 1784, writing as "A Jew Broker," Salomon protested allegations that Jewish merchants were profiteering, declaring it unjust that such charges were "cast so indiscriminately on the Jews of this city at large . . . for the faults of a few." His impassioned defense of his fellow Jews brought him national approbation. A year later, Salomon died, probably from a respiratory disease contracted while he was a British prisoner.

Within five years of his arrival in Philadelphia, Salomon advanced from penniless fugitive to respected businessman, philanthropist and defender of his people. He risked his fortune, pledged his good name and credit on behalf of the Revolution, and stood up for religious liberty. Despite financial setbacks at the end of his life, Salomon's name is forever linked to the idealism and success of the American Revolution and to the contributions Jews have made to the cause of American freedom.

Sponsored by Leslie Rose in memory of Edward and Lillian Rose

2

Francis Salvador:
Martyr of the American Revolution

When we think of Jewish heroes of the American Revolution, it is Haym Salomon, the financier of the patriot cause, who usually comes to mind. Rarely do we hear of South Carolina's Francis Salvador, the first identified Jew to be elected to an American colonial legislature, the only Jew to serve in a Revolution-era colonial congress, and the first Jew to die for the cause of America's freedom.

Francis Salvador was born in London in 1747. His great-grandfather Joseph, a merchant, established himself as a leader of England's Sephardic community and became the first Jewish director of the East India Company. When George III ascended the British throne, Joseph Salvador arranged an audience for a seven-man delegation that officially congratulated the king on behalf of the Jewish community.

Before Francis Salvador's birth, his family developed interests in America. Salvador's grandfather teamed with two other leaders of the London Jewish community to raise funds to send some of London's destitute Jews to the new British colony in Savannah. The Georgia trustees subsequently voted to ban Jewish immigration to Georgia, but not before grandfather Salvador and his two associates had landed forty-two Jewish settlers in Savannah in July 1733. When the founder of the colony, James

Oglethorpe, intervened on behalf of the Jews, the trustees decided to let them stay. The Salvador family then purchased personal land holdings in South Carolina.

As a young man, Francis Salvador was raised in luxury in London. He was well educated by private tutors and traveled extensively. At age twenty, he married his first cousin, Sarah, and took his place in the family shipping firm. The devastating effect of a 1755 earthquake in Lisbon, where the Salvadors had extensive interests, weakened the family's finances. The failure of the East India Company completed its ruin. By the early 1770s, virtually the only thing left of the Salvador family's immense wealth was the large plot of land they had purchased in the South Carolina colony.

In an attempt to rebuild the family fortune, in 1773 Francis Salvador moved to South Carolina. Intending to send for his wife, Sarah, and their children when he had prepared a proper home for them, Salvador arrived in Charleston in December and established himself as a planter on a 7,000-acre tract he acquired from his uncle. Salvador found himself drawn to the growing American movement against British rule and unhesitatingly threw himself into the patriot cause. Within a year of his arrival, at the age of twenty-seven, Salvador was elected to the General Assembly of South

Carolina, the first Jew to hold high elective office in the English colonies. He would retain the post until his sudden death.

In 1774, Francis Salvador was elected as a delegate to South Carolina's revolutionary Provincial Congress, which assembled in Charleston in January 1775. The Provincial Congress framed a bill of rights and prepared an address to the royal governor of South Carolina setting forth the colonists' grievances against the British crown. Salvador played an important role in the South Carolina Provincial Congress, which appointed him to a commission to negotiate with Tories living in the northern and western parts of the colony to secure their promise not to actively aid the royal government.

When the second Provincial Congress assembled in November 1775, Salvador urged that body to instruct the South Carolina delegation in Philadelphia to vote for independence. He played a leading role in the Provincial Congress, chairing its ways and means committee and serving on a select committee authorized to issue bills of credit to pay the militia. Salvador was also a member of a special commission established to preserve the peace in the interior parts of South Carolina, where the English superintendent of Indian affairs was negotiating an alliance with the Cherokees.

When the Cherokees attacked settlements along the frontier on July 1, 1776, massacring and scalping their inhabitants, Salvador, in an act reminiscent of Paul Revere, mounted his horse and galloped nearly 30 miles to give the alarm. He then returned to join the militia at the front, defending the settlements under siege. During a Cherokee attack early in the morning of August 1, Salvador was shot. He fell into some bushes, where the Cherokees subsequently discovered and scalped him. Salvador died forty-five minutes later. Major Andrew Williamson, the militia commander, reported, "When I came up to him after dislodging the enemy and speaking to him, he asked whether I had beaten the enemy. I told him 'Yes.' He said he was glad of it and shook me by the hand and bade me farewell, and said he would die in a few minutes."

A friend, Henry Laurens, reported that Salvador's death was "universally regretted," while William Henry Drayton, later chief justice of South Carolina, stated that Salvador had "sacrificed his life in the service of his adopted country." Dead at twenty-nine, never again seeing his wife or children after leaving England, Salvador was the first Jew to die in the American Revolution. Ironically, because he was fighting on the frontier, he probably never received the news that the Continental Congress in Philadelphia had, as he urged, adopted the Declaration of Independence.

Sponsored by Frangipane in loving memory of Murray Vidockler

3

Mordecai Sheftall
and the Wages of War

The war for America's independence posed great physical hardships for many on the patriot side: the heat of the Philadelphia summer that plagued the Founding Fathers as they gathered to declare independence, or the harsh cold endured by Washington's troops as they wintered at Valley Forge. Mordecai Sheftall, the leading Jewish citizen of Savannah, Georgia and an ardent patriot, also paid an extraordinary price for American independence.

Mordecai Sheftall's father, Benjamin, a deeply religious Jew, was one of the first European settlers of the Georgia colony. Benjamin Sheftall married his first wife, Perla, in 1734, and Mordecai was born in 1735.

Despite the opportunities presented by the new colony, Benjamin Sheftall never became wealthy; son Mordecai fared far better. By age twenty-one, Mordecai acquired land for cattle raising and, by twenty-five, he purchased a warehouse and wharf on the Savannah River.

Like his father, Mordecai Sheftall was a devoted and observant Jew. Savannah had only six Jewish families, but in 1771 Mordecai found a Jewish bride, Frances "Fannie" Hart, whom he "imported" from Charleston. Mordecai became a founding subscriber to Congregation Mickve Israel in Savannah and donated land for its first cemetery. Mordecai was the Jewish representative among the five incorporators of the

Union Society, a nondenominational philanthropic association founded by Savannah's religious bodies to assist widows and poor children.

Like a majority of his co-religionists, Mordecai Sheftall cast his lot with the revolt against British rule. In 1776, he was elected chairman of the revolutionary committee that assumed control of local government in Savannah. In 1777, he was appointed commissary general to the Georgia militia, responsible for supplying the colony's soldiers with food and matériel. Sheftall often reached into his own pocket to purchase supplies for the volunteers.

In 1778, impressed by his skill and selflessness as commissary general of Georgia, General Robert Howe appointed Sheftall to the post of deputy commissary general to the Continental troops stationed in Georgia and South Carolina. Before Congress could confirm him, however, Mordecai Sheftall was captured in December 1778, along with his fifteen-year-old son, Sheftall Sheftall, while fighting to defend Savannah against a British invasion force. Some of the outnumbered patriots escaped by swimming across the Savannah River, but the younger Sheftall could not swim and his father would not abandon him. With 185 other Americans, they were captured and imprisoned.

The British interrogated the Sheftalls under great duress, depriving them of food for two days. At one point, they were almost bayoneted by a drunken British soldier. Refusing to provide information about the Americans' sources of supplies or renounce the patriot cause, father and son were transferred to a dank prison ship, the *Nancy*, where the British deliberately offered Mordecai no meat other than pork, which he rejected. After several months, the elder Sheftall was paroled to the town of Sunbury, Georgia; his son remained on the *Nancy*.

Separation from family weighed heavily on Mordecai. He was finally able to arrange for his son's parole to Sunbury under the same restrictive conditions that governed his own freedom of movement. Things looked promising when American military pressure forced the British garrison to withdraw from Sunbury, but freedom for the Sheftalls did not follow. Local Tories beat and even killed patriots in Sunbury, especially parolees like the Sheftalls. Father and son fled on an American brig but were captured by a British frigate and transported to Antigua, where they remained prisoners until the spring of 1780. In June, both Sheftalls were paroled once more. They headed for Philadelphia, to which Mrs. Sheftall and the children had fled for safety. There, despite his own financial hardships, Mordecai helped fund a new synagogue for Congregation Mickve Israel.

Mordecai spent the remainder of the war in Philadelphia, seeking to help both the American cause and himself by financing a privateer to capture and loot British vessels. On its very first voyage, the ship ran aground. In 1783, when the war ended, Mordecai returned with his wife and children to Savannah. The state of Georgia granted Sheftall several hundred acres of land in recognition of his sacrifices on behalf of independence. When he died in 1797 at the age of sixty-two, Savannah buried him with full honors in the Jewish cemetery he had donated.

Sponsored by the children and grandchildren of Herman Levy

4

David Franks:
Vindication of an American Jewish Patriot

David Salisbury Franks was a hero of the American Revolution, but his reputation was tainted by his having served as aide-de-camp to the traitorous Benedict Arnold. Although cleared on all charges of complicity in Arnold's plot to surrender West Point to the British in 1780, Franks continued to be suspected of disloyalty. Thus, despite his formal exoneration, he never fully recovered his reputation. As a result, his name is rarely included in the pantheon of Revolutionary heroes.

David S. Franks was born in Philadelphia around 1740 into a large and highly respected Jewish merchant family. As a young man, Franks's father relocated his branch of the family to Quebec. In 1775, on the eve of the Revolution, David S. Franks was living in Montreal, serving in the distinguished position of *parnas* (president) of the Spanish and Portuguese synagogue in that city, though he was of German Jewish descent. According to historian Jacob Rader Marcus, Franks was jailed for sixteen days when he publicly defended the right of a protester to call King George III a fool and compare him to the pope. This experience converted him to the colonial cause and when the Continental Army invaded Quebec to liberate it from the British, Franks joined the revolutionaries. He was appointed paymaster of the Continental Army in Quebec

and apparently used his own money to pay the salaries of the American troops.

After the American campaign in Canada faltered, Franks joined the retreat to Philadelphia, reaching it in July 1776. He joined the Continental Army and in October 1777, because he spoke French, was assigned as liaison officer to the Comte d'Estaing, commander of the French naval forces fighting on the American side. Promoted to the rank of major, Franks was then assigned as aide-de-camp to Benedict Arnold, the military governor of Philadelphia. When Arnold alienated several of the city's leading merchants, General George Washington made him commander of the strategic garrison at West Point, which controlled access to the upper reaches of the Hudson River.

David Salisbury Franks naturally fell under suspicion of complicity once Arnold's treason became known. To make matters worse, he was probably confused with his Tory uncle David Franks of New York City. Eventually, a court martial found the charges against David Salisbury Franks unfounded and dropped them. Remarkably, Benedict Arnold himself wrote a letter from a British ship exonerating Franks. One can imagine, however, that a reference from Arnold did little to restore Franks's good name.

After Franks returned to active duty,

Washington had him assigned to his command. However, the other officers of Franks's regiment started a whispering campaign against him. Seeking to clear his name definitively, Franks asked General Washington to convene another court martial to investigate—rather than simply drop—the charges against him.

After a month-long investigation, the court issued a thorough report completely exonerating Franks. A promotion immediately followed. Franks was entrusted by the State Department to carry highly secret documents to diplomats Benjamin Franklin in Paris and John Jay in Madrid. In 1783, Franks returned to Philadelphia, but he soon left for Paris to deliver to Franklin the ratified peace treaty that ended the war and granted American independence. According to his accounts, Franks often paid more of his expenses than his beloved young nation could afford to reimburse.

At war's end, Franks was appointed American vice-consul in Marseilles, France. In 1786, he was appointed to the American diplomatic team that negotiated a trade treaty between the United States and the potentate of Morocco. Nonetheless, political opponents pursued David S. Franks. To a degree not comprehensible today, politics in the 1780s was a "blood sport" in which it was commonplace to attack opponents with accusations of vile moral corruption. Despite his exoneration, the Jeffersonian Republicans continued to attack Franks for his association with Benedict Arnold. In 1786, the attacks succeeded and Franks was dismissed from the diplomatic corps. He returned to the United States discredited and bankrupt.

Once more, Franks fought to restore his reputation. Several times, he petitioned President Washington for reappointment to the diplomatic service. Finally, in 1789, Congress granted Franks 400 acres of land in recognition of his service during the Revolutionary War. His last post was that of assistant cashier of the Bank of the United States in Philadelphia.

His fortune gone, David Salisbury Franks died of yellow fever in October of 1793 at the age of fifty-three. A Christian neighbor rescued his corpse from the coroner's wagon before it went to potter's field. Franks today lies buried today in Philadelphia's Christ Church Burial Yard, saved from the pauper's fate but not among his fellow Jews.

Like so may other "minor" patriots, Franks's name is not well known today. His courage, loyalty and willingness to expend his personal fortune for the cause of independence, plus his dogged determination to clear his name, deserve remembrance. Had he not had the bad fortune to be assigned to serve under the infamous Benedict Arnold, he might rank in fame with Haym Salomon as a Jewish patriot of the American Revolution.

Sponsored by Norman Klein and Ellie Black

5

Benjamin Nones:
"I am a Jew… I am a Republican… But I am poor"

Pollsters report that Americans are tired of political campaigns rife with smear tactics and attack ads. They long for candidates to focus on issues rather than personalities, to debate substance rather than mount character assassinations.

This preference for polite campaigning is relatively new to American politics and reflects a desire for civility in public life unknown in previous eras. In the early Republic, for example, the first two political parties, the Federalists and the Jeffersonian Republicans (now called the Democrats), routinely and falsely charged one another with corruption, sexual scandal and even treason. In Philadelphia in 1800, the Federalists introduced anti-Semitism into the political fray by attacking Benjamin Nones.

Born in France in 1757, Nones immigrated to Philadelphia around 1772. When the Revolutionary War broke out, Nones fought for his adopted nation. In 1777, he saw heavy action as part of the so-called Pulaski Legion, earning the rank of major with a citation for bravery. After the war, Nones returned to Philadelphia a war hero, but had to struggle to make a living. As a notary public and government interpreter, he barely earned enough to feed his growing family, which eventually numbered fourteen children. Nonetheless, he was active in civic and Jewish communal affairs, serving as an officer of the Society of Ezrath Orchim, the first organized Jewish charity in Philadelphia, and as president of Congregation Mikveh Israel. He was also an active member of an anti-slavery society.

Philadelphia was riven by political rivalries throughout the 1790s and Nones fought in the thick of the fray. The conservative Federalists, representing the interests of merchants and financial speculators, were battling the Jeffersonian Republicans, who presented themselves as the party of small businessmen, farmers, artisans, and laborers. Many Jews in the young nation leaned toward the Jeffersonians, considering them more favorable to religious liberty for minorities. The Federalists responded to the Jewish penchant for Jeffersonianism with a barrage of anti-Semitic attacks.

In August 1800, Benjamin Nones became a Federalist target. That summer, he participated in a Republican convention in Philadelphia. The city's leading Federalist newspaper, the *Gazette,* published a scurrilous account of the meeting, calling those who attended "the filth of society." It singled out Nones for its ugliest attack. The paper singled out Citizen N———," for being "a Jew, a Republican, and poor," the three worst epithets in the Federalist lexicon.

Nones immediately penned an impassioned response. When the *Gazette* refused to print it, even as a paid article, he took it to the *Aurora,* the city's Jeffersonian newspaper, which happily printed it. Although hot with indignation, Nones's reply conveys a dignity that transcends the two centuries since it first appeared.

> I *am* a *Jew.* I glory in belonging to that persuasion, which even its opponents, whether Christian, or Mahomedan [*sic*], allow to be of divine origin—of that persuasion on which Christianity itself was originally founded, and must ultimately rest—which has preserved its faith secure and undefiled, for near three thousand years, whose votaries have never murdered each other in religious wars, or cherished the theological hatred so general, so inextinguishable among those who revile them. . . .

> I am a *Republican!* . . . I have not been so proud or so prejudiced as to renounce the cause for which I have *fought,* as an American throughout the whole of the revolutionary war. . . . I am a Jew, and if for no other reason, for that reason am I a republican. . . . In republics we have *rights,* in monarchies we live but to experience *wrongs.* . . . How then can a Jew but be a Republican? . . .

> But I am *poor,* I am so, my family also is large, but soberly and decently brought up. They have not been taught to revile a Christian because his religion is not *so old* as theirs.

Nones's letter breathes the fire of pride in his religion and nation. His manifesto links American Jewry with the ideals of democratic government, individual liberty and toleration. His words establish Nones as both a distinguished Jew and a patriot.

In honor of Kenneth J. Bialkin

6

Uriah P. Levy:
From Cabin Boy to Commodore

In 1802, a ten-year-old boy ran away from his Philadelphia home and, against his parents' wishes, went to sea. Across the next six decades, Uriah Philips Levy (1792–1862) rose from cabin boy to become the first Jewish commodore in the United States Navy. His career placed him in the forefront of the struggle against anti-Semitism and class discrimination in the military. He, more than any other, brought an end to flogging as a mode of naval discipline. Uriah P. Levy's story is one of the most complex and compelling tales of nineteenth-century American Jewry.

Two years after running away, Levy returned to his family, reportedly to prepare for his bar mitzvah. After the ceremony, Levy's parents accepted his seagoing ambitions and apprenticed him to the owner of a commercial fleet. When the War of 1812 broke out, Levy volunteered for the U.S. Navy as a sailing master, a dangerous position that Levy thought "furnished the best proof . . . of love for my country." Captured after sinking more than twenty vessels in the English Channel, Levy and his surviving crewmates spent sixteen months in Britain's Dartmoor Prison.

Released from Dartmoor after the war, Levy returned to sea on the *U.S.S. Franklin*. In 1816, in recognition of his "extraordinary service and extraordinary merit," the Navy commissioned Levy as a lieutenant, a rare distinction for an ex-cabin boy and sailing master. Some of Levy's fellow officers spurned him as a "damned Jew." Others resented him because they had attained their rank via the traditional gentlemanly path, entering the service as commissioned midshipmen. To many of his naval colleagues, Levy, Jew and former cabin boy, could be neither an officer nor a gentleman. He would later introduce an apprentice system on his ships that opened greater democratic access to naval careers.

In 1837, despite discrimination, Levy was promoted to the rank of commander, and in 1838 he was made captain of the warship *Vandalia*. In this command, he pioneered a new approach to naval discipline that won his crew's loyalty through fairness rather than fear of corporal punishment. Most dramatically, he virtually abolished flogging aboard the *Vandalia*. In 1849, someone anonymously published a now-famous tract, "Essay on Flogging in the Navy . . . and Suggested Substitutes for the Discipline of the Lash." Historians consider Levy its author, especially because the following year he supported a congressional bill outlawing corporal punishment in the Navy. Since many sailors were young boys, Levy's advocacy of nonviolent discipline at sea was, in a sense, one of the nation's earliest public protests against child abuse.

Ironically, Levy himself was repeatedly disciplined. Though an excellent sailor, he was pugnacious, quick to anger, difficult to work with, and sensitive about his Judaism. Between 1827 and 1857, he was halled before six courts-martial and one disciplinary proceeding. Six guilty findings were returned against him, although the president of the United States personally overturned two.

In 1855, the Navy notified the sixty-three-year-old Levy and 200 other officers that they were no longer needed and summarily "stricken from the rolls" of active officers. When Congress reviewed this action, Levy testified that anti-Semitism had plagued his career. "I was raised in the faith of my ancestors," Levy told the committee, and "in deciding to adhere to it, I have but exercised a right, guaranteed by the Constitution . . . a right given to all men by their Maker—a right more precious to each of us than life itself." Congress restored him to active duty in 1858.

The high point in Levy's stormy career occurred soon afterwards. He took command of the *Macedonia*, then patrolling the Mediterranean. In 1859, the secretary of the navy named him commodore of the Mediterranean Squadron, the first Jew to hold so high a rank in the U.S. Navy. Upon his return to Washington in 1860, Levy authored the Navy's official rules of engagement, *A Manual of Rules for Men-of-War*.

Had Levy done no more than attain high rank after overcoming discrimination, he would deserve a place in American Jewish history. In 1836, however, Uriah P. Levy purchased Thomas Jefferson's former Virginia estate, Monticello, and the story of his and his family's efforts to preserve it earned Uriah P. Levy a place in the broader narrative of American history. (See the next chapter).

Sponsored by Eugene and Emily Grant in memory of Jack D. Weiler

7

The Levy Family and Monticello

J. M. Levy

Monticello in Virginia is remembered today as Thomas Jefferson's home and this nation's finest architectural expression of Enlightenment ideals. It is less well remembered that, for nearly a century, America's first Jewish naval commodore, Uriah Phillips Levy (1792–1862), and members of his family preserved Monticello.

Jefferson died in 1826, leaving a debt-burdened Monticello to his daughter. She sold it in 1831 to a private owner, who ran down the property. Around this time, the Marquis de Lafayette wrote Uriah P. Levy to ask what had become of Jefferson's beloved estate. Levy replied that he would find out. He made up his mind to acquire Monticello in tribute to Jefferson's ideals of religious liberty (see page 60).

When Uriah Levy purchased Monticello in 1836, almost no original fur-nishings remained and the grounds were overgrown. Levy restored the house and gardens and purchased back some of the original furnishings. He invited his elderly mother, Rachel Machado Phillips Levy (1769–1839), to spend her last years there. Today, visitors to Monticello visit Rachel's gravesite on the grounds.

Uriah P. Levy died in 1862, leaving Monticello to the "People of the United States" for use as an agricultural school for orphans of naval warrant officers. Uriah's wife, Virginia (1835–1925), and other members of his family contested the will.

In March 1863, Congress voted to accept Levy's gift, but subsequently renounced it because of cash shortages caused by the Civil War. That same year, Confederate soldiers occupied Monticello and despoiled it, further complicating matters. For nearly two decades, court battles pitted Virginia Levy against Uriah's brother Jonas (1807–1883) and several other family members. The courts ruled in favor of Jonas, but some members of the family battled on. In the early 1870s, Jonas's son Jefferson Monroe "J. M." Levy (1852–1924) began buying out the other heirs and by 1881 he owned Monticello outright.

J. M. Levy set about restoring the house and grounds. J. M. believed that private ownership of the home, with controlled visitor access, was the best way to preserve it. Others took a different view.

In 1911, Mrs. Martin Littleton, wife of a New York congressman, campaigned to establish Monticello as a national memorial. Mrs. Littleton testified vigorously in Congress against Levy's care of the estate and urged the government to expropriate it. She was particularly offended that the home contained portraits of the Levy family alongside those of the Jeffersons.

Levy proved a formidable defender of private property rights. He unequivocally told Congress he would not sell on both constitutional and sentimental grounds. The House Interior Committee nonetheless recommended taking Monticello by eminent domain. The story became front-page news. In scrapbooks he donated to the American Jewish Historical Society, J. M. Levy collected virtually every newspaper and magazine report of the campaign for and against him.

Reluctant to confiscate private property in peacetime, the House of Representatives voted down the Interior Committee's recommendation. Mrs. Littleton then offered to raise private funds to buy the estate. J. M. Levy remained firm. "When the White House is for sale," he curtly informed her, "then I will consider an offer for the sale of Monticello."

Two years later, in ill health, J. M. relented and offered to sell Monticello to the federal government to become a presidential summer home. In 1916, Congress approved the amicable purchase of Monticello. Once again, however, events intervened. With America's entry into World War I, the funds were diverted and never reappropriated. After the war, several foundations tried and failed to raise funds for the purchase. Finally, in 1923, the New York City–based Thomas Jefferson Memorial Fund united all the interested parties and raised enough to meet Levy's asking price. Felix Warburg, one of several Jewish philanthropists who contributed to the fund, wrote that the project reflected Jeffersonian ideals of "civil liberty, religious freedom and universal education."

J. M. Levy died a year later. As a matter of policy, the foundation "did not want [Monticello] to be a Levy shrine" and sold the family's pictures and furnishings at auction. Only the gravestone of Rachel Levy was left to mark the presence of the family that had owned and preserved Monticello for eighty-seven years.

In 1985, the Thomas Jefferson Foundation placed a marker at Rachel Levy's gravesite that reads: "At two crucial periods in the history of Monticello, the preservation efforts and stewardship of Uriah P. and Jefferson M. Levy successfully maintained the property for future generations." In 2001 the foundation published a full-length monograph on the topic, concluding a contentious episode in American history.

Sponsored by Mr. & Mrs. Joe Metz in memory of their parents, Rhetta and Barney Plough and Myrtle S. and Irving Metz, Sr.

8

Solomon Carvalho:
Artist-Hero of the Wild West

Born in Charleston, South Carolina, in 1816, Solomon Nunes Carvalho was descended from a famous Sephardic family. Devoted to fine art, literature, and the study of Judaic texts, Carvalho taught himself to paint and aspired to make his living as a portrait artist. He apprenticed as a daguerreotypist under Samuel F. B. Morse and became an innovative photographic pioneer. It comes as some surprise, therefore, that this urbane, scholarly easterner became a hero of the Wild West.

In 1853, Colonel John C. Frémont, a renowned explorer and Indian fighter, asked Carvalho to join his fifth and final expedition to map the American West. Frémont hoped to find a railroad route across the Continental Divide that could be crossed by transcontinental trains in the snowy depths of the Colorado winter. Frémont recruited Carvalho as the expedition's official photographer to record the route the railroad would follow. Without consulting his wife or children, Carvalho accepted.

Little did Carvalho know what hardships he would face. His daguerreotype equipment was heavy and cumbersome. The extremely cold temperatures, which sometimes dipped to 30 below zero, slowed the daguerreotype process so that making one image sometimes took more than an hour. Carvalho's twenty-one fellow trekkers resented waiting in the frigid temperatures while he finished. Despite the challenges, Carvalho was one of the first photographers of the Rockies and their Indian residents.

In December 1853, the party began to run out of supplies. To preserve the pack animals, Carvalho abandoned his photographic equipment. When the food was gone, the explorers slaughtered the horses and mules. Carvalho at first declined to consume their flesh because of his religious principles but finally decided that Judaism required him to eat rather than die. At one point, Frémont extracted a promise from each of the men that they would not cannibalize each other. Carvalho later wrote of one harrowing night in his best-selling account of the expedition, *Incidents of Travel and Adventure in the Far West* (1856):

> One of my feet was badly frozen, and I walked with much pain and difficulty. . . . I was the last man on the trail, and my energy and firmness almost deserted me. Alone, disabled, with no possible assistance from mortal man, I felt my last hour had come. . . . I [finally] came into camp about ten o'clock at night. It requires a personal experience to appreciate the intense mental suffering which I endured that night.

Carvalho weighed 150 pounds when the expedition began; he arrived in the Mormon settlement of Parawan, Utah, in February 1854, weighing less than 100. The residents of Parawan nursed Carvalho and the others back to health, and in April Carvalho traveled north to Salt Lake City to meet Brigham Young, the Mormon leader. The highly religious Young took an immediate liking to Carvalho, who was, like Young, a biblical scholar. Young asked Carvalho to join him at a meeting with Walkara, chief of the Ute Indians, with whom the Mormons had clashed. Carvalho sat sketching Young and Walkara as they discussed the tension between their communities. After an all-night session, the two leaders smoked a peace pipe together, a ceremony in which Carvalho joined.

Restored to health, Carvalho left Utah and journeyed to Los Angeles where he helped found the first Jewish organization in that city, the Los Angeles Hebrew Benevolent Society. Carvalho soon returned to his wife and family and settled in Baltimore, where he was instrumental in founding a synagogue, Beth Israel, which was one of the first in America to include prayers in English in its weekly ritual.

By 1870, eyesight failing, Carvalho could no longer paint. The artist-adventurer became an inventor and patented an innovative pressurized steam engine that reaped him great financial rewards. Carvalho lived until 1897 and is buried in the cemetery belonging to Congregation Shearith Israel in New York. His paintings and photographs are now treasured.

Ironically, the daguerreotypes from the Frémont expedition for which Carvalho and the others had sacrificed so much are lost, although a few were published in Carvalho's book. Frémont claimed that the originals were destroyed in a warehouse fire. Some experts suspect that they lie in an unopened crate in the Library of Congress. Despite Carvalho's later fame as a painter and his success as an inventor, no period of his life compared in excitement to his courageous months making those lost daguerreotypes.

Sponsored by the Jesselson Family

47

9

August Bondi:
The Jew Who Fought Beside John Brown

August Bondi

John Brown (1800–1859), the radical aboli-tionist, remains one of the most controversial figures in American history. Some see him as a principled freedom fighter, others as an outlaw. Brown led the anti-slavery Free State forces in "Bloody Kansas," which many historians define, in effect, as a rehearsal for the Civil War. Brown reached the height of his notoriety in a raid on the federal arsenal at Harpers Ferry, Virginia, in 1859, for which he was executed.

It is not well known that three immigrant Jews were among Brown's small band of antislavery fighters in Kansas: Theodore Wiener, from Poland; Jacob Benjamin, from Bohemia; and August Bondi (1833–1907),

from Vienna. Of the three, August Bondi left the most enduring mark on American Jewish history. None of the three accompanied Brown in the Harpers Ferry raid.

In contrast to Brown, whose ancestors arrived in America on the *Mayflower*, Bondi's family emigrated from Vienna to St. Louis in 1848, in the aftermath of an unsuccessful revolt in Austria. Bondi had been a member of the student revolutionary movement in Vienna and his idealism carried over to his adopted country. In 1855, he moved to Kansas to help establish the Free State movement. The Kansas-Nebraska Act of 1854 decreed that in 1855 the settlers in the Kansas Territory would decide by vote

48

whether Kansas would be a slave or free state. Pro-slavery Border Ruffians and anti-slavery Free Staters poured into Kansas Territory, each side hoping to capture the election.

At first, the anti-slavery forces appeared to hold the upper hand, but on election day some 5,000 heavily armed pro-slavery Missourians swarmed into the territory, overwhelmed the polling places, captured the ballot boxes, and elected a pro-slavery legislature. Once in control of the state government, the pro-slavery forces launched violent attacks against anti-slavery settlers.

John Brown moved to Kansas in 1855 and soon became enraged by the pro-slavery government's mistreatment of the anti-slavery majority. In May 1856, Brown led a raid on a company of Border Ruffians at Pottawatomie Creek and massacred more than a dozen of its members. The next day, Brown and his men captured forty-eight pro-slavery fighters at the Battle of Black Jack, a few miles from Palmyra, Kansas.

August Bondi, Jacob Benjamin and Theodore Weiner fought with Brown at Black Jack. In Bondi's account of the battle, which can be found in his papers at the American Jewish Historical Society, he recalls marching up a hill beside Brown, ahead of the other men:

> We walked with bent backs, nearly crawled, that the tall dead grass of the year before might somewhat hide us from the Border Ruffian marksmen, yet the bullets kept whistling. . . . Wiener puffed like a steamboat, hurrying behind me. I called out to him, "Nu, was meinen Sie jetzt" ["Now, what do you think of this?"]. His answer, "Sof odom muves" [a Hebrew phrase meaning "the end of man is death," or in modern phraseology, "I guess we're up against it"].

Bondi later wrote of Brown's leadership:

> We were united as a band of brothers by the love and affection toward the man who, with tender words and wise counsel . . . prepared a handful of young men for the work of laying the foundation of a free Commonwealth . . . . He expressed himself to us that we should never allow ourselves to be tempted by any consideration, to acknowledge laws and institutions to exist as of right, if our conscience and reason condemn them.

John Brown left Kansas to make his quixotic attack on Harpers Ferry. Captured, Brown was tried and hanged for treason. Benjamin only lived until 1866, and Weiner died in obscurity in 1906. August Bondi remained true to his convictions and continued to support the anti-slavery cause in Kansas. When the Civil War broke out, he was one of the first to enlist, serving as a first sergeant in the Kansas Cavalry. After the war, Bondi settled in Salina, Kansas, where he served as land clerk, postmaster, member of the school board, director of the state board of charities, a local court judge and as trustee of the Kansas Historical Society. He was known for his political integrity and idealism.

Bondi, who died in 1907, described himself as a "consistent Jew" throughout his life, although Salina was too much a frontier community to support a synagogue. When his daughters married, the family traveled to Leavenworth, Kansas, so that a rabbi could officiate. Although his funeral was held at the Salina Masonic Hall, a rabbi from Kansas City conducted the service.

August Bondi's life traced a remarkable path from guerrilla fighter against slavery to distinguished elected official and pillar of the community. Even in an age and place that could be inhospitable to Jews, Bondi always identified publicly and proudly with his heritage.

Sponsored by Jean and Sam Frankel

49

11

Judah Benjamin,
The Jewish Confederate

Confederate two dollar bill, 1862 with image of J. P. Benjamin.

One of the most misunderstood figures in American Jewish history is Judah P. Benjamin (1811–1884), whom some historians call the brains of the Confederacy, even as others blame him for the South's defeat. Born in the West Indies in 1811 to observant Jewish parents, Benjamin was raised in Charleston, South Carolina. A brilliant child, at age fourteen he entered Yale Law School and, on graduation, practiced law in New Orleans. A founder of the Illinois Central Railroad, a state legislator, a planter who owned 140 slaves until he sold his plantation in 1850, Judah Benjamin was elected to the United States Senate from Louisiana in 1852. When the slave states seceded in 1861, Confederate President Jefferson Davis appointed him attorney general, making Benjamin the first Jew to hold a cabinet-level office in an American government and the only Confederate cabinet member who did not own slaves. Benjamin later served as

the Confederacy's secretary of war and then as its secretary of state.

For a man of such prominence, Benjamin's kept his personal life and views somewhat hidden. In her autobiography, Jefferson Davis's wife, Varina, informs us that Benjamin spent twelve hours a day at her husband's side, tirelessly shaping every important Confederate policy. Yet Benjamin never spoke publicly or wrote about his role in the South's government and burned his personal papers before his death, allowing both his contemporaries and later historians to interpret him as they wished, usually unsympathetically.

During the Civil War, many Southerners blamed Benjamin for their nation's misfortunes. The Confederacy lacked the men and matériel to defeat the Union armies, and when President Davis decided in 1862 to let Roanoke Island fall into Union hands without mounting a defense rather than reveal the South's weakness, Benjamin, as Davis's loyal secretary of war, accepted responsibility and resigned. Anti-Semitism was an unpleasant fact, North and South, during the Civil War years, and Benjamin was falsely defamed as having weakened the Confederacy by transferring its funds to personal bank accounts in Europe.

After Benjamin resigned as secretary of war, Davis appointed him secretary of state. According to Eli Evans, Benjamin's most perceptive biographer, "Benjamin served Davis as his Sephardic ancestors had served the kings of Europe for hundreds of years, as a kind of court Jew to the Confederacy. An insecure President [Davis] was able to trust him completely because, among other things, no Jew could ever challenge him for leadership of the Confederacy." Near the end of the war, Benjamin privately persuaded Robert E. Lee that the South's best chance was to emancipate any slave who volunteered to fight for it. When Benjamin repeated this proposal to an audience of 10,000 in Richmond in 1864, his remarks lit a firestorm. Georgian Howell Cobb observed, "If slaves will make good soldiers, our whole theory of slavery is wrong." As Evans comments, "The South chose [instead] to go down in defeat with the institution of slavery intact."

When John Wilkes Booth assassinated Lincoln in 1865, Davis and Benjamin were suspected of having been involved in the plot, and with the martyred Lincoln being compared to Christ in the Northern press, Benjamin was pilloried as Judas Iscariot. Fearing that he would not be given a fair trial if charged with Lincoln's murder, Benjamin fled to England, where he lived out his life as a barrister, publishing a classic legal text on the sale of personal property.

Evans speculates that if Benjamin had been captured by Union troops, the United States might have had its own Dreyfus trial.

A solitary man, estranged from his wife, Benjamin died alone in England. His daughter buried him in the Catholic Père Lachaise Cemetery in Paris. Until 1938, when the Paris chapter of the Daughters of the Confederacy provided an inscription with his American name, his tombstone simply said "Philippe Benjamin."

While Judah Benjamin preferred obscurity, his prominence as a Jew ensured that he would come under harsh scrutiny during and after his life. For example, on the floor of the Senate, Ben Wade of Ohio once charged him, as a defender of slavery, with being an "Israelite in Egyptian clothing." Benjamin replied, "It is true that I am a Jew, and when my ancestors were receiving their Ten Commandments from the immediate hand of Deity, amidst the thundering and lightnings of Mount Sinai, the ancestors of the distinguished gentleman who is opposed to me were herding swine in the forests of Scandinavia."

In the epic poem *John Brown's Body*, Stephen Vincent Benét depicts Judah Benjamin as "other" in Confederate inner circles:

Judah P. Benjamin, the dapper Jew,
Seal-sleek, black-eyed, lawyer and epicure,
Able, well-hated, face alive with life,
Looked round the council-chamber with the slight
Perpetual smile he held before himself
continually like a silk-ribbed fan.
. . . [His] quick, shrewd fluid mind
Weighed Gentiles in an old balance . . .
The eyes stared, searching.
"I am a Jew. What am I doing here?"

Sponsored by Eli N. Evans

1

Isachar Zacharie:
Lincoln's Chiropodist and Spy

In early 1863, a friend discussed with Abraham Lincoln the idea of restoring European Jewry to its ancient homeland in Palestine. Lincoln agreed that a Jewish state in the Holy Land merited consideration. "I myself have regard for the Jews," he said. "My chiropodist is a Jew, and he has so many times 'put me on my feet' that I would have no objection to giving his countrymen 'a leg up.'"

Lincoln was referring to Isachar Zacharie, his foot doctor and confidant. Born in England, Zacharie never attended college or medical school but was trained in chiropody and called himself a doctor. He immigrated to America in the mid-1840s and worked in several cities before settling in Washington in 1862. Before mass-pro-duced shoes were perfected, many people suffered pain caused by ill-fitting footwear. Zacharie's reputation for treating foot pain brought him Secretary of War Edwin M. Stanton, Secretary of State William Henry Seward and eventually President Lincoln as clients.

Zacharie and Lincoln talked while Zacharie worked on the president's feet and in due course became good friends. Lincoln sought Zacharie's opinions, especially on Jewish affairs. At the end of 1862, Lincoln asked Zacharie to go to New Orleans, which had been captured by Union troops. Zacharie was to mingle with Southern whites and assess their sentiments toward General Nathaniel P. Banks, commander of the Department of the Gulf, which included

New Orleans, and toward the Union.

Zacharie recruited peddlers to gather information on Confederate troop movements and other matters. Zacharie met with local white people to gauge their feelings toward the Union (especially toward Union soldiers, some of whom were blacks) and watched for contraband shipments. He helped New Orleans Jews deal with the wartime shortages. He also advised Lincoln to rescind General Ulysses S. Grant's infamous expulsion of Jews from the Department of the Tennessee (see page 118).

In mid-1863, recognizing Zacharie's gift for diplomacy, General Banks enlisted him to open communication with Confederate leaders that might lead to a negotiated settlement of the war. After establishing contacts in Richmond, the Confederate capital, Zacharie reported to Lincoln and Seward on the possibility of initiating peace talks. Seward was enthusiastic, but other members of the cabinet strongly objected. Lincoln seized the initiative and, in the fall of 1863, personally issued Zacharie a pass to the Confederacy. In Richmond, Zacharie met with Confederate Secretary of State Judah P. Benjamin (like Zacharie, a Jew). He reported that the Confederates agreed to have General Banks represent the Union in peace talks, but once again members of Lincoln's cabinet rejected negotiations.

There is no archival copy of Zacharie's report, but according to the *New York Herald,* Zacharie proposed that the Federal government pardon the Confederates and transport them to Mexico, where they would expel the French-supported government of Emperor Maximillian and make Jefferson Davis president. The Southern states would then return to the Union. Whether any of this is true cannot be established, and whether such a remarkable idea would have been acceptable to North and South, much less the Mexicans, can only be surmised. In any event, nothing came of Zacharie's peace initiative.

Zacharie gave up being a peacemaker and returned to work as a chiropodist, opening a new office in Philadelphia. After briefly backing Banks for president in 1864, he campaigned for Lincoln, urging Jews to reelect the Great Emancipator. Using his influence with Lincoln to help his co-religionists, Zacharie persuaded the president to pardon Goodman L. Mordecai, a South Carolina Confederate, from a Union prison. Zacharie took Mordecai to the White House to personally thank the president.

A few months later, John Wilkes Booth assassinated Lincoln and Zacharie lost his White House access. In 1872, with Banks's support, Zacharie applied to Congress for $45,000 for having treated the feet of 15,000 Union soldiers. The Democratic press skewered Zacharie as a conniving "toe-nail trimmer." Zacharie insisted that he be paid for the value of the services he had performed. A congressional claims committee rejected his petition. He returned to England in 1874 and resided there until his death in 1897.

Whatever his political opponents thought of the chiropodist, Abraham Lincoln trusted Zacharie. In the words of the *New York World,* he "enjoyed Mr. Lincoln's confidence more than any other private individual . . . [and was] perhaps the most favored family visitor at the White House." Most important, Zacharie employed this privilege to aid his co-religionists, much to their benefit.
Sponsored by the Benjamin and Susan Shapell Foundation, Inc.

1

"To Bigotry No Sanction:" George Washington's Letter to the Newport Congregation

On August 17, 1790, Moses Seixas, the warden of Congregation Kahal Kadosh Yeshuat Israel, the Hebrew Congregation of Newport, Rhode Island, penned an epistle to George Washington, welcoming the newly elected first president of the United States on his forthcoming visit to that city. Invaded and occupied by the British and blockaded by the American navy, Newport had suffered greatly during the Revolutionary War. Hundreds of residents had fled, and many of those who remained were Tories. After the British defeat, the Tories fled in turn. The people of Newport were eagerly looking forward to the impending presidential visit but, as things turned out, the town's economy never recovered from the wartime interruptions and dislocations

Washington's visit to Newport was part of a goodwill tour the president was making on behalf of the new national government created in 1787. Newport had historically been a good home to its Jewish residents, who numbered approximately a hundred at the time of Washington's visit. The Newport Christian community accepted Jewish worship, even though at this time individual Jews did not possess full voting and office-holding rights in Rhode Island (see page 12). The Jews of Newport looked to the new national government, and particularly to the enlightened president of the United States, to remove the last of the barriers to religious liberty and civil equality confronting Rhode Island and American Jewry.

Moses Seixas's letter on behalf of the Newport congregation—he described them as "the children of the Stock of Abraham"—expressed the Jewish community's esteem for President Washington. They fervently believed, he said, that the God of Israel, who had protected King David in ancient times, had also protected Washington during the war, and that the same spirit which had resided in the bosom of the prophet Daniel and allowed him to govern over the "Babylonish Empire" now rested upon the new nation's president. While everywhere else in the world Jews lived under the rule of monarchs, potentates, and despots, the members of the congregation, as American citizens, were part of a great experiment: a government "erected by the Majesty of the People" to which Newport Jewry could look to ensure their "invaluable rights as free citizens."

Seixas elaborated his vision of the American polity in terms that have become a part of the national lexicon. He beheld in the United States

> A Government which to bigotry gives no sanction, to persecution no assistance—but

generously affording to All liberty of conscience, and immunities of citizenship: — deeming every one, of whatever nation, tongue or language equal parts of the great Governmental Machine: — This so ample and extensive federal union whose basis is Philanthropy, mutual confidence, and public virtue, we cannot but acknowledge to be the work of the Great God, who ruleth the Armies of Heaven, and among the Inhabitants of the Earth, doing whatsoever seemeth [to Him] good.

In closing, Seixas asked God to send the "Angel who conducted our forefathers through the wilderness into the promised land [to] conduct you [Washington] through all the difficulties and dangers of this mortal life." He concluded with the hope that "when like Joshua full of days, and full of honour, you are gathered to your Fathers, may you be admitted into the Heavenly Paradise to partake of the water of life, and the tree of immortality."

Not surprisingly, it is Washington's response, rather than Seixas's epistle, which is most remembered and reprinted. The president began by thanking the congregation for its good wishes and rejoicing that the hardships caused by the war had been succeeded by prosperity. Washington then borrowed ideas—and some words—directly from Seixas's letter:

> The Citizens of the United States of America have a right to applaud themselves for giving to Mankind examples of an

enlarged and liberal policy: a policy worthy of imitation. All possess alike liberty of conscience and immunities of citizenship. It is now no more that toleration is spoken of, as if it was by the indulgence of one class of people that another enjoyed the exercise of their inherent natural rights. For happily the Government of the United States, *which gives to bigotry no sanction, to persecution no assistance*, requires only that they who live under its protection, should demean themselves as good citizens.

> May the Children of the Stock of Abraham, who dwell in this land, continue to merit and enjoy the good will of the other Inhabitants; while every one shall sit under his own vine and fig tree, and there shall be none to make him afraid.

The president closed with an invocation: "May the father of all mercies scatter light and not darkness in our paths, and make us all in our several vocations useful here, and in his own due time and way everlastingly happy."

The letter, a foundation stone of American religious freedom and separation of church and state, is signed, simply, "G. Washington." Each year, Newport's Congregation Kahal Kadosh Yeshuat Israel, now known as the Touro Synagogue, rereads Washington's letter in a public ceremony. The words deserve repetition.

Sponsored by John, Diana, Mary and Sarah Herzog in loving memory of Robert and Norma Herzog

2

Jefferson and the Jews

Thomas Jefferson is deservedly a hero to American Jewry. His was one of the few voices in the early republic fervently championing equal political rights for Jews. Jefferson's Bill for Establishing Religious Freedom in Virginia is a classic statement of religious toleration. However, while Jefferson championed Jewish rights, he did so not out of respect for Judaism as a religion, but because he respected the right of the individual to hold whatever faith he or she wished.

Jefferson's advocacy of civic equality for American Jewry began as early as 1776, when he co-sponsored a bill—one the Virginia legislature ultimately defeated—that would have allowed Jews, Catholics, and other non-Protestants to be naturalized as Virginia citizens. During the debate, Jefferson quoted John Locke's argument that "neither Pagan nor Mahamedan [*sic*] nor Jew ought to be excluded from the civil rights of the Commonwealth because of his religion."

Four decades later, in 1820, Jefferson wrote to a Charleston Jewish physician, Dr. Jacob De La Motta, "Religious freedom is the most effectual anodyne against religious dissension." Jefferson told De La Motta that he was delighted to see American Jews assuming full social rights and hoped "they will be seen taking their seats on the benches of science as preparatory to their doing the same at the board of government." Subsequently, referring to the then-common practice of reading the King James version of the Bible in public schools, Jefferson expressed his belief that it was a "cruel addition to the wrongs" Jews had historically suffered "by imposing on them a course of theological reading which their consciences do not permit them to pursue." To Joseph Marx of Richmond, Jefferson expressed "regret . . . at seeing a sect [the Jews], the parent and basis of all those of Christendom, singled out for persecution and oppression."

While Jefferson advocated for the rights of Jews, he held certain aspects of Judaism in relatively low regard. In fairness, Jefferson opposed *all* religions that claimed to be based on divine revelation. He believed that God's existence had to be proven by reason and common sense, not asserted as an act of faith. A detractor of all priests, he found those of the Hebrew Bible "a bloodthirsty race, as cruel and remorseless as the being whom they represented as the family god of Abraham, of Isaac, and of Jacob, and the local God of Israel."

In 1787, Jefferson summed up his view of revelation in a letter to his nephew, warning him to be skeptical of "those facts in the Bible which contradict the laws of nature." As one example, he cited the assertion in the Book of Joshua that the sun stood still for several hours. Since that would have meant, in scientific terms, that the earth stood still, Jefferson asked his nephew to consider how the earth, spinning on its axis, could have stopped suddenly and started rotating again without enormous destruction to natural and man-made structures. Similarly, as a rationalist Jefferson doubted that God had personally inscribed the Ten Commandments on a tablet that Moses later destroyed and then rewrote.

It bothered Jefferson that the God of the ancient Hebrews was, in his words, "a being of terrific character, cruel, vindictive, capricious and unjust." He could not understand how Jews could believe that "the God of infinite justice" would "punish the sins of the fathers upon their children, unto the third and fourth generations." He agreed with John Adams that in respect to God, "the principle of the Hebrew is fear."

Moreover, Jefferson held that reason and logic demanded a belief in an afterlife, an area in which he found Judaism deficient. He argued that without fear of punishment beyond the grave, people lacked an incentive to behave well, and without hope of reuniting with loved ones, family commitments and friendships would lose their gravity. Since Judaism did not universally accept an afterlife, Jefferson thought it a religion without utility.

Despite his reservations about the "defects" of Judaism, Jefferson never wavered in his commitment to civil and religious freedom for Jews. His most notable achievement in establishing religious and civic toleration for American Jewry was his 1779 Bill for Establishing Religious Freedom in Virginia. Adopted in 1785, the bill proclaimed: "No man shall be compelled to frequent or support any religious worship, place or ministry whatsoever, nor shall be enforced, restrained, molested or burthened in his body or goods, nor shall otherwise suffer, on account of his religious opinions or belief; but that all men shall be free to profess . . . their opinions in matters of religion, and that the same shall in no wise . . . affect their civil capacities."

Two years later, in 1787, the citizens of the United States adopted the Constitution. Article VI contains the following Jefferson-inspired phrase: "No religious Test shall ever be required as a Qualification to any Office or public Trust under the United States."

Despite his attitude toward Judaism as a religion, Jefferson's advocacy of the rights of Jews—and of other religious minorities—has become the law and custom of the land. Toleration of all religions, the absence of an official religion, and the right to practice and express religious thought freely are Jefferson's legacy to America. Despite his private view of Judaism, Jefferson was indeed a most righteous Gentile.

Sponsored by Sandra and Norman Liss in memory of Michael Liss

3

The Jewish "Yentile" Governor of Utah

In 1916, Simon Bamberger ran for the office of governor of the state of Utah. Bamberger was the first non-Mormon, the first Democrat and the only Jew ever to seek that office. During the campaign, Bamberger visited a remote community in southern Utah that had been settled by immigrant Norwegian converts to Mormonism. The community's leader, a towering man, met Bamberger at the train and told him menacingly, according to historian Leon Watters, "You might yust as vell go right back vere you come from. If you tink ve let any damn Yentile speak in our meeting house, yure mistaken." Bamberger is said to have replied, "As a Jew, I have been called many a bad name, but this is the first time in my life I have been called a damned Gentile!" The Norwegian threw his arm around Bamberger and proclaimed, "You a Yew, an Israelite. Hear him men, he's not a Yentile, he's a Yew, an Israelite. Velcome my friend; velcome, our next governor." The Norwegian was right; Bamberger won the election.

From the founding of their religion in 1830, Mormons (or Latter-Day Saints, as they prefer to be called) have respected Judaism as a religion. Joseph Smith, the founder of Mormonism, proclaimed that "Lehi, a prophet of the tribe of Manasseh . . . led his tribe out of Jerusalem in the year 600 BC to the coast of America." The tenth Article of Faith of Mormonism proclaims, "We believe in the literal gathering of Israel and in the restoration of the Ten Tribes; that Zion will be built upon this [the North American] continent." In Mormon metaphor, the Utah desert was a latter-day Zion and the Great Salt Lake a latter-day Dead Sea. The Mormons who settled there under Brigham Young's leadership were, in their own minds, direct descendants of the ancient Hebrews. Accordingly, the early Mormons referred to all non-Mormons—regardless of their religion—as "Gentiles." Watters observed, "Utah is the only place in the world where Jews are Gentiles."

The pioneer Jews of Utah fared well under the Mormon majority. Because Mormon doctrine proclaimed agrarian pursuits the only respectable calling and commerce morally corrupting, the roles of shopkeeper, banker and businessman were left to Utah's Jews and other Gentiles. In early Utah, Jews and Mormons lived in symbiotic commercial harmony.

Simon Bamberger was one of the most successful Jewish Gentiles in the early history of Utah. Born in Hesse-Darmstadt, Germany, in 1846, he emigrated to America at age fourteen. After spending a few days in New York, the young Bamberger departed by train for Cincinnati. He fell asleep and missed his transfer at Columbus, Ohio. Instead, he disembarked in Indianapolis, where he had a cousin. After working in Indianapolis until the Civil War ended, Simon and his bother Herman, who had migrated after Simon, moved to St. Louis and became clothing manufacturers. On his way to Wyoming to collect a debt, Simon learned that the business had failed. He decided to travel on to Utah, as, in his own words, he "had no other objective in view."

Bamberger purchased a half-interest in a small hotel in Ogden, Utah. In his own words, "Soon thereafter an epidemic of smallpox broke out and the Union Pacific passengers were not permitted to come up to the town, so I gave up. I took the Utah Central to Salt Lake and there bought the 'Delmonico Hotel' . . . and renamed it the 'White House' in partnership with B. Cohen, of Ogden."

In 1872, Bamberger purchased an interest in a silver mine which, by 1874, made him wealthy enough to retire. However, the pioneering spirit in Bamberger was still strong. Two years later, he raised $1 million to construct a railroad to some coal mines in northern Utah and then built a second rail line to some small towns on the outskirts of Salt Lake City. Railroad competition was fierce, however, and Bamberger lost much of his fortune in the effort.

In 1910, Bamberger helped establish a Jewish agricultural colony in Clarion, Utah. In 1913 and again in 1915, when the immigrant Jewish farmers went bankrupt, Bamberger traveled east to raise funds to pay off their debts. His efforts could not save the colony, however, and it folded in 1915.

His Mormon friends noted Bamberger's civic-mindedness and urged him to run for governor. Although Bamberger was a Democrat, his policies paralleled those of Teddy Roosevelt and the Progressives. He insisted that the legislature balance the state budget, create a public utilities commission to regulate the price of electricity and gas and banned gifts by utility companies to public officials. He passed a modified line-item budget veto, created a state department of public health, instituted water conservation, and called for a longer school year, workers' compensation, the rights of unions and the nonpartisan election of judges. Bamberger, a teetotaler, supported Prohibition.

Bamberger died in 1926 and is buried in the cemetery of Congregation B'nai Israel, the first synagogue in Salt Lake City.

Sponsored by Constance and Harvey Kreuger

4

Teddy Roosevelt,
Jewish Avenger

Presidential campaign pamphlet, 1904.

In the 1890s, as Eastern European Jews poured into the tenements of New York's Lower East Side, Chicago's Maxwell Street area and similar neighborhoods in other cities, they were pressured by native-born Americans, most of whom were associated with the Republican Party, to abandon their ethnic loyalties and become "real Americans." Yet, when it was expedient, the Republicans, like the Democrats, appealed to Jewish voters on ethnic grounds. Today, we recognize that there is no conflict between being a proud Jew and a patriotic American. In the 1890s, this fact was still contested.

In late October 1899, New York's Lower East Side was flooded with handbills, printed in Yiddish, signed by "Jewish Members of the Republican State Committee." The fliers urged Jewish voters to cast their ballots for gubernatorial candidate Theodore Roosevelt, who the year before had led his Rough Riders in a courageous charge up San Juan Hill in Santiago, Cuba, during the Spanish-American War. The Rough Riders' victory combined with other American triumphs at sea and on land led Spain to surrender her empire in Cuba and the Philippines.

The Yiddish fliers bore the title, "WHO TAKES REVENGE FOR US?" Their opening sentence made the answer clear: "Every respectable citizen, every good American and every true Jew, must and will vote for the Republican gubernatorial candidate—*Theodore Roosevelt.*" In the symbolic calculus of American ethno-religious politics, America's victory over Spain was revenge for Spain's mistreatment of its Jews four centuries earlier, and candidate Roosevelt was the Jews' chief avenger.

Roosevelt was an unlikely hero for Yiddish-speaking tenement dwellers. Descended from patrician Dutch colonial forebears, Roosevelt was a wealthy, Harvard-educated outdoorsman. American politics has a way of making interesting bedfellows, however, and when Roosevelt campaigned for governor, the Republicans invoked the ghost of the fifteenth-century Spanish Inquisition to mobilize Jewish support for his candidacy.

The "Jewish Republicans" reminded (or taught) the Lower East Side "greenhorns" that, during the Inquisition, Jews had been the victims of unjust persecution. "Our ancestors," the flier noted, "were good and useful citizens."

> They made rich Spain's treasury; outfitted the ships which discovered America and gave Spain the power that made her a great nation. How did Spain reward them? Spain took away everything her Jews had, and she sent her Jews to the dungeons of the Inquisition and the fires of the auto da fé.

As if this were not enough, the flier continued, Spain's inquisitors had pursued their Jewish victims to the New World—to Brazil, Mexico, and especially Cuba—where, until its defeat in 1898, "there still rang in our ears the cries and screams of Spain's brutality." When William McKinley, the Republican president, "gave the word that Spain should move out of the New World," Secretary of the Navy Roosevelt "worked day and night until he worked out all the plans for our navy" and then, "at his

own expense organized a regiment of Rough Riders and went to the battlefield to meet the foe. . . . Under Roosevelt's command there were many Jewish Rough Riders. Roosevelt was like a brother to them. He recommended them to the president [McKinley] for promotions, and sang their praises to the world."

The flier warned that in this election, Roosevelt—and the war itself—now stood in judgment before the people of New York. Jewish voters, they made clear, had but one choice:

> Every vote for the COLONEL OF THE ROUGH RIDERS is approval of McKinley and the war. Every vote for Roosevelt's opponent . . . is a vote for Spain. . . . Can any Jew afford to vote against Theodore Roosevelt and thereby express disapproval of the war against Spain?

Roosevelt failed to carry the Lower East Side and lost New York City as a whole by 60,000 votes, but won election nonetheless, winning the rest of the state by 80,000 votes. A year later, he accepted the Republican nomination for vice president and succeeded to the presidency after McKinley's assassination in 1901. In 1904, when Roosevelt ran successfully for reelection, the Republicans once again appealed to New York's Yiddish-speaking voters to support the hero of San Juan Hill

It is the genius of America's two-party system that to win elections, Democrats and Republicans must both provide "big tents" to accommodate diverse constituencies. As the Jewish Republican campaign for Roosevelt illustrated, the need to build successful coalitions has eliminated the apparent conflict between retaining one's ethno-religious identity and being a patriot.
Sponsored by The Pumpkin Foundation

5

The Jewish Teddy Bear

Teddy bears are a symbol of gentleness and security the world over. It is well known that the teddy bear is named for President Theodore Roosevelt. Less well known are the inventors of the teddy bear, Rose and Morris Michtom, two Russian Jewish immigrants who lived in Brooklyn.

A bear is an unlikely symbol of gentleness. From time immemorial, bears have prompted fear, not affection. The teddy bear's namesake, Theodore Roosevelt, was a ferocious warrior and big game hunter—a man who killed for sport. However, an alliance between the rugged native-born Protestant president and the inventive immigrant Jewish couple from Brooklyn convert-

ed the bear into one of the most cuddly and enduring American icons.

The story begins in 1902. The states of Mississippi and Louisiana disagreed over the location of their common boundary, which bisected some of the least well developed land in the United States. The governors of the two states invited President Roosevelt to arbitrate the dispute. Roosevelt decided to combine his tour of the disputed territory with a five-day black bear hunt.

The president's foray attracted a large contingent of journalists who reported on his every move. Even more compelling to the reporters than the boundary dispute was his pursuit of a trophy bear. For four days, the press reported little about Roosevelt's arbitration of the boundary dispute and harped on the ability of the area's bears to elude his crosshairs. On the fifth and last day of the junket, apparently to redeem the president's reputation, one of his hunting companions caught and tied a bear cub to a tree so that the president could shoot it. When he came upon the cub, Roosevelt refused to kill it, saying that he only took prey that had a sporting chance to defend itself.

Roosevelt's demurrer took the nation by storm. America's most popular cartoonist, Clifford Berryman, published a drawing of Roosevelt turning his back on the young bear tied by its neck, and public response to the president's self-restraint was overwhelmingly favorable. The next day, the *Washington Post* published a second cartoon, depicting the bear as a more placid beast, cementing the docile image of the young bear even more firmly in the public imagination.

Enter the Michtoms. Morris had arrived penniless in New York in 1887, when only in his teens, a refugee from the pogroms. He married Rose and opened a small store that sold notions, candy and other penny items. In the evening, to help make ends meet, Rose sewed toys to be sold in the shop. Like millions of other Americans, the Michtoms avidly followed the press accounts of Roosevelt's journey into the Louisiana backcountry. Roosevelt's refusal to shoot the defenseless bear touched the Michtoms. Morris suggested to Rose that she sew a replica of the bear represented in Berryman's cartoons.

That night, Rose cut and stuffed a piece of plush velvet into the shape of a bear, sewed on shoe button eyes and handed it to Morris to display in the shop window. He labeled it "Teddy's bear." To his surprise, not only did someone come in and ask to buy the bear, but twelve other potential customers also wanted to purchase it. Aware that he might offend the president by using his name without permission, the Michtoms mailed the original bear to the White House, offering it as a gift to the president's children and asking Roosevelt for the use of his name. He told the Michtoms that he doubted his name would help its sales but they were free to use it if they wished.

The rest is an amazing—yet characteristic—American Jewish immigrant success story. The Michtoms churned out teddy bears, but the demand was so great they couldn't keep up. The couple concluded that teddy bears were more profitable than penny candy and dedicated full-time to producing them. Because of the doll's popularity, Roosevelt and the Republican Party adopted it as their symbol in the election of 1904, and Michtom bears were put on display at every public White House function.

The Michtoms' labor grew into the Ideal Toy Company, which remained in family hands until the 1970s. Although they sold millions of teddies throughout the world, the Michtoms were not spoiled by their good fortune. Ever mindful of their humble origins, they supported the Hebrew Immigrant Aid Society, the Jewish National Fund, the National Labor Campaign for Palestine and numerous other Jewish causes. While Ideal Toys could not obtain a patent on the teddy bear and many imitators entered the market, the Michtoms created an American—and worldwide—icon. Their original teddy bear, treasured and saved by Teddy Roosevelt's grandchildren, is now on display at the Smithsonian.

Sponsored by Mr. & Mrs. Jack Nash

6

An "Entirely Different" Jew in Congress

When Congressman Meyer London died in 1926, half a million New Yorkers attended his funeral. "For six hours," the *New York Times* reported, "the [Lower] East Side put aside its duties, pressing or trivial, to do honor to its dead prophet." Although a politician, London was so respected for his learning, even by his political opponents, that he was buried in the Writers' Lane section of Mount Carmel Cemetery, near the grave of Sholom Aleichem and other Jewish cultural heroes. London's working-class instincts and intellectual acumen made him a forceful advocate of the social legislation that later formed the heart of Franklin Roosevelt's New Deal.

Born in Russia in 1871, Meyer was the eldest son of Ephraim and Rebecca London. Both parents had strongly religious

upbringings, but Ephraim became enamored of the anarchistic and atheistic doctrines floating around tsarist Russia. He passed these radical ideas to Meyer, who later translated them, in the American political context, into moderate socialism.

A brilliant student in Russia, Meyer London received a Jewish education at home and secular education as one of the few Jewish boys chosen to attend a government-sponsored secondary school. He developed proficiency in six languages: Russian, Yiddish, English, German, French, and Italian. After the family emigrated to the Lower East Side of New York in 1888, the teenaged Meyer worked at a library, tutored students in English and attended law school at night. In 1896, at age twenty-five, Meyer London became a U.S. citizen, passed the bar exam and ran on the Socialist ticket for the Lower East Side seat in the New York State Assembly.

London entered politics in the heyday of the Tammany Hall Democratic machine, which employed bribery, fraud and pressure tactics to win elections. Running as a novice reformer on the Socialist ticket, London predictably lost to the Tammany candidate. He then focused his energies on providing legal services to Lower East Side trade unions like the ILGWU, the International Fur Workers, the Cloak Makers, and the United Hebrew Trades. According to one biographer, "London accepted only such clients and cases as would not interfere with his socialist principles, and he would never take a case involving an arrest." He preferred to work *pro bono* on union cases and, on one occasion, grateful striking union workers threatened to drop him as their lawyer if he continued to refuse the payment that they believed he deserved. From 1905 until his death, London served as legal counsel to the Workman's Circle.

London believed that workers were dehumanized by the capitalist system and that socialism offered their only chance for a better life. Running for Congress as a Socialist, he lost to Tammany-backed incumbent Henry Goldfogle in 1908, 1910, and 1912, but finally triumphed in 1914—becoming one of the few avowed Socialists ever to serve in Congress. In his native Yiddish, London told the crowd at a post-victory rally, with an implied swipe at uptown Jewry, "My person will represent an entirely different type of Jew from the kind Congress is accustomed to seeing."

Once in Washington, London sponsored legislation that met with defeat but later became an integral element of the New Deal program: minimum wage, unemployment insurance, increased taxes on the wealthy. He fought for such then-radical ideals as anti-lynching laws, larger immigration quotas and paid maternity leave. His civil rights proposals became law in the 1960s.

London's idealism was severely tested by America's entry into World War I. He viewed the war as a capitalist struggle for profits conducted at the expense of the working people on both sides. In 1917, he cast one of the few votes against entering the war. Nonetheless, when Congress approved American participation, London distressed his Socialist colleagues by voting to fund it. He explained, "I owe a duty to every man who has been called to the service of his country . . . to provide him with everything he needs [and] to get this fight over as soon as possible."

At the end of the war, London called for the "removal of the political and civic disabilities of the Jewish people wherever [they] exist." He supported the Balfour Plan and looked forward to a Jewish homeland in Palestine. As a Socialist, he once attended a congressional session on Yom Kippur. His Tammany opponent in the 1916 congressional race accused London of not being religious enough, but the Jewish voters of the Lower East Side overwhelmingly returned him to Congress for another term.

London was defeated in 1918, but won a final congressional term in 1920. At age fifty-five, he was struck by a taxicab as he crossed Second Avenue. In the ambulance, London made his wife promise not to sue the distraught cab driver. When he died shortly afterwards, his body lay in state at the Forward Building on East Broadway while tens of thousands marched by his coffin to pay their final respects.

Sponsored by Eugene and Emily Grant in memory of Jack D. Weiler

7

"Red Emma" Goldman's Jewish Anarchism

Emma Goldman was born in Kovno, Lithuania, in 1869 into a religiously traditional household. As a teenager, despite her father's wishes, she read the Russian anarchist writers Chernyshevski and Bakunin. When she expressed a desire for further education, her father told her, "Girls don't have to learn much! All a Jewish daughter needs to know is how to prepare gefilte fish, cut noodles fine and give the man plenty of children." In 1885 the strong-minded sixteen-year-old Goldman left home and boarded a ship for America, the land of freedom. By the 1890s, she had earned a reputation as "Red Emma," perhaps the most notorious radical lecturer in the United States.

Goldman spent a lifetime agitating for social justice for working people, the abolition of capitalism, freedom of spiritual and intellectual expression, free love and an end to war, racism, religious differences and ethnocentrism. However, she never forgot her Jewish identity. While she was still a child, Goldman's family had fled from Kovno to Königsberg, Germany, and then to St. Petersburg, Russia, because of anti-Semitic violence. Biographer Candace Falk notes that Judith, the heroic woman in the Apocrypha who cut off the head of Holofernes to avenge wrongs done to the Jewish people, was Goldman's female role model. Her experience of Russian violence against Jews informed her lifelong advocacy for social justice.

When she arrived in America in 1885, Goldman settled in Rochester, New York, where she worked in the garment industry and married Jacob Kersner. Soon afterwards, she was further radicalized by the hanging of seven anarchists who were convicted, on flimsy evidence, of killing two police officers by setting off a bomb in Chicago's Haymarket Square. For a time, Goldman tolerated near-starvation wages and marital strife, but in 1889 she divorced Kersner, packed her sewing machine and personal effects and moved to New York's Lower East Side in search of greater freedom and a larger platform for her anarchist views.

In New York City, anarchist newspaper editor Johann Most made Goldman a protégé. Most encouraged Goldman to agitate among Yiddish-speaking workers for a general strike and overthrow of the state. Beyond the usual anarchist protest against economic inequality, Goldman also called for "freedom, the right to self-expression [and] everybody's right to beautiful things." Goldman regularly invoked love of beauty and other higher instincts that she believed to be a common human heritage.

At this time, Goldman became involved with fellow anarchist Alexander Berkman. In 1892, the pair became incensed by the killing of strikers at Carnegie Steel's Homestead plant, near Pittsburgh. Goldman gave Berkman money to purchase a gun, which he used to wound Henry Clay Frick, the head of Carnegie Steel, in a failed assassination attempt. Berkman was sentenced to life in prison and federal authorities launched a crackdown on other anarchists. One year later, imprisoned for violating laws that prohibited anarchist speech, Goldman defiantly proclaimed that the government "can never stop women from talking."

After her release in 1895, Goldman ceased calling for assassinations and strikes and declared that "the key to anarchist revolution was a revolution in morality . . . a conquest of the 'phantoms' that held people captive," such as racism and religious intolerance. She avoided arrest until 1917, when she was jailed for speaking out against conscription in World War I. In 1919, the government deported her to Russia. Expecting to find freedom in the "workers' paradise," Goldman instead found Communist repression and lin-

gering anti-Semitism. She openly criticized Lenin for his anti-democratic policies. Disillusioned, she departed and spent her remaining days as a self-described "woman without a country." She lived for a time in Republican Spain but fled when Franco's fascists triumphed, moving to France. She continued to speak out against Stalin, Hitler, and all forms of totalitarianism.

In 1906, Goldman wrote, "Owing to a lack of a country of their own, [Jews] developed, crystallized and idealized their cosmopolitan reasoning faculty . . . working for the great moment when the earth will become the home for all, without distinction of ancestry or race." After her Soviet experience, she wrote, "When I was in America, I did not believe in the Jewish question removed from the whole social question. But since we visited some of the pogrom regions I have come to see that there *is* a Jewish question, especially in the Ukraine. . . . It is almost certain that the entire Jewish race will be wiped out should many more changes take place." Writing in 1937 after the rise of Hitler, Goldman concluded: "While I am neither Zionist nor Nationalist, I have worked for the rights of the Jews and [against] every attempt to hinder their life and development." Before she died in 1940 in Toronto, Emma Goldman—wandering Jew and anti-state radical—reluctantly acknowledged that her fellow Jews needed a refuge somewhere in the world: a nation of their own.

Goldman's speeches and writings inspired individuals as diverse as Leon Czolgosz, the 1901 assassin of President William McKinley, Roger Baldwin, founder of the American Civil Liberties Union and libertine novelist Henry Miller. In the 1960s and 1970s, her writings inspired a generation of feminists and New Left radicals. Goldman's legacy lives on.
In memory of Marvin Burko

8

Justice Cardozo, Sephardic Jew

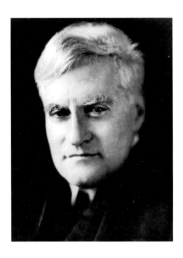

In 1932, President Herbert Hoover appointed Benjamin Nathan Cardozo to the Supreme Court of the United States. Cardozo was the second Jew, after Louis D. Brandeis, to serve on the nation's highest court. Previously, Cardozo had been a judge on the New York State Supreme Court and chief judge of the Court of Appeals. His background as a Sephardic Jew shaped his entire career.

The Cardozos were one of America's oldest and most distinguished families. Benjamin Cardozo's ancestors were numbered among the founders of Congregation Shearith Israel in New York. His eighteenth-century forebear Gershom Mendes Seixas served as the first Jewish incorporator and trustee of Columbia University; another helped found the New York Stock Exchange in 1792; and poet Emma Lazarus was his cousin.

Born in 1870, Benjamin Cardozo was the son of Judge Albert Cardozo and Rebecca Nathan. Albert Cardozo was vice president and a trustee of Congregation Shearith Israel, and Benjamin celebrated his bar mitzvah there. The family lived a life that might have been depicted in an Edith Wharton novel. However, the Cardozo family's image suffered a major setback when Albert, a Tammany Hall appointee to the bench, resigned his judgeship in 1872 just as a legislative committee was about to recommend impeaching him for nepotism.

Despite this taint of notoriety, Benjamin chose to enter the law and he proudly—one might say defiantly—entered his father's law firm upon graduation from Columbia University Law School. The young Cardozo distinguished himself as a commercial law litigator. Shy and reserved in his personal life, Cardozo was a powerful orator in the courtroom. Above all, perhaps driven to redeem his father's disgrace,

Cardozo developed a reputation for the utmost integrity.

After his bar mitzvah, Cardozo stopped attending religious services. In later life, he described himself as an agnostic but he never failed to identify himself as a proud Jew. He refused to allow pork and shellfish into his home and maintained the family pew at Shearith Israel. In 1895, at age twenty-five, he opposed the elimination of gender-segregated seating in the synagogue, a change that would have altered the Sephardic Orthodox *minhag*. Cardozo delivered a "long address," according to the congregational minutes, "impressive in ability and eloquence," which helped carry the day for the traditionalist side.

Other than serving as a trustee of Columbia University, all of Cardozo's volunteer activities were in the Jewish community. At a time when "polite" anti-Semitism was rampant among New York's social elite and Jews were virtually excluded from such venues as the New York Athletic Club and the Union League Club, Cardozo joined the Judean Club, an association "designed to gather together a body of cultured Jewish gentlemen . . . to advance the intellectual and spiritual aspirations of the Jews." Cardozo also served on the board of the American Jewish Committee and, despite his ambivalences joined the Zionist Organization of America. He wrote:

> I have signed the application with some misgiving, for I confess . . . that I am not yet an enthusiast. But today, the line seems to be forming between those who are for the cause and those who are against it, with little room for a third camp. I am not willing to join those who are against, so I go over to the others.

In the 1928 presidential contest, Cardozo privately favored Democratic candidate Al Smith against Herbert Hoover. While he respected Hoover, Cardozo wrote to a cousin, he felt that in the Republican camp "will be found all the narrow-minded bigots, all the Jew haters, all those who would make of the United States an exclusively Protestant government. . . . The defeat of Smith will be acclaimed as a great victory by . . . the friends of obscurantism." The victorious Hoover appointed Cardozo to the Supreme Court four years later, even though he had been elected to the New York bench as a Democrat.

Cardozo tried not to let his Jewish identity influence his judicial reasoning. Although an avowed opponent of the Hitler regime, he was distressed when, in 1935, New York City magistrate Louis Brodsky dismissed assault charges against five of six Jewish defendants who had stormed a German ship in New York harbor because it was flying the Nazi flag. Brodsky held that the lawbreakers were justified because the flag had provoked them, even though the U.S. government recognized Germany's National Socialist regime. Cardozo wrote:

> What is the use of striving for standards of judicial propriety if [one] condone[s] such lapses! It would have been bad enough if [Brodsky] had been a Gentile; but for a Jew it was unforgivable. Now our traducers will say—and with some right —that these are the standards of the race.

Professor Roscoe Pound of Harvard considered Cardozo one of the ten best legal minds in American history, and his writings made major contributions to the common law. As a jurist and committed Jew, Justice Cardozo brought honor to the United States and to his people.

Sponsored by Gumpel-Lurie Foundation in memory of Edgar J. Nathan, Jr.

73

9

Emanuel Celler:
A Voice for the Displaced

Congressman Emanuel Celler born in Brooklyn in 1888, embodied the American Jewish commitment to relieve the suffering of refugees and victims of persecution. His father, Henry, owned a whiskey business; during Emanuel's childhood, the Cellers' basement held a 25,000-gallon whiskey tank filled with the family brand, Echo Spring. When Henry Celler's whiskey business failed he was forced to find employment selling wine door-to-door. Soon after Emanuel graduated from public high school and entered Columbia College his father died and his mother passed away five months later. In his autobiography, *You Never Leave Brooklyn,* Emanuel Celler wrote, "I became the head of the household. . . . I took up [my father's] wine route. I went to school in the morning and sold wines all afternoon until seven o'clock in the evening." Despite these burdens, Emanuel Celler was a star student in college and in Columbia Law School, graduating from the latter in 1912.

From the very first, Manny Celler's career reflected his lifelong interest in the plight of refugees and immigrants. His earliest clients came from among his wine customers. Most of them were immigrants and more than one fell afoul of the immigration laws, but Celler worked hard to keep them from being deported for minor infractions.

During World War I, he served as an appeal agent for his local draft board. After the war, his law practice flourished and the successful attorney organized two banks and served as a director of two others.

In 1922, a political acquaintance persuaded Celler to run for Congress as a Tammany Hall Democrat. Celler enlisted friends, relatives and neighbors to canvass for him door-to-door. Although the district had never before elected a Democrat, Celler's stress on "the evils of Prohibition and the virtues of the League of Nations" enabled him to win the election by some 3,000 votes. In March of 1923, he assumed the seat that he would hold for forty-nine years and ten months, the second-longest term in congressional history.

Celler made his maiden speech on the House floor during the debate on the Johnson Immigration Act of 1924. Three years earlier, Congress had imposed a quota that restricted immigration for persons of every nationality to 3 percent of that nationality's presence in the United States in 1910, with an overall annual admission limit of 356,000 immigrants. This "national origins" system was structured to discriminate against Eastern and Southern European immigrants such as Italians, Russians, Poles, Slavs and, of course, Yiddish-speaking Jews. The Johnson Act of 1924, which Celler opposed, further cut the total annual number of immigrants and limited each nationality to 2 percent of its total number in 1890, virtually ending immigration from any country but England, France, Ireland and Germany.

The Johnson Act passed the isolationist Congress and was signed into law. Despite this setback, Celler had found his cause and, over the next four decades, he fought for the elimination of national origin as a basis for immigration restrictions. At no time were his efforts more critical than in the 1930s, when the United States, England and France, among others, proved unable or unwilling to open their doors to victims of Nazi persecution and—as was later discovered—genocide.

Celler's determination to fight immigration quotas was reinforced one Saturday during World War II, when a bearded rabbi came to his home. Celler always left the door unlocked on the Sabbath so his constituents could enter without ringing or knocking. The rabbi, in black hat and long coat, clutching a cane, spoke forcefully to Celler. "Don't you see, can't you see?" the rabbi asked, "Won't you see that there are millions—millions—being killed. Can't we save some of them? Can't you, Mr. Congressman, do something?" Celler equivocated, averring that President Roosevelt had told him that he sympathized with the plight of Europe's Jews but could not divert ships needed to transport war matériel and soldiers to bring in refugees. The rabbi's reply moved Celler to tears: "If six million

cattle had been slaughtered," the rabbi observed, "there would have been greater interest."

After the war, as chairman of the House Judiciary Committee, Celler resolved to liberalize the immigration laws. In 1946, Congress so restricted the number of displaced persons who could enter the United States that, despite the starvation in Europe, fewer than 3,000 DPs actually came to the U.S. Celler's determined efforts led to the passage in 1948 of a bill which allowed 339,000 DPs, many of them Jewish, to enter the country. Finally, in 1965, President Lyndon Johnson signed into law an act that eliminated national origins as a factor in immigration, culminating Celler's forty-one-year fight to overcome discrimination against Eastern European Jews and Catholics.

In 1981, at the age of ninety-three, Emanuel Celler passed away. Today, approximately 75 percent of American Jews are descended on at least one side of their family from Eastern European immigrants. Since 1965, the United States has been a haven for Jews escaping discrimination in the former Soviet Union. Their safe arrival, unfettered by discriminatory quotas, ratified Emanuel Celler's efforts to make America a promised land for Jewish immigrants, and for all victims of persecution.

In memory of Allen E. Elliott, father, and Ruth S. Elliott, sister, from Jeff, Audrey, Matthew and Alison Elliott

10

La Guardia 1, Hitler 0

Fiorello La Guardia chose not to wear his Jewish heritage on his sleeve. In fact, he allowed the public to identify him as Italian, not Jewish, even under the most tempting of political circumstances. When issues of Jewish interest came up in New York or national politics, however, the "Little Flower" was an ardent advocate for Jewish rights.

La Guardia was born in Greenwich Village in 1882 to a Catholic father, Achille Luigi Carlo La Guardia, and Irene Luzzato Coen, who had been raised in an observant Jewish home in Trieste. In 1880, the couple emigrated to the United States. After their third child was born, Achille joined the U.S. Army and was stationed at remote outposts in South Dakota and Arizona. In 1898, Achille became gravely ill from eating "embalmed" rations supplied to the Army and died four years later. When his son Fiorello was elected to Congress in 1922, the first bill he introduced called for the death penalty for "scavengers" who supplied tainted food to the military. The bill did not pass

but La Guardia never lost his Progressive disgust for government corruption and the ability of "the interests" to escape justice.

A superb linguist, the eighteen-year-old Fiorello became an American consular official in Budapest in 1900. Four years later, advised that his Jewish roots and lack of a Harvard degree would stunt his prospects in America's "white shoe" diplomatic service, La Guardia resigned and returned to New York. He worked for the Society for the Prevention of Cruelty for Children and as a translator for the U.S. Immigration Service while attending New York University Law School. On graduation, he specialized in protecting immigrant workers in the garment industry. Although he never earned much, La Guardia won numerous friends and a great reputation among the Lower East Side's immigrant Jewish garment workers and peddlers by representing them in court, free of charge.

In 1916, running as a Republican, La Guardia challenged the incumbent congressman from the Lower East Side, a Tammany-backed saloonkeeper named Farley. Speaking to crowds in Yiddish, Italian, and Serbo-Croatian, La Guardia defeated Farley by a narrow margin, becoming the first Italian American elected to Congress. In 1922, Tammany ran a Jewish candidate against La Guardia, circulating a flier that called him "a pronounced anti-Semite and Jew-hater." Advised to fight back by publicly announcing that his mother was Jewish, La Guardia rejected the tactic as "self-serving." Instead, he challenged his opponent to debate him in Yiddish—an offer his opponent could not accept. La Guardia won reelection.

Defeated for reelection in the Roosevelt landslide of 1932, La Guardia successfully ran for mayor of the City of New York in 1933 and became an implacable foe of Adolf Hitler and the Nazi regime. Before taking office, La Guardia called Hitler a "perverted maniac." In a public address in 1934, La Guardia warned, "Part of [Hitler's] program is the complete annihilation of the Jews in Germany." In 1937, speaking before the Women's Division of the American Jewish Congress, La Guardia called for the creation of a special pavilion at the upcoming New York World's Fair: "a chamber of horrors" for "that brown-shirted fanatic."

In response, the government-controlled press in Germany called La Guardia a "Dirty Talmud Jew," a "shameless Jew lout," and "a whoremonger." When the German ambassador officially protested to Secretary of State Cordell Hull about La Guardia's remarks, Hull replied that personally he "very earnestly deprecate[d] the utterances which have thus given offense to the German government." Nonetheless, he continued, in America the mayor of New York was free to speak his mind whatever the federal government might think. Hull complained privately to President Roosevelt that La Guardia was poisoning German-American relations, but Roosevelt asked Hull, "What would you say if I should say that I agreed completely with La Guardia?" Several months later, La Guardia visited Roosevelt and recorded the following scene:

> The president smiled as I entered his office. Then he extended his right arm and said, "Heil, Fiorello!" I snapped to attention, extended my right arm and replied, "Heil, Franklin!" And that's all that was ever said about it.

In May of 1937, news broke of a scandal in six Brooklyn public high schools in which bootleg contraceptives were being sold to students. The German press immediately blamed "the Jew La Guardia" for this episode of "hair-raising immorality." La Guardia fired back that he had no response to the charge: the only city official competent to deal with the German press allegations was the deputy sanitation commissioner in charge of sewage disposal!

In 1938, after the dismemberment of Czechoslovakia and Kristallnacht, La Guardia stepped up his attacks on the Hitler regime. At a rally of 20,000 anti-Fascists in Madison Square Garden, La Guardia proclaimed himself unable "adequately to describe the brutality of [Hitler] and his government" and called the Nazi regime a great threat to world peace. Historians David and Jackie Esposito write, "In the face of large-scale indifference to human rights violations abroad and growing isolationism at home . . . La Guardia reasserted a Progressive's faith in the rule of reason and the power of enlightened public opinion to face up to the Nazis and confront Hitler." When the United States entered the war in 1941, La Guardia's principled position was vindicated.

Sponsored by The Leo Rosner Foundation, Inc.

11

Stephen S. Wise
and the Anti-Nazi Boycott of 1933

In late January 1933, Adolf Hitler was appointed chancellor of the German Reich. Immediately, members of the Nazi Party began a campaign of violence against German Jews, socialists, communists and other opponents. Germany's Jewish Central Association (Verein) issued a statement asserting that "the responsible government authorities are unaware of the threatening situation" and the Verein had "dutifully apprised [the Hitler administration] thereof." The Verein's statement concluded, "We do not believe our German-fellow citizens will let themselves be carried away into committing excesses against the Jews." As early as 1933, however, Stephen S. Wise, founder of the American Jewish Congress, knew better.

The Central Verein's appeals did nothing to stop the terror against Jewish businesses. Stink bombs, picketing and shopper harassment by Nazi Party thugs continued for several days. Herman Goering announced, "I shall employ the police, and without mercy, wherever German people are hurt, but I refuse to turn the police into a guard for Jewish stores."

When word of the assaults reached America, representatives of the American Jewish Committee, B'nai B'rith and the American Jewish Congress met in New York to establish a joint committee to monitor the situation. They agreed that organized public protests in America would further undermine the already precarious position of German Jewry. Less than a month later, however, the American Jewish Congress changed its mind and called on its partners to help organize a protest campaign. On March 19, 1933, the organization convened an emergency conference of Jewish organizations.

At the meeting, the AJCongress announced a Madison Square Garden rally on March 27. The commander-in-chief of the Jewish War Veterans called for a boycott of German imports. The American Jewish Committee representatives counseled restraint because any rally in America "may add to the terrible dangers of the Jews in Germany." Irving Lehman pleaded, "I implore you in the name of humanity, don't let anger pass a resolution which will kill Jews in Germany."

Stephen S. Wise of the American Jewish Congress, had the final word:

> The time for prudence and caution is past. We must speak up like men. How can we ask our Christian friends to lift their voices in protest against the wrongs suffered by Jews if we keep silent? . . . What is happening in Germany today may happen tomorrow in any other land on earth unless it is challenged and rebuked. It is not the German Jews who are being attacked. It is the Jews.

The conference voted to hold the Madison Square Garden rally.

On March 27, the AJCongress and its allies convened simultaneous protest rallies at Madison Square Garden in New York and in seventy-five other cities. The New York rally was broadcast worldwide. A crowd of 55,000 inside the Garden and the streets outside heard AJCongress president Bernard Deutsch, American Federation of Labor president William Green, Senator Robert F. Wagner, former New York governor Al Smith and several Christian clergymen call for an immediate cessation to the brutal treatment of German Jewry.

The Nazis denounced the American complaints as slanders generated by "Jews of German origin." Goebbels announced a campaign of "sharp countermeasures"

against these attacks. He accused German Jewry of engineering a worldwide boycott of German goods to destroy the German economy. To give Jews a taste of their own medicine, Goebbels announced that the following Saturday, April 1, all good Aryan Germans would boycott Jewish-owned businesses. If, after the one-day boycott, the false charges against the Nazis in the overseas press stopped, there would be no further boycott of Jewish businesses. If worldwide Jewish attacks on the Nazi regime continued, Goebbels warned, "the boycott will be resumed . . . until German Jewry has been annihilated."

The boycott came off as planned. German police and S.S. troops enforced store closings. Hoodlums smashed the windows of some Jewish-owned stores and forced others to close by setting off stink bombs inside them.

Urged by Wise to protest to the German government, Secretary of State Cordell Hull issued a mild statement to the American ambassador to Berlin, complaining that "unfortunate incidents have indeed occurred and the whole world joins in regretting them." He expressed his personal belief, however, that the reports of anti-Jewish violence were probably exaggerated. Unimpressed by Hull's response, the Jewish War Veterans, the AJCongress, the American League for Defense of Jewish Rights, the Jewish Labor Committee, B'nai B'rith and others boycotted German goods.

Of course, the boycott did nothing to deter the Nazis, who steadily escalated their violence against Germany's. As Rabbi Wise observed, however, the boycott effort, whatever its effect, was a moral imperative. "We must speak out," he explained. "If that is unavailing, at least we shall have spoken."

Sponsored by Alan, Ilse, Robert and Charlotte Rosenberg

12

When the Rabbis Marched on Washington

"Make way for the rabbis!" It was probably the first time that a stationmaster at Washington's Union Station had ever shouted these words. But the crowd before him was unlike any ever seen before in the nation's capital. Four hundred rabbis converged on Union Station two days before Yom Kippur, 1943, in a united effort to rescue their fellow Jews from Nazi extermination.

The march was the brainchild of thirty-three-year-old Hillel Kook, a Jerusalem-born nephew of Abraham Isaac Kook, former chief rabbi of Palestine. Hillel Kook arrived in the United States in 1940 and he took the name Peter Bergson. Purchasing full-page ads in American newspapers criticizing Britain's restrictions on the number of Jews who could enter Palestine and pleading for Allied action to rescue European Jewry, Bergson and his associates, known as the Bergson Group, used the mass media to rouse public interest and press the Roosevelt administration to intervene against Hitler. Most provocatively, Bergson called for the formation of an international Jewish army that would fight under Allied auspices to liberate European Jewry.

One of Bergson's most spectacular initiatives was the 1943 March of the Rabbis. Despite his Orthodox background, Bergson himself was not observant. He

understood, however, the powerful visual impact of hundreds of Orthodox rabbis with their beards, black coats and black hats converging on Congress and the White House.

Gaining access to the Orthodox rabbinical leadership was no simple task. The elders of the American Orthodox community in the 1940s were mostly European-born talmudic scholars who spoke little English and were unfamiliar with the political ways of the New World. Few were accustomed to receiving national press coverage. Bergson and his associates used their fluent Yiddish and Bergson's family connections to win the trust of rabbis in the Hasidic and general Orthodox communities.

So it was that on October 6, 1943, more than 400 Orthodox rabbis, accompanied by marshals from the Jewish War Veterans of America, marched solemnly from Union Station to their first stop, the Capitol. Vice President Henry A. Wallace and a large bipartisan delegation of congressional leaders received them. While passers-by gawked and newsmen snapped photos, the rabbis recited the Kaddish, chanted the traditional prayer for the nation's leaders to the tune of the "Star Spangled Banner," and solemnly read aloud, in English and Hebrew, their petition calling for the creation of a special government agency to rescue European Jewry and expand the quota for

Jewish refugee immigration to the United States. *Time* magazine commented that on receiving the petition, Vice President Wallace "squirmed through a diplomatically minimal answer." The rabbis then marched from the Capitol to the White House.

On the advice of his aides, FDR, who was scheduled to attend a military ceremony, intentionally avoided the rabbis by leaving the White House through a rear exit while they marched silently in front. When Roosevelt's decision not to meet with the rabbis became known to the press, reporters interpreted it as a snub, adding a dramatic flair that transformed the protest rally into a full-fledged clash between the rabbis and the administration.

Capitalizing on the publicity from the march, Bergson's friends in Congress introduced a resolution asking FDR to create an agency that would find ways to provide a refuge for those Jews who remained in the Nazi grip. At Senate hearings on the resolution, a State Department official, Breckinridge Long, argued that America had absorbed more than its share of Jewish refugees. Arguing that Long's statistics were deliberately distorted, Treasury Secretary Henry Morgenthau drew up a stinging report to the president revealing the State Department's efforts to make Jewish immigration to the United States almost impossible. Within days, FDR announced the establishment of the War Refugee Board, which during the final year of the Holocaust was responsible for rescuing thousands of Jews and increasing Jewish immigration to America.

Bergson's skillful appeal to America's national conscience, including the rabbis' march, worked as nothing previously had to bring about a change in White House policy toward the Holocaust. Bergson's militancy, Morgenthau's insider access and the rabbis' willingness to take united political action combined to move FDR to act after three years of his claiming that only when the Allies defeated Hitler could European Jewry be saved.

Sponsored by Mr. and Mrs. Henry Kaplan in memory of those who perished at the World Trade Center

13

Davey Crockett of the New Frontier

Born on the West Side of Chicago in 1908, the last of the eleven children of Ukrainian Jewish immigrants, Arthur Goldberg began his life in poverty. Although he rose to high station, including a seat on the Supreme Court, he never placed his personal interests above his duty to public service. Goldberg's exemplary career was shaped by the liberal social ethics of Judaism and his experience of poverty as a young boy.

Goldberg's father was a fruit and vegetable peddler who drove a wagon drawn by a one-eyed horse through the streets of Chicago. When his father died at age fifty-one, eight-year-old Arthur, who had worked alongside him, was forced to keep working. He held jobs as a delivery boy, fish wrapper, shoe salesman and construction worker, all the while excelling at school. While in night school at De Paul University, Goldberg watched Clarence Darrow defend murderers Nathan Leopold and Richard Loeb and

determined to become an attorney. At age eighteen he entered Northwestern Law School, continuing to work and yet finishing at the top of the class of 1929, just as the Great Depression struck.

Goldberg accepted a job in a top Chicago law firm but resigned when he was assigned to foreclose mortgages on other people's property. Championing underdogs, Goldberg opened his own small office and began taking social justice cases. Among his clients was the American Newspaper Guild, which in 1938 struck against the Hearst newspapers in Chicago. For eight months, Goldberg represented the strikers without charge, spending countless days in court defending arrested picketers. In the end, Hearst recognized the union. Goldberg became a workingman's hero and eventually served as general counsel to the Congress of Industrial Organizations (CIO) and the United Steelworkers of America.

In 1955, Goldberg masterminded the legal aspects of the merger between the CIO and the American Federation of Labor, becoming chief counsel of the newly formed AFL-CIO. A brilliant negotiator and conciliator, he preferred compromise to resolve disputes. Goldberg drew the AFL-CIO into the emerging civil rights movement by filing *amicus* briefs with the Supreme Court in desegregation cases. Appointed secretary of labor by President John F. Kennedy in 1961, he came to be regarded as one the most energetic members of the cabinet. Some dubbed him the Davy Crockett of the New Frontier and Hubert Humphrey referred to him as the "vitamins" of the Kennedy administration. A year later, Kennedy nominated Goldberg for a seat on the Supreme Court.

After confirmation, Goldberg provided the fifth liberal vote on the Warren Court. He wrote the *Escobedo* opinion, which preceded *Miranda*, establishing the constitutional right of a suspect to have a lawyer present during interrogation. He answered critics of the ruling, "If the exercise of constitutional rights will thwart the effectiveness of a system of law enforcement, then there is something very wrong with that system." Goldberg's great theoretical contribution was his revitalizing of the Ninth Amendment, which states that if a right is not enumerated in the Constitution, the people retain it. He applied this principle in *Griswold v. Connecticut*, which overturned a law prohibiting married couples from obtaining birth control devices or information. *Griswold* paved the way for *Roe v. Wade* and other decisions confirming that individuals have a right to be left alone by government, even if that right is not specifically stated in the Constitution.

In 1965, President Lyndon Johnson asked Justice Goldberg to replace Adlai Stevenson, who had died suddenly, as ambassador to the United Nations. To the surprise, if not shock, of many, Goldberg accepted. Pundits maintained that Johnson was killing two birds with one stone: filling the UN vacancy and clearing the "Jewish seat" on the Supreme Court for his close friend Abe Fortas. Less clear is why Goldberg agreed to step down, since the judicial post carried life tenure and great prestige. Perhaps the court's slow pace bored him, or he may have believed that by applying his negotiating skills at the UN he could help end the Vietnam War. The only public explanation Goldberg gave was that he could not refuse his president's request. Goldberg was only the fourth Supreme Court justice in the twentieth century to resign from active service to take another job.

Of course, Goldberg was frustrated by not being able to end the war. In 1968, when Fortas's nomination to the post of chief justice ran into Senate opposition, the lame-duck Johnson contemplated nominating Goldberg. He later urged his successor, Richard Nixon, to appoint Goldberg as chief justice, a step that the more conservative Nixon never seriously contemplated.

When Goldberg retired from government in 1968 and became president of the American Jewish Committee, he said, "I'm proud of my Jewish heritage; I don't like any American who's not proud of his heritage." The link between his Judaism and his liberalism appeared particularly at Seders, where he retold the story of the Israelites in a way that made their struggle sound like the civil rights struggle of the 1960s. A friend once remarked, "He makes the whole thing the story of all the oppressed and outcast of the world, as if he were presenting a brief before the Supreme Court of History that will forever put Pharaoh in outer darkness."

In honor of Sheldon S. Cohen

Part V

Judaism in America

1

Isaac Harby and the Americanization of Reform Judaism

Silhouette of Isaac Harby

The introduction of Reform into American Judaism is usually associated with the arrival of intellectual German-speaking Jews fleeing Europe's failed republican revolutions of 1830 and 1848, and with German-born rabbis such as David Einhorn of Baltimore and Isaac Mayer Wise of Cincinnati. However, the first stirrings of American Reform had native roots.

In December 1824, led by Isaac Harby, forty-seven Charleston, South Carolina, Jews petitioned the leaders of Congregation K. K. Beth Elohim for changes in the Shabbat service. At that time, Beth Elohim followed the Sephardic *minhag* (ritual), which its leadership considered the service used by observant Jews since the time of the Second Temple. The dissidents asked that Hebrew prayers in the service be immediately followed by an English transla-

tion, that new prayers reflecting contemporary American life be added, that the rabbi offer a sermon in English that applied the scriptures to everyday life, and that the services be shortened.

An unlikely Reformer, Isaac Harby was descended from an Orthodox Sephardic family that fled Spain for Portugal and then lived in Morocco, London and Jamaica. His father, Solomon, settled in Charleston in 1782, where he married Rebecca Moses, the daughter of one of South Carolina's leading Jewish families. Born in 1788, Isaac became a teacher, playwright, literary critic, journalist and newspaper editor.

Harby demonstrated little interest in religion in his younger years, but in the early 1820s he became alarmed by Protestant efforts to convert American Jews and by the emergence of anti-Semitism in politics. He wanted Charleston Jewry to defend Judaism against its critics and themselves against proselytizers but worried that they would be unable to resist the Protestant challenge because they knew too little about their religion and could not understand the traditional liturgy at Beth Elohim.

Harby thought that services at Beth Elohim had to become more "American"—in other words, more like the services in Protestant churches. He wished to worship, as he put it, as part of the "enlightened world." The leaders of Beth Elohim refused to consider the reformers' petition because it lacked support from two-thirds of the membership. In response, the reformers created a competing "Reformed Society of Israelites for Promoting True Principles of Judaism According to Its Purity and Spirit."

The Reformed Society of Israelites obtained a site, wrote its own prayer book, introduced music into the service and prayed without head coverings. Harby served as orator and, in 1827, as president. On the first anniversary of the reform petition, he delivered an address explaining the Society's goals, which he circulated widely as a pamphlet. Understandably, the pamphlet received a mixed reception in the Jewish community, but many non-Jewish readers praised it. Even octogenarian Thomas Jefferson wrote to say that he found the reforms proposed "entirely reasonable," while confessing that he was "little acquainted with the liturgy of the Jews or their mode of worship."

While the Reformed Society flourished for a few years, the leaders of Beth Elohim never ceased their relentless criticism of the reformers. Many members became discouraged as their families split on religious grounds. Harby left Charleston for New York in 1827, profoundly affected by the premature death of his wife (Harby

himself died suddenly in 1828). Other reform leaders either died or drifted away. Although the Society never officially disbanded, it disappeared sometime after the mid-1830s. Most of its members rejoined Beth Elohim.

The spirit of reform in Charleston did not die with Harby. When a fire destroyed Beth Elohim in 1838, thirty-eight members petitioned the trustees, requesting that "an organ be erected in the [new] synagogue to assist in the vocal part of the service." The "Great Organ Controversy" split the congregation as nothing previously. The leadership again refused, claiming that playing an organ during services violated the injunction against labor on Shabbat. Following the by-laws, the reformers convened a general meeting of the congregation. A two-thirds majority reversed the leadership's decision.

Beth Elohim became the first American synagogue with an organ. This opened the way for other changes in the ritual, many of which had been requested a decade earlier by the Reformed Society: confirmation classes for boys and girls, abandoning the second day of festival observances and, eventually, family seating rather than the separation of men and women. The defeated traditionalists split away to form a new congregation. Beth Elohim thereafter evolved at the forefront of American Reform Judaism.

Harby and his associates sincerely believed that Judaism in America had to modernize to combat the proselytizing forces of conversion. The traditionalists argued that watered-down Judaism was assimilated beyond recognition. In many ways, the debate between American reformers and traditionalists begun in Charleston in 1824 continues.

In memory of Jacob Rader Marcus

87

2

Rebecca Gratz's "Unsubdued Spirit"

Of the many contributions Jewish women have made to American life, one of the most enduring is the volunteer institutions they created to serve their fellow Jews in need and to educate Jewish children. Without their efforts, Jewish life in America would have a much diminished face. Among the countless thousands of women who helped found, sustain and serve American Jewish charitable institutions, none looms larger than Rebecca Gratz (1781–1869). Critics speculate that Gratz's selfless devotion to humankind, and particularly to her fellow Jews, inspired Sir Walter Scott to model the character Rebecca in his novel *Ivanhoe* after her.

The sixth of twelve children born to Michael and Miriam Gratz, the young

Rebecca was well educated, both formally and through considerable reading in her father's extensive library. Members of the extended Gratz family were leading merchants of early nineteenth-century America, and their commercial activities helped settle western Pennsylvania, Kentucky and the Ohio Valley. The Michael Gratz family belonged to Philadelphia's social and economic elite and Rebecca's friends included many of the city's most important cultural figures.

Historian Diane Ashton tells us that Gratz once expressed the belief that, through her "unsubdued spirit," she could overcome any obstacle. Not believing she would find a man who might become an "agreeable domestic companion," Gratz never married.

Family lore has it that the beautiful Rebecca turned down a proposal from the son of the president of the University of Pennsylvania because she would not marry outside the Jewish faith. Instead, she became a Judaic scholar and chose a life of service to her family, her community and the cause of Jewish education—especially for women.

Gratz began devoting her life to others at age nineteen, when her mother recruited her to care for her father, who had been felled by a stroke. Although not poor, after Michael Gratz's stroke the Gratz women developed a newfound empathy for families whose breadwinner could no longer work. Rebecca, her mother and her sister joined with twenty other women to found Philadelphia's Female Association for the Relief of Women and Children in Reduced Circumstances. Her stint at this organization taught Gratz that some Christian women tried to use their philanthropic work to proselytize among the Jewish needy. She became convinced that Jewish women and children should receive services from their own charitable organizations.

In 1819, Gratz spearheaded the founding of Philadelphia's Female Hebrew Benevolent Association, the first Jewish charity in America formed outside a synagogue. The society provided food, shelter, fuel, clothing, an employment bureau and travelers' aid to Jews in distress. In the 1850s, Gratz helped found an orphanage and a foster home for Philadelphia's Jewish children that later became the basis for Philadelphia's Association for Jewish Children.

It was in Jewish religious education for children, however, that Gratz best showed her skill as an institution builder. Rebecca insisted that her many Christian friends respect her Jewish beliefs. She understood, however, that if Judaism was to be respected by the wider society, Jews themselves would have to be knowledgeable about—and observant in—their faith. Adapting to mid-nineteenth-century American life, however, Gratz gave Jewish education a form resembling the religious instruction received by America's Christian majority.

In 1838, she founded Philadelphia's coeducational Hebrew Sunday School, which she served as superintendent and secretary well into her eighties. Adopting the Sunday school format was only one innovation; she also limited membership on the faculty to females who had graduated from the school, providing American Jewish women with their first public roles in religious training. The school served students ranging from early childhood through the teens. Gratz recruited Philadelphia's illustrious rabbi Isaac Leeser to write the first curriculum for the Hebrew Sunday School. Quickly, the school expanded to several branches throughout the Philadelphia area and continued as an independent citywide institution until the close of the nineteenth century.

In her long life, Rebecca Gratz outlived all but one sibling and many of her nieces and nephews. Despite her losses, she never surrendered her "unsubdued spirit" or her deep Jewish faith. With great honor, Rebecca Gratz was buried in Congregation Mikveh Israel's historic cemetery. Her lasting monument, however, was American Jewry's Hebrew Sunday school movement, which endures to this day, reflecting Gratz's unique blend of Judaism and American culture.

Sponsored by Nancy and Martin Polevoy

3

Penina Moïse

When Penina Moïse was born in 1797, American Jewish women—like women in general—had only limited cultural and career opportunities. Moïse spent her adult life overcoming these cultural limitations, as well as her own physical disabilities. She left her mark as America's first female Jewish poet and hymnist, and her hymns, written mostly in the 1830s and 1840s, are still sung in Reform congregations today.

Penina Moïse was the sixth of nine children born to Abraham and Sarah Moise. The Moïses moved to Charleston, South Carolina, from the Caribbean five years before Penina was born and their French Jewish background strongly influenced her. Moïse would later impress her students with the "gayety, contentment, and joyous philosophy of her French temperament."

When Penina was twelve, Abraham Moïse died, leaving his family impoverished. Penina's formal education ended but she continued to read on her own. Legend has it that she sometimes stayed up late, reading by moonlight. Isaac Harby—dramatist, teacher, editor, and bright star in Jewish Charleston's intellectual firmament—became her intellectual mentor. He also nurtured her Judaism. Moïse began writing Jewish hymns, poems and odes in English and did so until her death in 1880.

When Moïse's synagogue, K. K.

Beth Elohim, burned in a fire in 1838, the Charleston Jewish community rebuilt it. When the new building opened in 1841, the choir sang an original ode Moïse composed for the event. Her hymns were collected together in a volume, the first Jewish hymnal printed in English on American soil.

Moïse's first published poem appeared in a Charleston newspaper in 1819. For the next six decades, her prodigious output of stories, poems and essays appeared in national magazines such as *Godey's Ladies' Book* and in newspapers from New Orleans to New York. She was a regular contributor to Isaac Leeser's *Occident and American Jewish Advocate*, an early English-language Jewish newspaper. In the 1840s, she was also the head teacher in K. K. Beth Elohim's Sunday school.

Unfortunately, Moïse never earned a satisfactory living from her writing or teaching. She nursed her mother until the latter died in 1842. Moïse supplemented the household's income by making fine lace and embroidery but always lived modestly. Penina was the only Moïse sibling not to marry. Her niece recalled, "Although Penina had many eligible offers, she refused all, considering nothing sufficient inducement to marry except love for a worthy object, and . . . this, it was said, was never given where it could be reciprocated." Historian Solomon

Breibart interprets this to mean that Moïse disapproved of interfaith marriage and the only man she was ever attracted to was not Jewish.

Moïse first won national artistic acclaim in 1833 when she published *Fancy's Sketch Book,* a collection of her poems. Breibart notes that the work was unusual in several respects: it was the first published book of verse by an American Jewish woman; it appeared under her own name when, conventionally, most women authors used pseudonyms; and it broke female boundaries by addressing serious political themes, such as Southern secession and states' rights, the Turkish oppression of the Greeks and Irish home rule.

Most important, Moïse's poems advocated for Jewish rights around the world. She prefigured the writings of Emma Lazarus in "To Persecuted Foreigners," a poem in which she proposed that Europe's oppressed Jews "come to the homes and bosoms of the free," to "Plenty's flowering bed," where "a Western Sun would gild their future day." In 1833, when the House of Lords denied full extension of rights to Jews in the British Isles, the outraged Moise composed "The Rejection of the Jew Bill, by the House of Lords," in which she characterized its action as an "Aristocratic Inquisition." Moïse also protested the killing of Jews in Damascus in 1840 and the kidnapping by Catholic priests in 1858 of Edgar Mortara, an Italian Jewish boy. Moïse was also an

early Zionist: her poetry looked forward to a day when "Captive Judah" would again be "ingathered" in the Holy Land. She wrote,

> The world hath not a link as strong
> As that which chains us to her sod.
> We cherish thee through scorn and wrong
> Land that first heard the voice of God!

During the Civil War years, Moïse moved to Sumter, South Carolina, for safety. By then, she was suffering from near-total blindness, painful neuralgia and insomnia, but her spirits never wavered and her mind remained active. At war's end, Moïse returned to Charleston and opened a private school where she taught, from memory, all the literature she had memorized while sighted. With her niece Jacqueline as scribe, Moïse continued to write verse.

Penina Moïse's last will and testament dictated that, in keeping with her modesty, she be buried in a plain pine box in Charleston's Jewish cemetery and that no flowers be strewn over her grave. Flowers, she wrote, "Are for those who live in the sun." (One does not know whether she meant this as a reference to her lost eyesight or to her death.) Moïse's hymns are still sung, but her poems are rarely read nowadays. In 1999, she was posthumously inducted into the South Carolina Academy of Authors. Perhaps her time in the sun still lies ahead.

In honor of Ruth B. Fein

4

Gershom Kursheedt, Institution Builder

In 1848, Gershom Kursheedt of New Orleans wrote to Rabbi Isaac Leeser of Philadelphia, "I have but one ambition in life, and that is to elevate the character of our people in the eyes of God and man." Historian Kenneth Libo observes that "no American did more in his day to build Jewish congregational life at home . . . and raise funds for [the Jews of] Palestine than Gershom Kursheedt."

Born in 1817 in Richmond, Virginia, Gershom Kursheedt had a distinguished Jewish pedigree. His grandfather was the first American-born rabbi, Gershom Mendes Seixas of New York, and his parents were Rabbi Israel Baer Kursheedt and Sarah Abigail, daughter of Gershom Mendes Seixas. The seventh of Israel Baer and Sarah Abigail's nine children, Gershom is reported to have absorbed "a passionate love of Jewish learning and a profound concern for Jewish causes" from both his parents. He was challenged to put both of these commitments to work when he moved to New Orleans at age twenty-one to work in an uncle's retail business.

The Jewish community of New Orleans established its first synagogue, Shanaria-Chasset, in 1828, ten years before Kursheedt's arrival. By that time, the young congregation had fallen to precarious depths. A German Jewish periodical reported that Shanaria-Chasset's rabbi, Albert "Roley" Marks, was disgracing the community:

> This stigma in the ranks of the Jewish ministry eats whatever comes before his maw, never keeps the feast of Passover, indeed, has none of his boys circumcised. . . . At Purim, the book of Esther could not be read since . . . the rabbi-reader was preoccupied with his duties as [part-time] fire chief. When challenged by a pious member of the congregation, the rabbi, beside himself with wrath, pounded the pulpit and shouted, 'By Jesus Christ, I have a right to pray!' After his death the rabbi's widow, a Catholic, was restrained only with difficulty from putting a crucifix on his grave.

Considering the situation at Shanaria-Chasset hopeless, Kursheedt helped organize a new congregation, Nefutzoth Yehudah, which elected him its first president. To fund construction of a synagogue for the congregation, Kursheedt turned to one of New Orleans's wealthiest men, Judah Touro, who until that time had only weakly identified with his Judaism and had done relatively little philanthropically to help his fellow Jews. Kursheedt tutored Touro into a practicing Jew and America's first great philanthropist.

Kursheedt persuaded Touro, who was unmarried and childless, to use his fortune to continue the Jewish traditions so beloved by Touro's father Isaac, hazzan of the synagogue in Newport, Rhode Island. Thanks to his efforts, Touro purchased an abandoned neoclassical church in downtown New Orleans and renovated it into a 470-seat sanctuary. On the advice of Kursheedt and Isaac Leeser, Touro funded the salary of Rabbi Moses Nathan to serve the congregation. Kursheedt made all the arrangements for dedicating the building in 1849 and, according to historian Bertram Korn, the ceremony had a powerful impact on Touro. After the dedication, Touro "seemed to have returned to Judaism," Korn observed, "in a most determined way. He attended services regularly, built a schoolhouse next to the synagogue in 1851 and provided rooms there for Gershom Kursheedt to live."

As part of his commitment to the Jewish community of New Orleans, Kursheedt organized the city's Hebrew Benevolent Society, the forerunner of today's Jewish community federation. A yellow fever epidemic in 1853 left the Hebrew Benevolent Society with responsibility for supporting four Jewish widows and twenty orphans. Kursheedt persuaded Touro to fund the construction of a home for Jewish widows and orphans.

Before the home could be built, Touro died. Just before his passing, Kursheedt influenced Touro to write a will leaving most of his estate to Jewish causes. Touro's bequests were at that time the largest ever left by an American citizen to charitable institutions. His estate of $200,000 provided funds for every existing traditional synagogue in America and $50,000 for the relief of poor Jews in Palestine. Until the very end, Kursheedt reported that he struggled to get Touro to provide for these Jewish charities. After Touro's death, Kursheedt wrote to Leeser, "If you knew how I had to work to get that will made . . . you would pity me. . . . [There were] arguments, changes and counterchanges in the sums for institutions, till my heart sickened."

Despite these struggles, Touro named Kursheedt co-executor with Sir Moses Montefiore of a $50,000 bequest for the poor Jews of Palestine. Kursheedt traveled to England to meet with Montefiore, from whence the two men traveled to Jerusalem to determine how best to use the Touro bequest. Montefiore proposed constructing a hospital, an idea to which Kursheedt instantly consented. When the two men returned to Jerusalem in 1857 they discovered that in the interim the Rothschild family had built such a hospital. The two men decided instead to build almshouses for the "worthy" Jewish poor. The colony of houses became the first Jewish neighborhood outside the walls of the old city.

Montefiore wrote to Kursheedt, "It must be a great happiness to you to know that with your great influence with the late Mr. Touro . . . you have been the means to directing the eyes and hearts of many of our Brethren toward the Holy Land and contributing to the welfare of our coreligionists now dwelling in that land of our Fathers." Kursheedt had indeed achieved his "one ambition": elevating the character of his people in the eyes of God and man.
In honor of Abigail Kursheedt Hoffman

5

The Fight for Jewish Chaplains

For Jews who wish to observe the rituals of their faith, war poses seemingly insurmountable challenges. The exigencies of war can make the observance of the Sabbath, holy days and kashrut rules very difficult. As the Arab attack on Israel during Yom Kippur of 1973 made clear, Jewish soldiers must, on occasion, subordinate religious observance to combat. Despite the priority of combat over religious observance, there have been times when Jewish religious observance shaped American military policy.

At the outbreak of the Civil War, for example, Jews could not serve as chaplains in the U.S. armed forces. When the war commenced in 1861, Jews enlisted in both the Union and Confederate armies. The Northern Congress adopted a bill in July of 1861 that permitted each regiment's commander, on a vote of his field officers, to appoint a regimental chaplain so long as he was "a regularly ordained minister of some Christian denomination."

Representative Clement L. Vallandigham of Ohio, a non-Jew, protested this clause because it discriminated against soldiers of the Jewish faith. Vallandigham argued that the Jewish population of the United States, "whose adherents are . . . good citizens and as true patriots as any in this country," deserved to have rabbis minister to Jewish soldiers. In his view, the law was blatantly unconstitutional because it endorsed Christianity as the official religion of the

United States. However, no organized national Jewish protest supported Vallandigham and the bill sailed through Congress.

Three months later, a YMCA worker visiting the field camp of Cameron's Dragoons, a Pennsylvania regiment, discovered to his horror that the officers had elected a Jew, Michael Allen, as regimental chaplain. While not an ordained rabbi, Allen was fluent in the Portuguese minhag (ritual) and taught at the Philadelphia Hebrew Education Society. As Allen was neither a Christian nor an ordained minister, the YMCA representative filed a formal complaint with the Army. Obeying the recently enacted law, the Army forced Allen to resign his chaplaincy post.

Hoping to create a test case based strictly on a chaplain's religion and not his lack of ordination, Colonel Max Friedman and the officers of Cameron's Dragoons then elected an ordained rabbi, the Reverend Arnold Fischel of New York's Congregation Shearith Israel, to serve as regimental chaplain-designate. When Fischel, a Dutch immigrant, applied for certification as chaplain, the secretary of war, none other than the Simon Cameron for whom the regiment was named, complied with the law and rejected his application.

The rejection of Fischel finally stimulated American Jewry to action. The American Jewish press let its readers know that Congress had limited the chaplaincy to Christians and argued for equal treatment for Judaism before the law. This initiative irritated a handful of Christian organizations, including the YMCA, which resolved to lobby Congress against the appointment of Jewish chaplains. To counter their efforts, the Board of Delegates of American Israelites, one of the earliest Jewish communal defense agencies, recruited Reverend Fischel to live in Washington, minister to wounded Jewish soldiers in that city's military hospitals and lobby President Abraham Lincoln to reverse the chaplaincy law. Although today several national Jewish organizations employ representatives to make their voices heard in Washington, Fischel's mission was the first lobbying effort of this type.

Armed with letters of introduction from Jewish and non-Jewish political leaders, Fischel met on December 11, 1861 with President Lincoln to press the case for Jewish chaplains. Fischel told the president that, unlike many others who were waiting to see him that day, he came not to seek political office, but to "contend for the principle of religious liberty, for the constitutional rights of the Jewish community, and for the welfare of the Jewish volunteers." According to Fischel, Lincoln asked several questions about the chaplaincy issue, "fully admitted the justice of my remarks . . . and agreed that something ought to be done to meet this case." Lincoln promised Fischel that he would submit a new law to Congress "broad enough to cover what is desired by you in behalf of the Israelites."

Lincoln kept his word, and seven months later, on July 17, 1862, Congress adopted his proposed amendments to the chaplaincy law to allow "the appointment of brigade chaplains of the Catholic, Protestant and Jewish religions." In historian Bertram Korn's opinion, Fischel's "patience and persistence, his unselfishness and consecration . . . won for American Jewry the first major victory of a specifically Jewish nature . . . on a matter touching the Federal government." Korn concluded, "Because there were Jews in the land who cherished the equality granted them in the Constitution, the practice of that equality was assured, not only for Jews, but for all minority religious groups."

Sponsored by Mr. and Mrs. Burton G. Greenblatt

6

Of Civil Seders in the Civil War

For Jewish soldiers fighting for the North during the Civil War, the Passover story was especially powerful. These men saw clear parallels between the Union freeing the South's slaves and Moses leading the ancient Hebrews out of Egypt. Celebrating the Seder helped them remember the purpose for which they risked their lives. However, holding a Seder in a war zone requires flexibility and creativity.

In 1862, the *Jewish Messenger* published an account by J. A. Joel of the 23rd Ohio Volunteer Regiment of a Seder celebrated by Union soldiers in Fayette, West Virginia. Joel and twenty other Jewish soldiers were granted leave to observe Passover. A soldier home on leave in Cincinnati shipped *matzot* and *Haggadot* to his colleagues. Joel wrote:

> We . . . sen[t] parties to forage in the country [for Passover food] while a party stayed to build a log hut for the services. . . We obtained two kegs of cider, a lamb, several chickens and some eggs. Horseradish or parsley we could not obtain, but in lieu we found a weed whose bitterness, I apprehend, exceeded anything our forefathers "enjoyed."
>
> We had the lamb, but did not know what part was to represent it at the table; but Yankee ingenuity prevailed, and it was decided to cook the whole and put it on the table, then we could dine off it, and be sure we got the right part.
>
> The necessaries for the *choroutzes* we could not obtain, so we got a brick which, rather hard to digest, reminded us, by looking at it, for what purpose it was intended.

Yankee ingenuity indeed! Historian Bertram Korn observes, "It must have been quite a sight: these twenty men gathered together in a crude and hastily-built log hut, their weapons at their side, prepared as in Egypt-land for all manner of danger, singing the words of praise and faith in the ancient language of Israel." The Seder proceeded smoothly until the eating of the bitter herbs. Joel recounted:

> We all had a large portion of the herb ready to eat at the moment I said the blessing; each [ate] his portion, when horrors! What a scene ensued. . . . The herb was very bitter and very fiery like Cayenne pepper, and excited our thirst to such a degree that we forgot the law authorizing us to drink only four cups, and . . . we drank up all the cider. Those that drank more freely became excited and one thought he was Moses, another Aaron, and one had the audacity to call himself a Pharaoh. The consequence was a skirmish, with nobody hurt, only Moses, Aaron and Pharaoh had to be carried to the camp, and there left in the arms of Morpheus.

More problematic was the situation of Union soldiers who, unable to hold their own Seders, were forced to "fraternize" with local Southern Jews. Myer Levy of Philadelphia, for example, was in a Virginia town one Passover late in the war when he saw a young boy sitting on his front steps eating a piece of *matzoh*. According to Korn, when Levy "asked the boy for a piece, the child fled indoors, shouting at the top of his lungs, 'Mother, there's a damn Yankee Jew outside!'" The boy's mother invited Levy to Seder that night. One wonders how the Virginian family and the Yankee soldier interpreted the Haggadah portions describing the evils of bondage.

On the eve of the fifth day of Passover (April 14), 1865, Abraham Lincoln was shot and died of his wounds in the early morning of April 15, which had already been scheduled as a national day of prayer to mark the end of the Civil War. Jews across the land were gathering in synagogues to give thanks. When news of Lincoln's death arrived, Korn notes, the synagogue altars were quickly draped in black and, instead of Passover melodies, the congregations chanted Yom Kippur hymns. Rabbis set aside their sermons and wept openly in their pulpits, as did their congregants. Lincoln had been protective of American Jewry, overturning General Grant's infamous General Order No. 11 expelling Jews from the Department of the Tennessee and supporting legislation allowing Jewish chaplains to serve in the military (see pages 94 and 118). The *Jewish Record* drew an analogy between Lincoln not having lived to see the reconciliation of North and South and Moses dying on Mount Pisgah before he saw the Israelites enter the Promised Land.

At times when no American armed forces are in combat anywhere in the world, it is easy to forget how difficult it can be for Jewish soldiers to serve their country while maintaining the traditions that beautify Judaism. Nevertheless, for Jewish Union soldiers fighting between 1861 and 1865 to free others from slavery, the Passover parallels must have made each Seder particularly sweet and meaningful.

Sponsored by The Gottesman Fund

7

Isaac Mayer Wise, the "Trefa Banquet" and the Dream of Jewish Unity

On a humid Cincinnati evening in July 1883, over 200 distinguished guests, Jews and non-Jews alike, gathered at Cincinnati's exclusive Highland House restaurant to celebrate a milestone in the history of American Judaism: Hebrew Union College, which Rabbi Isaac Mayer Wise founded, had just ordained its initial graduating class. America finally produced four home-grown ordained rabbis. Most of the diners had just attended the eighth annual meeting of the Union of American Hebrew Congregations (UAHC), the first association of American Jewish synagogues, which Rabbi Wise had also organized. The graduates and guests looked forward to an evening of gastronomical pleasure. What they witnessed was the beginning of the end of Wise's dream of American Jewish religious unity.

For nearly four decades after his arrival from Bohemia, Isaac Mayer Wise envisioned a unified American Judaism that balanced European tradition and New World realities. He built the Hebrew Union College to train American rabbis and organized the Union of American Hebrew Congregations as a forum for traditional and Reform-minded rabbis and congregations to resolve their differences.

By 1883, some traditionalists had introduced a degree of modernization, such as English sermons and English prayers, into their services, and the more liberal ones even allowed organ music and mixed choirs of men and women. This encouraged Wise to hope for convergence. His close friend, Reverend Isaac Leeser of Philadelphia, the leading traditionalist figure, aided him. Like Wise, Leeser was willing to focus on uniting American Jewry.

Other rabbinical voices were not so united. Especially contentious were the so-called Eastern radical reformers, led by Rabbi David Einhorn of Baltimore. Veterans of the radical Reform German rabbinical conferences of the 1850s, the liberals intended to expunge what they deemed outmoded religious practices, such as kashrut, derisively called "kitchen Judaism," and the second day of holiday observances. Some radicals even advocated observing Shabbat on Sunday.

Wise himself damaged the reform-traditionalist détente in 1855 by introducing, at a meeting intended to demonstrate the harmony of American Judaism, his prayer book, *Minhag America*. Though moderate in its reforms, the book distressed the traditionalists, including Leeser, and did not go far enough for some of the radicals.

Wise's diplomatic genius contained these differences. By creating the UAHC in 1873 and founding Hebrew Union College in Cincinnati in 1875, he maintained the fragile traditionalist-reformer détente into the beginning of the 1880s. As historian Abraham J. Karp states, Wise "understood that congregations could be united through participation in a project rather than through agreement on resolutions." Wise proposed the seminary to develop an American rabbinate and, thus, an American Judaism.

The banquet for the first Hebrew Union College graduating class on that fateful July evening tangibly confirmed for Wise the efficacy of his strategy. Reformers and traditionalists were breaking bread together. The first course, however, was "Little Neck Clams (half shell)." According to the memoirs of Rabbi David Phillipson, the clams provoked "terrific excitement" and "two rabbis rose from their seats and rushed from the room." While leaders gave unity speeches from the podium, a number of traditional rabbis sat stoically through the meal, failing to applaud and refusing to taste even one morsel of the "Soft-shell Crabs" and "Salade of Shrimps," or the ice cream and cheese that followed the meat courses.

Historians debate whether Wise approved the menu, the Jewish caterer acted on his own, or the Einhorn faction surreptitiously ordered the *tref* courses to force a showdown. Wise claimed no knowledge of how the shellfish got on the menu. He personally kept a kosher home and claims to have ordered Gus Lindeman, the caterer, to serve kosher food. Lindeman did serve kosher meat but "supplemented" it with the shellfish and dairy desserts. A later investigation by a panel of UAHC rabbis cleared Wise of wrongdoing, but the damage was done.

The "trefa banquet" helped lead to the formal break between tradition and reform. In the three years after the banquet, a series of debates between reformer Kaufmann Kohler and traditionalist Alexander Kohut crystallized positions in each camp. In 1885, the UAHC conference in Pittsburgh, dominated by radicals, adopted a platform of Reform Jewish theology that defined the movement for over half a century. In 1886, some change-oriented rabbis who could not go as far as the Pittsburgh radicals established the Jewish Theological Seminary of America, laying the foundation for Conservative Judaism. In 1888, New York City's Orthodox community decided to recruit a chief rabbi from Eastern Europe to serve as a regnant authority. After these events, there was no turning back. American Judaism had divided into organized movements, each claiming its right to define Jewish religious practices. The "trefa banquet" did not cause the division, but most colorfully symbolized the sensibilities and principles that led to it.

Sponsored by Betsy and Ken Plevan in memory of Rabbi Henry Messing

8

Modern Orthodoxy Builds a Cathedral

In 1887, Congregation Kahal Adath Jeshurun (KAJ) of New York City opened the doors of its new synagogue on Eldridge Street on New York's Lower East Side. This towering structure was adorned with elaborately carved woodwork, glistening brass fixtures and luminous stained-glass windows. Artists stenciled its vaulted ceilings, painted its walls with *trompe l'oeil* murals and elaborately carved its ark. For grandeur, architectural critics argued, only the great Reform synagogues—Temple Emanu-el on Fifth Avenue and Central Synagogue, an elaborate Moorish structure on Lexington Avenue—could compare.

Between 1880 and 1920, the Jewish population of the United States increased tenfold to 2 million people. Much of the growth occurred on the Lower East Side. Our image of the newcomers, indelibly engraved by Emma Lazarus, is of "poor,

huddled masses, yearning to breathe free." Indeed, many of the new immigrants were impoverished and unskilled. However, the life they built on the Lower East Side—and especially the grand Eldridge Street Synagogue—indicates that the Jews of the Lower East Side were a more accomplished group than is sometimes imaged.

Founded under the name Congregation Beth Hamedresh (House of Study) in 1853, KAJ suffered through a number of controversies and schisms. In 1856, Congregation Beth Hamedresh purchased the Welsh Chapel on Allen Street and converted it into a synagogue. Three years later, the congregation fought over whether the rabbi or congregants would control services. When the rabbi's adherents seceded, the president's followers remained in the Allen Street building, kept the name Beth Hamedresh until 1890, then took the new name Congregation Kahal Adath Jeshurun. The congregation viewed itself as Americanized, that is, democratically controlled by its lay leaders and not its rabbinate.

Congregation KAJ was Americanized in other ways as well. Unlike many of the other congregations on the Lower East Side, membership in KAJ was not primarily based on *landsmen* from a particular Eastern European town. Attracting upwardly mobile but ritually traditional middle- and working-class immigrants from various parts of Eastern Europe, Congregation KAJ disapproved of Reform Judaism's decision to alter halachic tradition. KAJ's challenge was to maintain traditional Jewish practice without rejecting the freedom and modernity provided by the American context. The congregation sought to construct a modern "cathedral" to their religion, but one still dedicated to traditional observance. KAJ was thus one of the first "modern Orthodox" congregations in America, and its elegant Eldridge Street Synagogue the first major American house of worship built from the ground up by Eastern European Jews.

At the opening of the imposing new sanctuary, Rabbi Bernard Drachman enjoined his congregants to "make a battlement for the roof of their house . . . otherwise they might stand before their mirrors some morning and not recognize themselves as orthodox any more." Drachman, who favored the use of English in Orthodox services as a way to encourage participation, was concerned that young American Jews who went to college would note the "beauty and dignity maintained in the Christian Church and even in the Reformed Temples . . . to the detriment of the down-town synagogues," which they might perceive as "primitive, untutored, undignified and un-American." The grandeur and adornment of the Eldridge Street Synagogue was meant to compete with uptown allures.

Following Drachman to the *bimah*, Pereira Mendes, rabbi of New York's Congregation Shearith Israel, declared that "beauty and outward form and decorum were essential if Orthodoxy was to maintain itself, and retain the loyalties of its youth." Accordingly, Congregation KAJ's officers made rules of decorum and appointed ushers to enforce them. The "Contract for the Sale of Seats" at Eldridge Street stipulated that individuals purchasing seats "must adhere strictly to the rules for maintaining peace and order of the service." The minute books cite frequent fines imposed on congregants for interrupting the service, loud talking (especially during the reading of the Torah), late arrival, unclean language and spitting on the floor. Between 1885 and 1909, the decorum committee purchased dozens of spittoons.

Despite the grandeur of its building, Congregation KAJ has been unable to keep the Eldridge Street Synagogue full. After reaching a membership peak of 300 families in the 1920s, most of its congregants—like the Jewish immigrant population of many American cities—died or moved to more affluent neighborhoods. The remaining members of Congregation KAJ, reinforced by younger Jews gentrifying the Lower East Side, now meet in the basement of the Eldridge Street Synagogue. Upstairs, the ornate murals and hand-carved wood are undergoing restoration by a private foundation formed to preserve this once-elegant monument to a people who balanced tradition and change.

Sponsored by Michael Steinhardt

9

Chanukah, American Style

Jewish postcard, ca. 1915

Chanukah, the Festival of Lights, celebrates the victory in 164 B.C.E. of armed Jewish rebels led by Judah the Maccabee over the army of the Syrian despot Antiochus IV. Against all odds, the courageous, resourceful and badly outnumbered Jewish freedom fighters, David-like, slew the Syrian Goliath. Since then, Jews around the world marked Chanukah as a "minor" holiday, meaning that, while not an observance commanded by Scripture, it is nonetheless traditional. Chanukah has allowed Jews who were oppressed or under pressure to assimilate to look back to a golden age in which militant, assertive Jews maintained their religious freedom and independence. Lighting candles, playing cards and gambling with *dreidels* recall the prowess of the Maccabees and the miracle of the oil that burned for eight days, a sign that Jews are indeed God's chosen people.

For the millions of Jewish immigrants who came to America at the end of the nineteenth and beginning of the twentieth centuries, Chanukah took on new, ambiguous and conflicted meanings. Chanukah's proximity on the calendar to Christmas posed particular challenges. By the 1890s, Christmas was firmly established as America's premiere season for gift giving. For Americans of all faiths, consumerism and general feelings of "good cheer" supplemented, if not replaced, the religious basis for Christmas. The holiday was rapidly becoming a national, rather than purely Christian, tradition.

For Jewish immigrants feeling pressure to shed their European ways, exchanging gifts with neighbors at Christmas time signaled their adaptation to their new home. In 1904, the *Forward* quoted Jewish Christmas shoppers who, when challenged, asked (in Yiddish), "Who says we haven't Americanized?" The paper observed, "The purchase of Christmas gifts is one of the first things that proves one is no longer a green-horn."

As historian Jenna W. Joselit notes, some Jewish leaders criticized the tendency of immigrant Jews to accept Christmas as an American consumer ritual. In 1890, Rabbi Kaufmann Kohler asked, "How can the Jew, without losing self-respect, partake in the joy and festive mirth of Christmas? Can he without self-surrender, without entailing insult and disgrace upon his faith and race, plant the Christmas tree in his household?"

Yet, Kohler admitted, Chanukah as then celebrated by American Jewry could not hold a candle (so to speak) to Christmas. Kohler said of the comparison, "How humble and insignificant does one appear by the side of the other" and suggested that Chanukah needed more pizzazz. Jewish homemaking advisor Esther Jane Ruskay lamented in 1902 that Christmas's focus on family celebrations, gift-giving, decorations and Santa Claus "gives a zest to life that all the Chanukah hymns, backed by all the Sunday-school teaching and half-hearted ministerial [rabbinic] chiding, must forever fail to give."

Joselit notes that it was not until the late 1920s, when Congress effectively ended mass Jewish immigration to America, that Chanukah "began to come into its own as a Jewish domestic occasion and an exercise in consumption." Merchandisers to Jews began advertising their wares as ideal Chanukah gifts. *Der Tog* carried an ad in Yiddish for Hudson automobiles, which were proclaimed "A Chanukah Present for the Entire Family— The Greatest Bargain (*metsiah*) in the World." Colgate promoted toiletries as

Chanukah gifts and food purveyors such as Loft's and Barton's candies marketed chocolates wrapped in gold foil to simulate Chanukah *gelt.* Aunt Jemima flour proclaimed itself "the best flour for latkes" and the *Hadassah Newsletter* advised that "mah-jongg sets make appreciated Chanukah gifts."

With the creation of the State of Israel in 1948, Chanukah took on a new, or rather renewed, meaning. In the aftermath of the Holocaust, the valor and success of Israel's military forces helped rebuild the image of the Jew as fighter. Zionists proudly identified the Haganah and Irgun as descendants of the Maccabees. Loft's Chocolate Company issued a board game called "Valor Against Oppression" that featured General Moshe Dayan. Not to be outdone, Barton's produced what Joselit calls "an Israelized version of Monopoly whose board featured a map of Israel, miniature Israeli flags [and] menorahs."

Despite the shift in the meaning of Chanukah in light of Israeli military success, the holiday remains ambivalent for many American Jews. For younger Jewish children, December can still be a difficult month of dealing with the omnipresent lures of Santa Claus. Yet Chanukah seems to grow in popularity as the observance of traditional Jewish ritual becomes more widespread and intense. In 1951, a California Jewish woman advised her fellow Jews: "Let this be our guiding principle: Keeping within the framework of our own tradition, using a color scheme of blue and silver and yellow and gold, let us adorn our homes inside and out as beautifully as we can for Chanukah, enlarging upon the old-time Feast of Lights."

Sponsored by Betsy amd Walter Stern

103

10

Beyond Seltzer Water:
Rabbi Geffen and the Kashering of Coca-Cola

As a symbol of American culture, Coca-Cola has penetrated every nation in the world and is served at kosher events. While Coke has been on the market since 1886, only since 1935 has it been certified kosher, including *kosher le-Pesach*. Gaining that certification was a complicated task.

Rabbi Tobias Geffen, an Orthodox rabbi who served Atlanta's Congregation Shearith Israel from 1910 until his death in 1970 at the age of ninety-nine, was responsible for kashering Coke. Rabbi Geffen was an unlikely contributor to the worldwide success of the beverage. Born in Kovno, Lithuania in 1870, he emigrated to Canton, Ohio in 1903 and accepted his Atlanta pulpit seven years later. During his long tenure at Shearith Israel, Geffen became the dean of Southern Jewish Orthodoxy.

As the millions of Jews who migrated to the United States from Poland, Lithuania, Russia, Ukraine, and elsewhere in Eastern Europe before World War I became more Americanized, they wanted increasingly to partake of "real" American life, including consuming American foods and beverages. While seltzer water might have been the preference of many traditional Jewish immigrants, their rapidly assimilating children and grandchildren demonstrated their Americanization by drinking Coke.

Because the Coca-Cola Company was headquartered in Atlanta, Rabbi Geffen received letters from several Orthodox colleagues around the nation asking whether it was halachically permissible to consume Coca-Cola. Uncertain of the answer, Geffen contacted the company to ask for a list of Coke's ingredients.

At the time, Rabbi Geffen did not know that the formula for Coca-Cola is a closely guarded trade secret, one of the best-kept trade secrets in American history. Only a handful of individuals know the formula. Once Rabbi Geffen inquired, the Coca-Cola Company made a corporate decision to allow him access to the list of ingredients in Coke's secret formula *provided he swore to keep them absolutely secret*. Geffen agreed to the terms. The company did not tell Geffen the exact proportions of each ingredient, but gave him a list of contents by name.

When Geffen received the list of ingredients, he discovered that one of them was glycerin made from non-kosher beef tallow. Even though a laboratory chemist told Geffen that the glycerin was present in only one part per thousand (one part in sixty is dilute enough to earn kosher certification), Geffen informed the Coca-Cola Company that since the glycerin was a planned rather than accidentally added ingredient, observant Jews could not knowingly tolerate its inclusion. Thus Coke failed to meet the standards of kashrut.

Back at the company's laboratories, research scientists went to work finding a substitute for tallow-based glycerin and discovered that Proctor and Gamble produced a glycerin from cottonseed and coconut oil. When the scientists agreed to use this new ingredient, Geffen gave his *hechsher*, or seal of approval, for Coke to be marketed as kosher.

A second problem still vexed Geffen: the formula for Coke included traces of alcohol that were a by-product of grain kernels. Since anything derived from grains is *chametz*, or forbidden at Passover, Coca-Cola could not be certified kosher for use at Passover. Coke's chemists experimented and found that during the Passover season they could substitute sweeteners produced from beet sugar and cane sugar for grain-based ones without compromising Coke's taste. They agreed to start manufacturing Coke with the new sugars several weeks before Passover each year.

Rabbi Geffen was pleased to have performed this service for American Jewry and the Coca-Cola Company. In his papers, which are housed in the archives of the American Jewish Historical Society, researchers can find a *teshuvah* (rabbinic response) that Geffen wrote which includes the following:

> Because Coca-Cola has already been accepted by the general public in this country and Canada and because it has become an insurmountable problem to induce the great majority of Jews to refrain from partaking of this drink, I have tried earnestly to find a method of permitting its usage. With the help of G-d I have been able to uncover a pragmatic solution in which there would be no question nor any doubt concerning the ingredients of Coca-Cola.

Thanks to Rabbi Geffen, even the most observant Jew can feel comfortable that "things go better with Coke."

Sponsored by Judge and Mrs. Chester J. Straub

11

Alice Davis Menken: Faith Beyond the Synagogue Door

Born to privilege in 1870 and married into wealth in 1893, Alice Davis Menken dedicated her life to helping Jewish women less fortunate than herself. Menken belonged to the Daughters of the American Revolution and was a great-granddaughter of the legendary *hazzan* Moses Levi Maduro Peixotto of New York's Sephardic Congregation Shearith Israel. At a time when upper-class women were, for the most part, denied careers, independent ownership of property and the right to vote, Menken could have been content to live the life of a clubwoman. Instead, she forged her Sephardic Jewish values to a progressive social philosophy to change the face of women's correctional theory. Even more, she mobilized the other "ladies" of Shearith Israel into joining her crusade to rescue delinquent Jewish women. Judge Judith S. Kaye has said of Menken,

"Led by a faith that did not stop at the synagogue door, Alice Menken went out to help those who had been dealt a much harsher hand in life."

Alice Menken helped found the Shearith Israel Sisterhood in 1896 and presided over it from 1900 to 1929. The sisterhood's initial undertaking was Neighborhood House, a settlement that served immigrant families on the Lower East Side that helped 300 poor Jewish families obtain clothing, coal, food, and medical care. In 1908, a sudden influx of "Oriental" Sephardic refugees from the Balkans, Turkey, Greece and Syria flooded the Lower East Side and looked to Neighborhood House for help. Under Menken's leadership, the sisterhood balanced "Americanization" of these immigrants with retention of their Sephardic heritage. On the Fourth of July,

106

1912, for example, the Sisterhood distributed 500 copies of the Declaration of Independence in Ladino translation.

Menken's enduring contribution to Jewish social service, however, was in the field of delinquency and corrections, particularly among Jewish females. Menken served as director of the Department of Court, Probation and Parole for the Jewish Board of Guardians women's division. In 1907, she helped create the Jewish Board of Guardians, which took responsibility for supervising Jewish youth during and after court-imposed probation.

In 1908, at the request of New York City magistrates, Menken organized a committee of Shearith Israel women to work with the probation department of the Women's Night Court of New York City. This court handled the criminal cases of numerous immigrant Jewish women who were homeless, substance addicted or prostitutes. The magistrates asked Menken and the sisterhood to organize a support system so that the delinquent women might have an alternative to incarceration, or be assisted upon their release. Menken recruited many sisterhood members to volunteer on behalf of these unfortunates.

Characteristically, Menken worked harder than anyone else in this cause. In their jointly authored history of Congregation Shearith Israel, David and Tamar de Sola Pool offer an insight into Menken's dedication: "After a full day's work she would go late at night to the Night Court for Women, sit with the poor victims dragged in by the police, sustain them in their difficulties at court, and follow through with their problems and those of their family." In 1920, Governor Alfred E. Smith appointed Menken to the Board of Managers of the New York State Reformatory for Women. She later served on the Bureau of Social Service of the New York State Board of Parole.

In 1911, Menken helped found the Jewish Big Sister Association and, according to historian Felicia Herman, stimulated the creation of several local chapters around the United States. Menken demonstrated her commitment to personal involvement with Jewish delinquent girls by taking several of them into her home over the years.

Today, conservatives and "realists" might consider Menken's attitude toward corrections fuzzyheaded liberalism. However, Menken made a meaningful contribution to society's recognition that women's penology requires different approaches than men's, and that prevention is better than punishment. In her 1936 obituary, the *New York Times* called Menken a pioneer in "the evolution of penology from an attitude of sentimentality and punishment to the broader conception of mercy and rehabilitation." In her published writings and personal papers, which reside at the American Jewish Historical Society, Menken argued that community involvement and improved social service delivery systems could prevent more poor women from stumbling into trouble than punishment could deter. Menken's ideas came into ascendancy during the 1920s, when separate juvenile courts and correctional facilities for women became commonplace throughout the United States.

At her funeral, Rabbi David de Sola Pool reflected on the connection between Menken's Sephardic Jewish faith and her social activism. "Her religion was not limited to the forms of the ritual which she loved," he said, "but was an outward example to those who may doubt the value of religion."

Sponsored by George and Mildred Weissman

Part VI

THE FIGHT AGAINST ANTI-SEMITISM

1

Turks, Jews and Infidels Need Not Apply

In 1776, the very year that the Declaration of Independence proclaimed that "all men are created equal," the voters of Maryland adopted a constitution that set the standard for holding state office. It read in part:

> No other test or qualification ought to be required on admission to any office of trust or profit than such oath of support and fidelity to the State . . . and a declaration of belief in the Christian religion.

Cecilius Calvert, Lord Baltimore, founded Maryland to provide a haven for England's persecuted Catholics. Ironically, by the time of the Revolution, Catholics had become a small and unpopular minority in Maryland. The new state's Catholics intended the provision allowing any Christian to hold public office as a guarantee of their own equality.

With the adoption of the Bill of Rights in 1787, which ensured freedom of religion to all American citizens, the restrictions on the holding of public office in Maryland, including military service and the practice of law, became blatantly unconstitutional. At least it seemed that way to Maryland's Jewish leaders, Solomon Etting and Jacob Cohen of Baltimore, who, along with other petitioners, appealed to the state assembly in 1797 on behalf of "a sect of people called Jews" who "are deprived of invaluable rights of citizenship" and want to be "placed on the same footing as other good citizens."

Etting, whose silhouette is above,

had fought in the Revolution and been active in public life in Pennsylvania before moving to Baltimore. An energetic man who held the distinction of having been the first American-born *shochet* (ritual slaughterer), Etting served as a director of the first American railroad company, the Baltimore and Ohio. Cohen was a banker and Jewish communal leader. Both men were Jeffersonian Democrats and had influential friends in the legislature.

Their 1797 petition initiated a thirty-year fight to repeal the religious require-ments for participation in Maryland's public life. A committee of the Assembly found the Etting-Cohen petition "reasonable" but the legislature took no subsequent action. Etting and Cohen submitted several more petitions between 1798 and 1804, each of which was supported by the Jeffersonians. Maryland's upper chamber, which was controlled by Federalists representing conservative, anti-immigrant, rural areas, blocked passage of any reform act. The Federalists argued that lifting the restrictions in the constitution would open office-holding to "Turks and infidels" as well as Jews.

In the early 1820s, Etting and Cohen found a legislative champion for their peti-tion: Thomas Kennedy, an Irish Catholic state representative. As a Catholic, Kennedy wanted to broaden the spirit of toleration in Maryland, both for Catholics and Jews. Kennedy made a plea for fairness: as citi-zens, Jews—and even Turks and infidels if they were citizens—must have the same right to serve as other citizens. Having seen their proposal defeated before, Etting and Cohen realized that Kennedy's bill was too broad to win conservative support. They per-suaded him to focus, at least for the time being, on winning political rights specifical-ly for Jews.

In 1822, Kennedy and his allies launched a campaign to "extend to the sect of people professing the Jewish religion, the same rights and privileges enjoyed by Christians." Kennedy's proposed legislation came to be known as the "Jew Bill." Maryland's conservative rural newspaper editors and legislators opposed it. When the bill came up for a vote in the upper house of the state legislature in 1823, it was defeated and Kennedy lost his seat in the legislature. Reelected in 1824, Kennedy, with the help of the Baltimore Jewish community, resumed the fight. In 1825, the Democrats won a majority in the upper house and had a chance to pass his bill.

In the end, the Maryland Assembly heeded Kennedy's pleas for justice and his argument that failure to pass his bill would drive Jews out of the state, to the detriment of the local economy. In 1826, the Maryland Assembly finally adopted a bill allowing Jews to hold office. Its key provision stated that:

> Every citizen of this state professing the Jewish religion . . . appointed to any office of public trust [shall] make and subscribe a declaration of his belief in a future state of rewards and punishments, in the stead of the declaration now required.

The "Jew Bill" adopted in 1826 did not directly amend or strike the offending clause from the Maryland constitution. Rather, the bill circumvented it. The Maryland Assembly saw fit only to allow Jews who affirmed their belief in an afterlife to sit as members. Today, while the Maryland constitution still formally limits public office to Christians, the clause is not enforced and religious tests are never applied to lawyers or elected officials.

Sponsored by Richard and Rosalee C. Davison

2

David Seixas Stands Accused: 1821

Scandal clouds David Seixas's contributions to American history. The oldest of the twelve children born to Gershom Mendes Seixas (*hazzan* of Congregation Shearith Israel in New York) and his second wife, David Seixas became an inventor, businessman and teacher of the deaf. None of these undertakings went smoothly, however. In an 1864 obituary, Isaac Leeser wrote that David Seixas's life "was as varied as the figures of a kaleidoscope, shadow and sunshine alternating with him ceaselessly . . . his biography . . . a picture remarkable for variety and strange vicissitudes."

In 1804, at age sixteen, David Seixas left New York for New Orleans. Seven years later, he moved to Philadelphia and became an agent for Harmon Hendricks, American Jewish pioneer in the importation and manufacture of copper. David then went into his own business, manufacturing English-style crockery, the importation of which was interrupted by the War of 1812, and gained renown for his innovations in this field.

Historian Kenneth Libo notes that David Seixas's inventiveness made a number of existing products more useful, such as an improved sealing wax and a less costly printer's ink. Seixas built a brewery, pioneered the daguerreotype process (an early form of photography) and discovered a method for igniting anthracite coal, which to

that point had been considered too dense to burn. This high-intensity coal became a key ingredient in steel manufacturing.

Like many inventors, Seixas never made a substantial living from his creations. What he lacked in business acumen, however, he made up for in social conscience. Around 1816, Seixas attended a lecture by Thomas H. Gallaudet on the latest innovations in teaching the deaf. Inspired by what he heard, according to Libo, "Seixas became acquainted with a number of deaf waifs on the streets of Philadelphia whose shabby appearance and wild gestures frequently excited laughter and ridicule." Seixas brought eleven of them to his home, which he shared with his widowed mother and two unmarried sisters. In Seixas's words, these children had been "thrown aside as useless lumber," but it was his "hope to restore [each one] to society as a useful and happy member."

Seixas gave up his businesses to teach the children a sign language he had invented. Rebecca Gratz, a contemporary Jewish altruist who worked to improve the lives of Philadelphia's poor children (see page 88), wrote, "David Seixas is distinguishing himself among the benefactors of mankind, and is likely to reap the reward due his talent and humanity." Indeed, Seixas's efforts made such a favorable impression that in 1820, Philadelphia's leading philanthropists established the Pennsylvania Institution for the Deaf and Dumb, promising that "indigent children, resident anywhere within the State, shall be received into the school and asylum, maintained and educated gratuitously as far as the funds of the institution shall permit." They named Seixas the school's headmaster.

The school's first graduates included Albert Newsam, who became a leading lithographer, and John Carlin, who became a successful portraitist and advocate for deaf education. In 1821, the Pennsylvania legislature, much impressed, voted to fund the annual attendance of fifty indigent students at the school.

If Rebecca Gratz thought that David Seixas was "likely to reap the reward due his talent and humanity" she was wrong. Instead, in November of 1821, Seixas was ignominiously dismissed from his post. The preceding summer, the mother of a female student had confided to Mrs. Cowgill, the school's matron, that she had dreamed that her daughter was at risk of being molested. Three months later, Mrs. Cowgill somehow got the mother, who could neither read nor write, to pen a note about her dream. Cowgill then passed it to a school trustee. A committee of trustees, in the presence of Mrs. Cowgill, met with the girl, who accused Seixas of visiting her in her sleeping quarters and hugging and kissing her. There were inconsistencies in the girl's story and the mother admitted that she would have forgotten the dream if Mrs. Cowgill had not urged her to record it. Yet the investigation continued.

In his defense, Seixas wrote of his feelings toward his students, "Already, before their entrance into the Asylum, I had fed many, clothed some, and instructed all. . . . I had raised them to partial habits of mental and physical industry; I beheld them elevated by my own personal sacrifices." Seixas asked, "Could I contemplate their former state of degradation . . . without experiencing a solemn responsibility . . . for them? Who cultivates a vegetable—who rears an animal —a brute—and yet feels not a kindred like sensation?"

The committee found Seixas guilty.

As with many child-abuse allegations, we will probably never know the full facts. The case against Seixas was based on the solicited testimony of a girl influenced by adults, but she did say that Seixas had molested her. Isaac Leeser labeled Seixas's removal an act of anti-Semitism. Rebecca Gratz and other prominent Philadelphians, in a vote of confidence, established Seixas as the head of newly created Philadelphia Asylum for the Deaf and Dumb, which they funded. Still, the blot sullied Seixas's reputation during his lifetime and still shadows it.

Perhaps the final word belongs to the Pennsylvania legislature, which in 1824 voted David Seixas "the thanks of the people of this Commonwealth for his unremitting zeal and success in improving the children under his tuition."

Sponsored by Frances and Harold S. Rosenbluth

4

Isaac Lesser
and the Blood of Damascus

*Whoever preserves a single soul of Israel . . .
it is as if he preserved an entire world.*
—Babylonian Talmud

The earliest collective action by American Jewry on behalf of their overseas brethren came in 1840 in response to a "blood libel" charge in Damascus. That year, in the ancient capital of Syria, an Italian friar and his Muslim servant mysteriously disappeared. The Capuchin order of Catholic monks charged that Jews had kidnapped and ritually murdered the two men to fulfill a reputed injunction that non-Jewish blood had to be used in making Passover matzoh. Under torture, two "witnesses" named sev-eral prominent Damascus Jews as the "killers." The accused were arrested, tortured, and sentenced to death. Knowing the suggestibility of child witnesses, local officials then seized sixty-three Jewish children to compel them to "reveal" where the blood was hidden.

Word of these outrages reached the United States in the summer of 1840. American Jews were dismayed that the ancient blood libel—the charge that ritual murder of Christians was a part of the Passover ritual—had reared its ugly head. What was American Jewry, so few in number and weak in international influence, to do? While the English and French Jewish communities sent delegations to the Ottoman sultan protesting the treatment of Damascus's Jews, American Jewry—numbering no more than 15,000 individuals scattered across a vast nation—had no national organization to speak for it, no experience at presenting a united front on any issue of national or international moment.

Rabbi Isaac Leeser of Philadelphia, America's foremost traditionalist rabbi, joined by communal leaders from other major cities, filled the breach. Leeser helped organize public rallies, meetings of synagogue congregations and committees of correspondence in New York, Philadelphia, Richmond, and Cincinnati, among other cities. The rallies called on President Martin Van Buren to intervene on behalf of the Jews of Damascus.

The American Jewish petitions argued, "The moral influence of the Chief Magistrate of the United States would be, under Heaven, the best aid we could invoke for the protection of our persecuted brethren under the Mohammedan domain." The New York protesters did "most emphatically and solemnly deny as well in our own name as in that of the whole Jewish people, that murder was ever committed by the Jews of Damascus, or those of any other part of the world, for the purpose of using the blood or any part of a human being in the ceremonies of our religion."

Van Buren ordered American diplomats in Constantinople and Alexandria to inform the Ottoman government of the "horror" felt by all Americans at the "extravagant charges strikingly similar to those which, in less enlightened ages, were made pretexts for the persecution and spoliation of these unfortunate people." The president cited America's liberal institutions, which "place upon the same footing, the worshipers of God, of every faith and form." American values compelled Van Buren to protest "in behalf of an oppressed and persecuted race, among whose kindred are found some of the most worthy and patriotic of [American] citizens."

Bowing to pressure from the United States, Britain and France, Pasha Muhammed Ali, the Ottoman overlord of Syria, ordered an end to the torture and confinement of the Jewish prisoners and instructed officials in Damascus to protect the city's Jewish community. The American ambassador helped Sir Moses Montefiore, who represented English Jewry, to secure from the Ottoman sultan an imperial decree in November declaring that the blood libel had "not the least foundation in truth" and that Jews "shall possess the same advantages and enjoy the same privileges" as his other subjects, especially the free exercise of their religion.

American Jewry had experienced its first taste of successful united action on behalf of its brethren overseas. Rabbi Leeser expressed the thinking of many American Jews of the time, as well as the spirit of the Babylonian Talmud, when he observed, "As citizens we belong to the country we live in; but as believers in one God, as the faithful adorers of the Creator, as the inheritors of the law, the Jews [of other lands] are no aliens among us, and we hail the Israelite as brother, no matter whether his home be the torrid zone, or where the poles encircle the earth with impenetrable fetters of icy coldness." These words remain the credo of American Jewry to the present day.

Sponsored by Ruth and Sid Lapidus

5

General Grant's Infamy

In 1862, in the heat of the Civil War, General Ulysses S. Grant initiated the most blatant *official* episode of anti-Semitism in nineteenth-century American history. In December of that year, Grant issued his infamous General Order No. 11, which expelled all Jews from Kentucky, Tennessee and Mississippi.

The immediate cause of the expulsion was the raging black market in Southern cotton. While enemies in war, the North and South remained dependent on each other economically. Northern textile mills needed Southern cotton. The Union Army itself used Southern cotton for tents and uniforms. Although the Union command preferred an outright ban, President Lincoln decided to allow limited trade in Southern cotton.

To control the trade, Lincoln insisted that the Treasury Department and the Army license it. As commander of the Department of the Tennessee, Grant was charged with issuing trade licenses in his area. With cotton prices soaring in the North, unlicensed traders bribed Union officers to allow them to buy Southern cotton without a permit. As one exasperated correspondent told the secretary of war, "Every colonel, captain or quartermaster is in a secret partnership with some operator in cotton; every soldier dreams of adding a bale of cotton to his monthly pay."

In the fall of 1862, Grant was under pressure to capture the heavily defended city of Vicksburg, thereby enabling the Union to control the Mississippi River and cut the Confederacy in half. Grant resented having to divert his attention from Vicksburg to the cotton trade, and especially the corruption it was causing. Merchants seeking trade permits besieged his headquarters. When Grant's own father appeared one day seeking licenses for a group of Cincinnati merchants, some of whom were Jews, Grant's frustration boiled over.

Only a handful of the corrupt traders were Jews, but in the emotional climate of the war zone, ancient prejudices flourished. The terms "Jew," "profiteer" "speculator," and "trader" began to be employed interchangeably. The Union's commanding general, Henry W. Halleck, linked "traitors and Jew peddlers." Grant had a similar mentality, describing the "Israelites" in the war zone as "an intolerable nuisance."

In November 1862, convinced that the black market in cotton was organized "mostly by Jews and other unprincipled traders," Grant ordered that "no Jews are to be permitted to travel on the railroad southward [into the department] from any point," nor were they to be granted trade licenses. The illegal commerce continued, and on December 17, Grant issued Order No. 11: "The Jews, as a class violating every regulation of trade established by the Treasury Department . . . are hereby expelled from [Kentucky, Tennessee, and Mississippi] within twenty-four hours."

Subordinates enforced the order at once in the area surrounding Grant's headquarters in Holly Springs, Mississippi. Some Jewish traders had to trudge 40 miles on foot to evacuate the area. In Paducah, Kentucky, Union officers gave the town's thirty Jewish families—all long-term residents, none of them speculators, and at least two of them Union veterans—twenty-four hours to leave.

Several of Paducah's Jewish merchants, led by Cesar Kaskel, dispatched an indignant telegram to President Lincoln condemning Grant's order as an "enormous outrage on all laws and humanity . . . the grossest violation of the Constitution and our rights as good citizens under it." Jewish leaders in St. Louis, Louisville and Cincinnati organized protest rallies and telegrams reached the White House from the Jewish communities of Chicago, New York, and Philadelphia.

Cesar Kaskel arrived in Washington on January 3, 1863. Two days earlier, the Emancipation Proclamation had gone into effect. Kaskel conferred with Adolphus Solomons, an influential Jewish Republican, and then went with Cincinnati Congressman John A. Gurley directly to the White House. Lincoln received them promptly. After studying Kaskel's copies of General Order No. 11 and the specific order expelling Jews from Paducah, Lincoln commanded Halleck to order Grant to revoke General Order No. 11. Grant complied three days later.

On January 6, a delegation led by Rabbi Isaac M. Wise of Cincinnati called on Lincoln to express its gratitude. Lincoln received the delegation cordially, told them he was surprised that Grant had issued such a command, and stated his conviction that "to condemn a class is, to say the least, to wrong the good with the bad." He drew no distinction between Jew and Gentile, the president said, and would allow no American to be wronged because of his religious affiliation.

After the war, by deed and word, Grant overcame his anti-Semitic reputation. A subordinate had drafted General Order No. 11, he said, and he had signed the document without reading it. Grant carried the Jewish vote in the presidential election of 1868, formed close friendships with individual Jews and named several Jews to high office. General Order No. 11 remains one of the few blights on the brilliant military career of the general who saved the Union. *Sponsored by Eli Blach*

6

Thanksgiving and the Jews: Pennsylvania, 1868

The first Thanksgiving was held in Plymouth, Massachusetts, in 1621, attended by ninety Native Americans and fifty English Pilgrim settlers. The idea of a feast to offer thanks for agricultural bounty mirrored ancient harvest celebrations, such as the Jewish Sukkot, the Greek mid-June Thesmophorian celebration and the Roman Cerealian rites of mid-April. The Pilgrims' day of thanksgiving was not an annual event and did not become an American ritual for more than 200 years. To mark the adoption of the Constitution and the establishment of a new government, President George Washington declared November 26, 1789 a day of thanksgiving and prayer. However, he did not renew his declaration in subsequent years and it was not until 1863, in the midst of a terrible Civil War, that President Abraham Lincoln fixed the last Thursday of each November as a "day of thanksgiving and praise to our beneficent Father." After the Union triumphed, Thanksgiving Day became an even more significant observance in the northern states.

It was in this context that Governor John W. Geary of Pennsylvania, in 1868, issued a proclamation to the citizens of his state urging them to celebrate Thanksgiving. Geary's proclamation read in part:

> Unto God our Creator we are indebted for life and all its blessings. It therefore becomes us at all times to render unto Him the homage of grateful hearts . . .and I recommend that the people of this Commonwealth on [November 26] refrain from their usual avocations and pursuits, and assemble at their chosen place of worship, to "praise the name of God and magnify Him with thanksgiving."

While these sentiments were not offensive, some of what else Geary said was: "Let us thank Him with Christian humility for health and prosperity," he urged, calling on Pennsylvanians to pray that "our paths through life may be directed by the example and instructions of the Redeemer, who died that we might enjoy the blessings which temporarily flow therefrom, and eternal life in the world to come."

The terms Geary used roused a unified protest from Philadelphia's rabbis because, in the words of America's first English-language Jewish newspaper, the *Occident*, the governor "apparently intended to exclude Israelites" from the celebration. According to the *Occident,* a week after Geary's proclamation the "Hebrew Ministers" of Philadelphia "deemed it their duty" to draft a powerful petition in response. Their "solemn protest" was signed by all seven of the city's rabbis, including Sabato Morais, who later played a central role in establishing the Conservative movement's Jewish Theological Seminary of America in New York, and Morris Jastrow, a major Reform figure. Regarding Geary's choice of words, the rabbis, regardless of affiliation, agreed that:

> An [elected] official, chosen by a large constituency, as the guardian of inalienable rights, ought not to have evinced a spirit of exclusiveness. He should have remembered that the people he governs are not of one mind touching religious dogmas, and that by asking all to pray that "their paths through life may be directed by the example and instruction of the Redeemer" . . . he casts reflections upon thousands, who hold a different creed from that which he avows.

In his private capacity, the rabbis said, Governor Geary would certainly resent being told by a Catholic priest that on a national holiday he should go make confession, and so too he would resent it if another public official told him to perform some religious observance. "The freedom-loving authors of the American Constitution," declared the rabbis, "opened indiscriminately to all the avenues of greatness, so that the position now filled by a follower of . . . [Protestant theologians] Calvin or Wesley may tomorrow be occupied by the descendant of Abraham, or, perchance, by a freethinker." Geary's proclamation was "an encroachment upon the immunities we are entitled to share with all the inhabitants thereof; and we appeal to the sense of justice which animates our fellow-citizens, that a conduct so unwarrantable may receive the rebuke it deserves, being universally stigmatized as an offence against liberty of conscience, unbecoming a public functionary, and derogatory to the honor of the noble state he represents."

Despite this outspoken rabbinical indictment, Geary did not revoke the proclamation, and Pennsylvania officially celebrated a Christianized Thanksgiving that year. In the decades since, however, Thanksgiving has retained little of its Christian origin. Today, signs in the windows of butcher shops in Jewish neighborhoods advertise kosher turkeys for Thanksgiving. Most American Jews have absorbed the holiday, shorn of its Christian trappings, and made it a nonreligious time for family gathering. In 1868, Pennsylvania's rabbis expressed what would become the majority American view: "a government-declared holiday should—with the possible exception of Christmas—be totally devoid of religious content, and we may all bring to it whatever, if any, spirituality we wish."

Sponsored by Louise P. and Gabriel Rosenfeld in memory of Miriam and Maxwell W. Passerman

7

American Jewry's Man in Romania

In 1870, President Ulysses S. Grant and his secretary of state, Hamilton Fish, interviewed H. Z. Sneerson, great-grandson of the founder of Lubavitch Hasidism. Arriving from Palestine, the black-frocked Sneerson hoped to persuade Grant and Fish to remove the incumbent American consul in Jerusalem, whom many considered an anti-Semite. Some months later, Sneerson again contacted Grant, this time to ask that Benjamin Franklin Peixotto be appointed as unpaid consul in the newly independent principality of Romania. At Sneerson's bidding, Peixotto, the scion of an American Sephardic dynasty whose personal papers reside at the American Jewish Historical Society, abandoned his budding legal career to help his afflicted co-religionists in Romania.

Peixotto's pursuit of political equality for Romania's Jews, once he obtained the post, seemed quixotic at the time but proved prescient in hindsight.

Under its 1858 constitution, Romania granted equal political rights to all of its Christian citizens. The constitution proclaimed that "the enjoyment of these rights may [also] be extended to other religions by legislative arrangements." In other words, if Jews were to vote or hold public office, the legislature would have to grant such rights explicitly. Grant understood that Peixotto's primary mission would be to advocate on behalf of Jewish political rights in Romania. Grant was trying to live down his reputation for anti-Semitism acquired during the Civil War (see page 118), and American public opinion at the time mildly supported humanitarian battles for Jewish rights in countries overseas.

Peixotto arrived in Bucharest, the Romanian capital, with expectations characteristic of other "enlightened" American and Western European Jews of the time. He assumed that Great Power diplomatic efforts could persuade the government to emancipate the country's Jews, most of whom were traditionally Orthodox, and that progressive secular education would help them to assimilate and modernize so that they would appear worthy of the same rights American Jews enjoyed. Peixotto hoped, in his own words, to start schools that would begin "disseminating modern thought, liberalizing the mind, reaching into [Romanian Jewry's] hearts by showing them how they may still be Jews without the frightful social costumes and customs which they persist in retaining."

At first, Peixotto did not attain his goals. The Romanian legislature's refusal to act thwarted his efforts to win citizenship for Jews, as did the unwillingness of the handful of successful, assimilated French-speaking Romanian Jews to stand up for their Yiddish-speaking brethren. Nor was Peixotto able to raise the funds to organize secular schools for Jewish students. After two years of unsuccessfully begging his American and European friends to reimburse the personal expenses he incurred while lobbying and for his outlays on Romanian Jewish schools, Peixotto was bankrupt and discouraged.

Pogroms in two cities in 1872, plus attacks on his character in the local press, persuaded Peixotto to abandon hope that Romania's nationalist government would do anything for the country's Jews. Instead, he decided to encourage emigration to the United States. Without consulting Washington, Peixotto broached the topic in a letter to the Romanian government, which greeted the proposal with enthusiasm. However, the Grant administration and many European and American Jewish lead-

ers opposed the idea. Some argued that Romania's Jews would not want to leave, others that Peixotto's proposal would make things worse for the Jews, since their Christian neighbors would consider them disloyal. Still others worried that few Romanian Jews could afford the passage, and they might not be welcome in America. Secretary Fish considered recalling Peixotto but refrained because he feared that doing so would signal indifference to the fate of Romanian Jewry.

However unpopular Peixotto's plan was elsewhere, Romania's Jews strongly embraced it. Thousands applied when they heard a rumor that he would pay the passage of any Jew wishing to emigrate to America. Peixotto had no such resources but encouraged local Jewish communities to establish emigration societies that could send individuals to America to earn enough money to bring others over. American railroads and steamship lines encouraged the dream by sending agents to Romania to promote emigration.

Assessing his efforts to encourage Jewish emigration, Peixotto wrote, "I, a free man, knowing my country and its inhabitants as I do—knowing how she has assimilated hundreds of thousands—nay—millions before, of foreign birth and equally inferior in every way to these poor people—hope that [the United States] might at least hope to rescue *some* and possibly promote the safety of *all*."

Peixotto's encouragement of emigration anticipated America's role as haven to the Jews of Europe, who emigrated by the millions between 1887 and 1920. It also reminds us of the role the United States might have played in saving at least a portion of the Holocaust victims in the 1930s and 1940s.

Sponsored by Samson Bitensky

8

Emma Lazarus,
Lost and Found

The stirring words of "The New Colossus," now inscribed at the base of the Statue of Liberty, are almost as familiar to most Americans as the national anthem.

> Give me your tired, your poor,
> Your huddled masses yearning to breathe free,
> The wretched refuse of your teaming shore.
> Send these, the homeless, tempest-tossed to me.
> I lift my lamp beside the golden door.

American Jewish poet Emma Lazarus penned the sonnet in November 1883. Today, it is considered a classic document of American history. In 1976, the only surviving version of the sonnet written in Lazarus's own hand, which is preserved in the archives of the American Jewish Historical Society, traveled across the nation with originals of the Declaration of Independence and the Constitution, as part of the nation's bicentennial celebration.

It was only by happenstance that the poem became an American icon. Lazarus wrote the sonnet at the request of a friend, Constance Cary Harrison, who was chairing an art exhibition to raise funds to construct the pedestal on which the Statue of Liberty now stands. The statue itself was a gift from the people of France to the people of the United States, but individual Americans had to voluntarily fund construction of the pedestal. Neither New York State nor the federal government was willing to do so.

As a component of the charity art exhibition, Harrison gathered a portfolio of original literary works by leading American authors, which she planned to auction as part of the fund-raising effort. Harrison asked Lazarus, already a poet of growing reputation, to write a sonnet for the occasion. Lazarus replied that she could not "write to order." Harrison knew that Lazarus had been doing volunteer work with Jewish immigrants at a Lower East Side settlement house, so she asked the poet to think of them for inspiration. Several days later, Lazarus sent Harrison "The New Colossus."

Lazarus's poem was the only offering read aloud at the opening-night gala. The literary portfolio brought a disappointing $1,500 in the auction, and its present whereabouts are unknown. Lazarus died in 1887 at the age of thirty-eight, after which her sonnet—and her poetry in general—fell into obscurity. In 1901, Lazarus's friend Georgina Schuyler decided to install a plaque inscribed with "The New Colossus" at the statue.

Schuyler's campaign to enshrine her friend's poem was not easy. Richard Watson Gilder, a friend of Lazarus and editor of the respected *Century Magazine*, helped Schuyler cut through bureaucratic red tape and the sensitivities of the Lazarus family to obtain government approval for the project. Just before the plaque was cast, however, a suggestion by Samuel Ward Gray, head of the American branch of Baring Brothers Bank, almost changed the course of history. In a letter to Gilder, Gray objected to the terms "huddled masses" and "wretched refuse." To Gray, huddled masses suggested that most immigrants were slum dwellers from big cities, but such people were not "what America has received from Europe, nor, above all, what she invites."

Gray cited America's Irish, Scandinavian, and German immigrants as examples of immigrants from predominantly rural backgrounds. Jews were the exception, in Gray's mind, since they were "town livers" and could thus be called huddled masses, but he saw the Jews who emigrated not as wretched refuse but as "strong and able." To correct Lazarus's "error," Gray offered substitute lines: "Your stirring myriad, that yearn to breathe free / But find no place upon your teeming shore."

While there is no written record of Gilder's response to Gray, he must have held firm against any changes. In 1903, Lazarus's words were cast in their original form and the plaque installed on a second-story landing inside the pedestal building. The poem remained there, once again relatively unnoticed, until an immigrant journalist of Slovenian origin, Louis Adamic, incorporated verses from "The New Colossus" into virtually everything he wrote in the 1930s and 1940s on the plight of Eastern European Jewry. Adamic's writings elevated the poem into national consciousness and, in 1945, the tablet was moved to the main entrance of the Statue of Liberty, where visitors see it today.

Despite these precarious beginnings, it is now difficult to imagine the statue without the sonnet, or the sonnet without the statue. Aside from the flag, Lady Liberty is the most recognizable symbol of America. And Emma Lazarus, Jewish author, has truly become the poet laureate of America's immigrants.

Sponsored by The Leo Rosner Foundation, Inc.

9

Mark Twain and the Jews: Part I

Mark Twain, widely regarded as America's greatest writer, was far more than a humorist. After the Civil War, he served as America's conscience on ethnic and racial issues. Twain defended Jews, blacks and Indians against prejudice. While many of his contemporaries negatively stereotyped the Jewish people, Twain defended them in word and deed. Ironically, his major published protest against anti-Semitism alienated some of the very people he was trying to defend. The story of Twain's attitude toward Jews and anti-Semitism is enlightening and requires two chapters to tell.

In his youth, Twain held the same negative views of Jews that his neighbors embraced, seeing them as acquisitive, cowardly and clannish. Hannibal, Missouri, his hometown, had only one Jewish family, the Levys, and Twain joined in hazing the young Levy sons. In 1857, Twain wrote an uncomplimentary, ironic article about Jewish coal dealers for a Keokuk, Iowa, newspaper, portraying them as money-hungry.

Twain's attitude apparently changed around the time of the Civil War. He confided to his daughter Suzy that "the Jews seemed to him a race to be much respected . . . they had suffered much, and had been greatly persecuted, so to ridicule or make fun of them seemed to be like attacking a man when he was already down."

A key moment came in 1860, when a trusted Mississippi River captain, George Newhouse, told Twain a story (the veracity of which cannot be established) about a courageous Jew who had boldly saved a slave girl in a poker dispute between a desperate planter and a cheating, knife-yielding gambler. The Jew killed the cheater in a duel and returned the slave girl to the planter's daughter, who had been her mistress as well as her friend and companion from birth. Twain later reported hearing other versions of this story from other "eye-witnesses," indicating that the story may have been apocryphal.

In the moral world of 1860, Twain saw no contradiction in returning a slave girl to her mistress rather than freeing her. The story led Twain to conclude that the Jewish hero was "an all-around man; a man cast in a large mould." These same words found their echo in Twain's reaction upon learning in 1909 that his daughter Clara was engaged to a Russian-Jewish pianist, Ossip Gabrilowitsch. Twain told Clara, "Any girl could be proud to marry him. He is a man— a real man."

Twain had replaced his earlier negative stereotype of the Jewish people with another, more positive one. In 1879, he wrote privately:

Samson was a Jew—therefore not a fool. The Jews have the best average brain of any people in the world. The Jews are the only race who work wholly with their brains and never with their hands. There are no Jewish beggars, no Jewish tramps, no Jewish ditch diggers, hod-carriers, day laborers or followers of toilsome, mechanical trades. They are peculiarly and conspicuously the world's intellectual aristocracy.

In truth, there were indeed impoverished Jewish beggars, as there were sweated Jewish toilers in the garment and cigar industries and Jews who lifted and carried in the construction trades. Just a year earlier, in fact, New York's Jewish cigar makers conducted a bitter five-month strike for higher pay and shorter hours. While Twain had meant to pay the Jewish people a compliment, his facts were inaccurate. Some of these inaccuracies would later haunt him.

Twain's personal view of Jews meant little until March 1898, when he wrote an article titled "Stirring Times in Austria." He had been living in Europe to gather material for his writings and settled in Vienna in 1896. Two years later, as part of a complicated attempt to hold together the Austro-Hungarian Empire in the face of ethnic nationalist fervor, the imperial Hapsburg family designated Czech as the official language of Bohemia (now the Czech Republic), displacing German. This policy triggered rioting by German-speaking members of the Austrian parliament, who wanted German language and culture to prevail in the empire. To distract the populace, according to Twain, the Austrian government stirred up anti-Semitic feelings, and Vienna's Jews became the victims of widespread attacks, both political and physical.

In March 1898, *Harper's Magazine* published an essay by Twain describing these events. As historian Philip Foner relates, "At the very close of the lengthy article, [Twain] mentioned, without comment, the attacks on the Jews, pointing out that, although they were innocent parties in the dispute, they were 'harried and plundered.' Twain noted, 'In all cases the Jew had to roast, no matter which side he was on.'"

The *Harper's* article generated several letters, and in particular a poignant response from an American Jewish lawyer who asked Twain to explain "why, in your judgment, the Jews have been, and are even now, in these days of supposed intelligence, the butt of baseless, vicious animosities." The lawyer further asked, "Can American Jews do anything to correct [this prejudice] either in America or abroad? Will it ever come to an end?" In response, Twain penned "Concerning the Jews," which *Harper's* also published. In the next chapter, we will examine his answers and the controversy they stirred up.

Sponsored by Norman Klein and Ellie Black

10

Mark Twain and the Jews: Part II

In March 1898, *Harper's Magazine* published Mark Twain's "Stirring Times in Austria," an account of the anti-Jewish rioting in Vienna. An American Jewish reader wrote to Twain inviting him to speculate on the causes of anti-Semitism. Twain answered with a lengthy essay titled "Concerning the Jews." He expected the article to please almost no one, a prediction that turned out to be accurate.

Twain argued that prejudice against Jews derived neither from their public conduct nor their religion, but from Christian envy of Jewish economic achievements. He cited a speech by a German lawyer who claimed that "eighty-five percent of the successful lawyers of Berlin were Jews" and therefore wanted the Jews expelled from the city. Twain observed that envy "is a much more hate-inspiring thing than is any detail connected with religion."

Twain thought Jewish success a product of the Jews' good citizenship, family loyalty, intelligence and business acumen. Crime and drunkenness, he said, were nonexistent among Jews; they cared for their needy without burdening the larger community and were honest in business. Yes, honest in business. Twain knew that most of his contemporaries viewed Jewish businessmen as crooked, but he cited the very success of the Jews as proof of their integrity.

A business cannot thrive where the parties do not trust each other. In the matter of numbers, the Jew counts for little in the overwhelming population of New York, but that his honesty counts for much is guaranteed by the fact that the immense wholesale business of Broadway, from the Battery to Union Square, is substantially in his hands.

Twain mistakenly criticized world Jewry for not taking an active role in the Dreyfus Affair, even though it had. He suggested that Jews could become a political force by using their votes in their collective interest, and that they should organize military companies to raise their prestige. He believed that Jews exhibited an "unpatriotic disinclination to stand by the flag as a soldier" and had made no significant contributions to American independence.

Commenting on the recent first World Zionist Congress in Basel, Twain noted that Theodor Herzl had enunciated a plan to "gather the Jews of the world together in Palestine, with a government of their own—under the suzerainty of the Sultan, I suppose." He observed,

I am not the Sultan, and I am not objecting; but if that concentration of the cunningest brains in the world are going to be made into a free country (bar Scotland), I think it would be politic to stop it. It will not be well to let that race find out its strength. If the horses knew theirs, we should not ride any-more.

Twain concluded:

> The Egyptian, the Babylonian, and the Persian rose, filled the planet with sound and splendor, then . . . passed away. The Greek and the Roman followed. The Jew saw them all, beat them all, and is now what he always was, exhibiting no decadence, no infirmities of age, no weakening of his parts. . . . All things are mortal but the Jew; all other forces pass, but he remains. What is the secret of his immortality?

Twain described "Concerning the Jews" as "my gem of the ocean," but predicted that "neither Jew nor Christian will approve it." He proved prescient. Jewish critics acknowledged Twain's respect for Jews but bemoaned his factual errors. They denied that Jews had played a minimal role in gaining American liberty, dominated commerce or shirked military service. Several were especially offended by Twain's saying that Jews had done nothing to win the acquittal of Captain Dreyfus.

His friendliest critics believed that Twain was innocently ignorant of the facts. Simon Wolf, a founder of the American Jewish Historical Society, sent Twain a copy of his book, *The American Jew as Patriot, Soldier and Citizen*, to correct some of his misconceptions. Others, like Rabbi M. S. Levy, thought Twain's observations were actually "tinged with malice and prejudice." Levy cited Jewish participants in the American Revolution who had "fought and bled" for the new nation. He called Twain's assertions "a libel on [the Jew's] manhood and an outrage historically." Levy also challenged Twain's assertion that Jews were "money-getters." Levy replied, "Money-getters? The Vanderbilts, Goulds, Astors, Havemeyers, Rockefellers, Mackays, Huntingtons, Armours, Carnegies, Sloanes, Whitneys, are not Jews, and yet they control and possess more than twenty-five per cent of all the circulated wealth of the United States."

Twain took the criticisms to heart. In 1904, he wrote "The Jew as Soldier," an essay conceding that Jews had indeed fought in the Revolution, the War of 1812 and the Mexican War in numbers greater than their percentage of the population. This meant that "the Jew's patriotism was not merely level with the Christian's but overpassed it." Twain did not respond to Levy's charges about Jews in the economy, but he never again raised this stereotype in print.

When Twain died in 1910, the American Jewish press mourned. Many of the obituaries reprinted the words of the president of New York's Hebrew Technical School for Girls: "In one of Mr. Clemens's works he expressed his opinion of men, saying he had no choice between Hebrew and Gentile, black men or white; to him, all men were alike." By the time of his death, Mark Twain was recognized as a true friend of the Jewish people.

Sponsored by Norman Klein and Ellie Black

11

Henry Ford Invents a Jewish Conspiracy

Henry Ford, the industrial genius who perfected the mass production of automobiles before World War I and thereby revolutionized the way we live, was a reclusive man who brooked no opposition or criticism. Ford's determination to prevent unionism at his plants produced violence, mostly initiated by his own strikebreakers. He opposed many facets of twentieth-century social and cultural change, including Hollywood movies, out-of-home childcare, government regulation of business, immigration from Eastern Europe, and new fashions in dress and music. For the most part, Ford's fame, wealth, and power insulated him against any need to apologize for his views. In 1927, his anti-Semitism brought him, for one of the few times in his life, to humiliation.

In an age that celebrated industrial heroes, Ford was a true giant. In 1922, he considered running for the presidency and public opinion polls reflected widespread support for his candidacy. Despite the fact that he apparently hoped to occupy the most scrutinized and public position in the nation, historian Keith Sward says that Ford was "inaccessible as the Grand Lama" and an anti-democrat. One of the few individuals Ford trusted was his personal secretary, Ernest Liebold, described by historian Leo Ribuffo as "an ambitious martinet" who took advantage of Ford's dislike of paper-

work and refusal to read his mail to control access to the great man. Ford would later blame Liebold for his Jewish woes.

In the period from 1910 to 1918, Ford grew increasingly anti-immigrant, anti-labor, anti-liquor, and anti-Semitic. In 1919, Ford purchased a newspaper, the *Dearborn Independent,* as a platform for these views. He hired a journalist, William J. Cameron, to listen to his ideas and write a weekly column in his name.

Ford believed there was a Jewish conspiracy to control the world economy. He blamed Jewish financiers for fomenting World War I so that they could profit from supplying both sides. He suspected Jewish automobile dealers of conspiring to undermine his company's sales policies. Ford wanted to vent his distorted beliefs about Jewish power in the pages of the *Dearborn Independent.* For a year, the editor refused to run his anti-Jewish articles and finally resigned rather than publish them. Cameron, Ford's personal columnist, took over the editorship and, in May 1920, published the first of a series of articles titled "The International Jew: The World's Problem."

Over the next eighteen months, Cameron ran "The International Jew" as a series, later collecting the articles and publishing them as a book. Liebold hired former military intelligence investigators to assist

Cameron in gathering so-called evidence which "proved" that Jews controlled world finance, were the secret organizers of radical political movements and manipulated diplomacy to cause wars in which Christians died to enrich Jews. The investigators unearthed "evidence" purportedly showing that President Woodrow Wilson had taken secret orders over the phone from Justice Brandeis and that a Jewish member of the Federal Reserve Board had personally thwarted Ford's plan to purchase nitrate mines from the federal government.

A few months after the series began, Ford's operatives introduced him to a Russian émigré, Paquita de Shishmareff. She showed Ford a copy of the *Protocols of the Elders of Zion*, a document forged by the Russian tsar's secret service at the turn of the century that purportedly recorded a series of lectures by European Jewish leaders outlining a plan by Jewish communists and bankers to overthrow the governments of Europe. Ford passed a copy of the *Protocols* to Cameron, and the *Independent* began publishing excerpts from this "blueprint" for Jewish world domination.

As historian Ribuffo noted, "It was clear [to Ford] that Jews used these ideas [in the *Protocols*] to 'corrupt Public Opinion,' [that Jews] controlled finance, sponsored revolution, and were 'everywhere' exercising power." The *Independent* charged that the Jewish-inspired national debt was enslaving Americans and that German Jewish financier Paul Warburg had emigrated to America to create the Federal Reserve "for the express purpose of changing our financial system." As an "international nation" of people who cooperated with each other, the *Independent* argued, Jews had an unfair advantage in business over Christians, who relied on individualism to get ahead. The paper even described American Jewish aid for Jewish victims of Russian pogroms as part of the conspiracy.

The *Independent* published anti-Semitic articles for seven years until the target of one series, California farm cooperative organizer Aaron Sapiro, sued Ford for libel. Sapiro was the third Jew to sue Ford and the first to get to trial. Ford refused to testify and apparently staged an automobile accident so he could hide in a hospital. The judge finally declared a mistrial, but Ford decided to settle with Sapiro out of court. During the trial, Jewish leaders had called for a boycott of Ford cars, and slumping sales may have played a role in Ford's decision to settle the case.

The American Jewish Committee and the B'nai B'rith Anti-Defamation League negotiated an agreement whereby Ford publicly announced that "articles reflecting on the Jews" would never again appear in the *Independent.* Ford claimed he was "mortified" on learning that the *Protocols* had been forged, described himself as "fully aware of the virtues of the Jewish people" and offered them his "future friendship and good will." Claiming to have been too busy to read the pieces, he implicitly blamed Liebold and Cameron for printing them. Louis Marshall, chairman of the American Jewish Committee, described Ford's statement as "humiliating."

Ford closed the *Independent* in December 1927. Years later he claimed that his signature on the agreement with the Jewish organization had been forged and that Jewish bankers had caused World War II. Ford died in 1947, apparently unchanged and unrepentant.

Sponsored by Irene and Arnold Rabinor

12

Rabbi Brennglass
and the Massena Blood Libel

Massena is a quiet city in upstate New York. It sits beside the St. Lawrence River across the water from Canada. The Jewish populace is small and supports one synagogue. Massena seems an unlikely location for a major event in American Jewish history, but it was.

In 1928, a "blood libel" accusation against the hundred or so Jews then living in Massena tore the city apart. Blood libels have been a part of Jewish history at least since 1144, when the Jews of England were accused of having purchased a Christian boy—the child martyr William of Norwich—to torture and crucify him. At the heart of the blood libel is the canard that Jews murder Christian children to procure their blood, or more rarely their internal organs, for use in making matzoh at Passover. Geoffrey Chaucer, author of the *Canterbury Tales*, accused the "cursed Jewes" of infanticide in "The Prioress's Tale." The myth of Jewish ritual sacrifice persisted through the centuries and occasionally resonated on the fringes of American society, nowhere more openly and angrily than in Massena, New York.

On Erev Yom Kippur, 1928, the New York State Police brought in Rabbi Berel Brennglass of Massena's Orthodox congregation Adath Israel for questioning. Four-

year-old Barbara Griffiths of Massena had disappeared and Albert Comnas, a Greek immigrant from Salonika, charged that, as the highest of Jewish holy days was at hand, the Jews of Massena might have kidnapped little Barbara and ritually murdered her for her blood. The police interrogated Rabbi Brennglass for more than an hour about Jewish practices in respect to human sacrifice and the use of blood in food. Fortunately, during the interrogation, Barbara emerged from the woods, where, having become lost, she had spent the night in the tall grass.

Her reappearance did not fully calm some of the townspeople. They suggested that the Jews had released her only because their plot had been discovered. Choosing to believe this was true, Mayor W. Gilbert Hawes organized a boycott of Massena's Jewish-owned businesses. Massena's dismayed Jewish community leaders called on Rabbi Stephen S. Wise, chairman of the American Jewish Congress, to intervene. Wise called on his friend Al Smith, New York's governor, who was running for president on the Democratic ticket that year, to speak out in defense of Massena's Jews. Smith assured Wise that while he could do nothing about the mayor's actions, which were not under his jurisdiction, he would make certain that the actions of the state trooper in the case were thoroughly investigated.

The incident ended during the next two or three weeks. The *New York Times* picked up the story and made it a national event. Mayor Hawes, a Republican with his eyes on his pending reelection campaign and apparently under pressure from the national Republican Party, issued a public apology. His statement read in part, "In light of the solemn protest of my Jewish neighbors, I feel I ought to express clearly and unequivocally . . . my sincere regret that by any act of commission or omission, I should have seemed to lend countenance . . . to what I should have known to be a cruel libel imputing human sacrifice as a practice now or at any time in the history of the Jewish people." Hawes was reelected for a sixth consecutive term.

Historically, blood libels have not been leveled exclusively at Jews. Ironically, in Roman times the early Christians were accused of practicing infanticide and baby eating. Perhaps this was a residual charge associated with the Jewish origins of early Christianity. The Spanish explorers of the New World justified their conquest of Mexico on the grounds that the Aztecs performed "ritual crucifixions" at Easter (a logical impossibility, since the Aztecs knew nothing of Christian theology). As recently as the Bosnian war, Serbian militiamen accused their Muslim opponents of crucifying and decapitating Christian children and floating their corpses down the Drina River.

However, the blood libel charge has clung consistently to Jews for at least a millennium. That it could arise in the United States in the twentieth century gives pause. As Rabbi Brennglass reminded his congregation at the Kol Nidre service in 1928, "We must forever remind ourselves that this happened in America, not tsarist Russia, among people we have come to regard as our friends. We must show our neighbors that their hatred originates in fear, and that this fear has its roots in ignorance. . . . We must show them they have nothing to fear from us. We must tell the world this story so it will never happen again."

In memory of Edward B. Schilder

13

The Myth of Ben Franklin's Anti-Semitism

The economic despair of the 1930s spawned a number of right-wing journalists who blamed Jews for the Great Depression. One of the most influential was a Nazi sympathizer, William Dudley Pelley (1890–1965), whose magazine, *Liberation*, was a significant source of anti-Semitic venom. The isolationist Pelley boldly—and falsely—invoked words supposedly spoken by Benjamin Franklin to stir resentment against Jews, whom Pelley claimed had deliberately caused the depression for their own benefit. Pelley's libel of Franklin, although declared by experts to be false, continues to emerge from time to time to blemish that great man's reputation.

Pelley "quoted" Franklin from the purported private diary of Charles Pinckney, a South Carolinian and one of the framers of the Constitution. Pinckney supposedly kept the diary during the Constitutional Convention in 1787. Pelley claimed to have in his possession one of the few copies of the diary that had survived General Sherman's order to destroy private libraries during his Civil War march through the South. Pelley may have written the diary himself, or perhaps a copy of the forged document was given to him. We do know that Franklin never uttered the words attributed to him in the forged diary.

Pelley claimed that Pinckney's diary quoted Franklin addressing the Constitutional Convention as follows:

> We must safeguard this young nation . . . from the insidious influence and impenetration of the Continental religions which pauperize and degrade all countries and peoples over whom they hold sway. But there is a greater menace to these United States of America than the strictly Roman [Catholic threat].
>
> This greater menace, gentlemen, is the Jew!
>
> In whatever country Jews have settled in any great numbers they have lowered its moral tone; they have depreciated its commercial integrity; have segregated themselves; have not assimilated; have sneered at, and tried to undermine, the Christian religion upon which this nation is founded, by objecting to its restrictions; have built up a State within a State, and when opposed have tried to strangle that country to death financially, as in the case of Spain and Portugal.

Paradoxically, after accusing Jews of segregating themselves and not assimilating into the nations in which they lived, Franklin supposedly called them hypocrites for proclaiming their desire for a homeland in Palestine. Pelley quotes Franklin as saying that Jews do not want to live in their own nation "because they are vampires, and vampires do not live upon vampires. They cannot live among themselves only. They must subsist on Christians, and other peoples not of their race."

Franklin allegedly warned the convention: "If you do not exclude [Jews] from the United States in the Constitution, in less than two hundred years they will have swarmed here in such great numbers that they will dominate and devour the land, and change our form of government for which we have shed our blood, given our lives, our substance, jeopardized our liberty, and put into it our best thoughts." Pelley italicized Franklin's final words on the subject: *"If you do not exclude the Jews for all time, your children's children will curse you in your graves!"*

Franklin has been frequently quoted elsewhere as saying, "There is much difference between imitating a good man, and counterfeiting him." Pelley's Franklin was clearly a counterfeit, not an imitation, but it took on a life of its own. Rumor circulated that a copy of Pinckney's diary could be found at the Franklin Institute in Boston. In 1938, the institute's director published a rebuttal of Pelley's canard, a copy of which resides in the archives of the American Jewish Historical Society. The director denied that the institute had a copy of the diary and noted that "historians and librarians have not been able to find it or any record of it having existed. The historians have further said that some of the words and phraseology used in the quoted speech cast grave doubt upon its colonial origin." One of the most notable anachronisms is the charge that colonial American Jews were calling for a homeland in Palestine, for the movement to resettle the Holy Land did not begin until the nineteenth century. The director summed up the historians' view of the diary by saying, "In plain English, they have deemed it a fake."

The director accused the forger of having a "hellish desire to fan the flame of racial hatred." The truth of Franklin's feelings toward Jews, he noted, was quite different. For example, he observed, "When the Hebrew Society of Philadelphia sought to raise money for 'a religious house,' or synagogue, in Philadelphia, Franklin signed the petition of appeal for contributions to 'citizens of every religious denomination,' and gave five pounds personally to the fund. . . . We suggest to our benighted friends that they read what Franklin thought about Honesty, Peace, Virtue, Religion, Industry and Citizenship."

The director concluded by quoting Franklin's own Poor Richard: "A lie stands on one leg, truth on two." Even though this lie about Franklin only stands on one leg, it apparently continues to stand. In 2001, an Egyptian general invoked Pelley's version of Franklin's "warning" about American Jewry as part of a verbal attack on the State of Israel.

Sponsored by Samson Bitensky

14

Rabbi Gittelsohn's Iwo Jima Sermon

The fight for Iwo Jima in 1945 was one of the bloodiest of World War II. A tiny island in the Pacific dominated by a volcanic mountain and pockmarked with caves, Iwo Jima was the setting for a five-week, non-stop battle between 70,000 American marines and an unknown number of deeply entrenched Japanese defenders. The courage and gallantry of the American forces, climaxed by the dramatic raising of the American flag over Mount Suribachi, is memorialized in the Marine Corps monument in Washington, D.C. Less remembered, however, is that the battle occasioned an eloquent eulogy by a Marine Corps rabbi that has become an American classic.

Rabbi Roland B. Gittelsohn (1910–1995), assigned to the Fifth Marine Division, was the first Jewish chaplain in the history of the Marine Corps. The American invasion force at Iwo Jima included approximately 1,500 Jewish marines. Rabbi Gittelsohn was in the thick of the fray, ministering to marines of all faiths under fire. He shared the fear, horror and despair of the fighting men, each of whom knew that each day might be his last. Roland Gittelsohn's tireless efforts to comfort the wounded and encourage the fearful won him three service ribbons.

When the fighting ended, Division Chaplain Warren Cuthriell, a Protestant minister, asked Rabbi Gittelsohn to deliver the memorial sermon at a combined religious service dedicating the Marine Cemetery on Iwo Jima. Cuthriell wanted all the fallen marines—black and white, Protestant, Catholic and Jewish—honored in a single nondenominational ceremony.

Unfortunately, racial and religious prejudice was still strong in the Marine Corps, as it was then in America. According to Rabbi Gittelsohn, most of the other Christian chaplains objected to having a rabbi preach over predominantly Christian graves. The Catholic chaplains in particular, in keeping with church doctrine, opposed any form of joint prayer service.

To his credit, Cuthriell refused to alter his plans. Gittelsohn, on the other hand, wanted to save his friend further embarrassment and so decided it was best not to deliver his sermon. Instead, three separate religious services were held. At the Jewish service, to a congregation of seventy or so who attended, Rabbi Gittelsohn delivered the powerful eulogy he had originally written for the combined service:

> Here lie men who loved America because their ancestors generations ago helped in her founding, and other men who loved her with equal passion because they themselves or their own fathers escaped from oppression to her blessed shores. Here lie officers and men, Negroes and whites, rich men and poor . . . together. Here are Protestants, Catholics and Jews together. Here no man prefers another because of his faith or despises him because of his color. Here there are no quotas of how many from each group are admitted or allowed. Among these men, there is no discrimination. No prejudices. No hatred. Theirs is the highest and purest democracy. . . .
>
> Whosoever of us lifts his hand in hate against a brother, or who thinks himself superior to those who happen to be in the minority, makes of this ceremony and the bloody sacrifice it commemorates, an empty, hollow mockery. To this, then, as our

> solemn duty, sacred duty do we the living now dedicate ourselves: to the right of Protestants, Catholics, and Jews, of white men and Negroes alike, to enjoy the democracy for which all of them have here paid the price. . . .
>
> *We here solemnly swear that this shall not be in vain. Out of this and from the suffering and sorrow of those who mourn this will come, we promise, the birth of a new freedom for the sons of men everywhere.*

Among Gittelsohn's listeners were three Protestant chaplains so incensed by the prejudice of their colleagues that they boycotted their own service to attend Gittelsohn's. One of them borrowed the manuscript and, unknown to Gittelsohn, circulated several thousand copies to his regiment. Some marines enclosed the copies in letters to their families. An avalanche of coverage resulted. *Time* magazine published excerpts, which the wire services spread even further. The entire sermon was inserted into the *Congressional Record*, the Army released the eulogy for shortwave broadcast to American troops throughout the world and radio commentator Robert St. John read it on his program and on many succeeding Memorial Days.

In 1995, in his last major public appearance before his death, Gittelsohn reread a portion of the eulogy at the fiftieth commemoration ceremony at the Iwo Jima statue in Washington. In his autobiography, Gittelsohn reflected, "I have often wondered whether anyone would ever have heard of my Iwo Jima sermon had it not been for the bigoted attempt to ban it."

Sponsored by Sally F. Broido in memory of Theodore Broido, who loved and trusted Roland B. Gittlesohn

Part VII

Sports

1

"The Great Bennah": Pride of the Jews

Growing up in New York's Greenwich Village before World War I, Benjamin Leiner, the son of Russian Jewish immigrants, and his friends fought against Irish, Italian and other ethnic youth gangs for neighborhood "turf." As he later recalled, "In the winter we fought with snowballs packed tightly around pieces of coal and soaked with water until they were hard as cannon balls. Then we used baseball bats, stones and loaded canes. . . . There was many a boy who suffered permanent injury from an encounter with the warriors from the next block."

After Leiner lost one of these street fights, his uncle took him for boxing lessons. According to historian Peter Levine, the slender young Leiner became the undisputed champion of his block and began fighting for prize money at local gyms.

Leiner's mother deeply opposed his fighting, which she considered dangerous and unseemly for an Orthodox Jewish boy. To protect her feelings, Leiner began fighting under the name Benny Leonard, but he could not keep his secret for long. Confronted after returning home with a black eye, Benny admitted that he had been hurt in the ring. Then he put his $20 winnings on the kitchen table. "My mother," he later said, "looked at my black eye and wept. My father, who had to work all week for

$20, said, 'All right Benny, keep on fighting. It's worth getting a black eye for $20; I am getting *verschwartzt* [blackened] for $20 a week.'"

This anecdote tells much about how boxing helped assimilate East European Jewish immigrants and their children into the American mainstream. For successful fighters like Leonard, it offered a chance to escape from low-wage sweatshops and factories. By 1916, Benny could afford to move his parents to a larger home in Harlem, where he continued to live.

In 1917, Leonard won the lightweight championship of the world. That night, his immigrant Jewish followers proudly marched through Harlem waving American flags. Leonard held the title for eight long years, despite the fact that the lightweight division was probably the most competitive in boxing. Known as "the Great Bennah," Leonard was so skillful that he could boast of going through fights without his opponent mussing his hair. Sportswriter Al Lurie wrote that when Leonard was the champion, he was "the most famous Jew in America . . . beloved by thin-faced little Jewish boys who, in their poverty, dreamed of themselves as champions of the world."

One of those little boys was Budd Schulberg, who later became a famous novelist and screenwriter. Schulberg said of

Leonard, "To see him climb in the ring sporting the six-pointed star on his fighting trunks was to anticipate sweet revenge for all the bloody noses, split lips and mocking laughter at pale little Jewish boys who had run the neighborhood gauntlet."

Leonard's reign as champion was about more than revenge, however. It conveyed respect and recognition. In a burst of hyperbole, the *New Warheit,* an American Jewish paper, compared "the Great Bennah" to Albert Einstein and concluded that the boxer "is perhaps even greater than Einstein, for when Einstein was in America only thousands knew him but Benny is known by millions. It is said that only twelve people or at the most twelve times twelve the world over understand Einstein, but Benny is understood by tens of millions in America." The paper drew a Zionist conclusion from Leonard's success: "Just as we need a country so as to be the equal of other people, so we must have fists to become their peers."

Ever mindful of his mother's concern, Leonard retired in 1925. "My love for her," he told the press, "is greater than my love for the game that has made me independently wealthy, and to which I owe all I now possess." Unfortunately, the stock market crash of 1929 wiped out Leonard's wealth. By 1930, he felt he had to return to the ring to recoup his fortune.

Sadly, age and inactivity had taken their toll. After a series of tune-up fights against weaker opponents, Leonard was matched against a tough Irish boxer, Jimmy McClarnin. "There is scarcely a Jew whose blood runs red," the sportswriter for the Los Angeles *B'nai B'rith Messenger* wrote, "who is not vitally interested in the outcome. . . . Win, lose or draw, this compatriot of mine will have shown the world that he was a true fighting man."

McClarnin knocked out Leonard in six rounds, the first time Leonard lost by a KO. He retired again and assumed a career in vaudeville and as a boxing referee. In 1947, while refereeing a fight, he had a heart attack and died in the ring, a fitting place for his life to end. Al Lurie mourned Leonard with the following words:

> When a people is beaten, persecuted and frustrated, it finds more than mere solace in its champions. . . . When Leonard was accepted and admired by the entire fair-minded American community, the Jews of America felt they, themselves, were being accepted and admired. Leonard, therefore, symbolized all Jewry.

Since Leonard's time, Jews have earned America's admiration in such fields as science, medicine, business, entertainment and politics. Like other immigrants groups, however, Jews had to fight their way into respectable society. Benny Leonard did his fighting in the ring, on behalf of an entire generation.

Sponsored by Judge Lawrence Ashley

2

Arnold Rothstein:
J. P. Morgan of the Underworld

Nothing gave a stronger boost to organized crime in America than Prohibition, which took effect on January 16, 1920. The ban on the manufacture and sale of drinking alcohol did nothing to dry up the demand for whiskey and wine. Some observers speculated, in fact, that banning alcoholic beverages made them more appealing to those who might otherwise not have indulged. In 1989, retired Detroit gangster Hershel Kessler told historian Robert Rockaway that during Prohibition, "People wanted booze, they wanted dope, they wanted to gamble and they wanted broads. For a price, we provided them with these amusements. We only gave them what they wanted."

Historians speculate that Jews comprised half of the nation's leading bootleggers, and that Jewish gangsters like Meyer Lansky and Bugsy Siegel dominated organized crime in certain cities. As the city with the largest Jewish population, New York produced the largest number of Jewish gangsters. The kingpin of the New York Jewish underworld was not a street-tough gangster but a refined gambler named Arnold Rothstein. According to Rockaway, "Rothstein is recognized as the pioneer big businessman of organized crime in the United States." Of his various escapades, Rothstein is best remembered for his impact on American sports.

Historian Leo Katcher described Rothstein as "the J. P. Morgan of the underworld; its banker and master of strategy." Meyer Lansky, a man of some intelligence himself, observed, "Rothstein had the most remarkable brain. He understood business instinctively and I'm sure that if he had been a legitimate financier he would have been just as rich as he became with his gambling and the other rackets he ran."

Rothstein was born with a business pedigree. New York governor Al Smith dubbed his father, wealthy businessman Abraham Rothstein, "Abe the Just." A pious man with a reputation for philanthropy and honesty, Abraham Rothstein served as chairman of the board of New York's Beth Israel Hospital. His older son became a rabbi. Younger son Arnold was interested in business, but not his father's. After flunking out of school because he spent his time gambling, Arnold Rothstein figured that "if anyone was going to make money out of gambling he had better be on the right side of the fence. I was on the wrong end of the game." In his late twenties, Rothstein opened a gambling parlor. By 1912, when he was thirty, Rothstein was a millionaire from the profits of his gambling parlors and the racetracks he owned.

Rockaway observed, "With gambling as his base, Rothstein had access to the cash and political protection needed to make big deals in many other spheres," notably bootlegging. He was among the first to purchase fine liquor in England, smuggle it to America by the boatload and distribute it to the speakeasies and "blind pigs" that replaced legal taverns during Prohibition.

Rothstein did not stay in liquor smuggling for long. The business was too decentralized for him to control and the profit margins were small. He turned his experience as an "importer" to narcotics smuggling, a far more lucrative and less competitive business. By 1926, Rothstein was the financial overlord of the American narcotics trade.

Rothstein had an eye for talent. His henchmen during the 1920s included celebrity thugs such as "Legs" Diamond, "Lucky" Luciano, Dutch Schultz, and Frank Costello. Luciano worshipped Rothstein. "He taught me how to dress . . . how to use knives and forks and things like that at the dinner table, about holdin' a door open for a girl," Luciano reminisced. "If Arnold had lived a little longer, he could've made me pretty elegant."

Rothstein's style captured the public imagination. Damon Runyan modeled the character Nathan Detroit in *Guys and Dolls* on him. In *The Great Gatsby*, F. Scott Fitzgerald called his Rothstein-based character Meyer Wolfsheim. Nothing Rothstein accomplished in his life of gambling, bootlegging and dealing drugs compares, however, with his fixing the World Series—the Black Sox Scandal of 1919.

In 1919, baseball was truly America's pastime. Because they considered themselves grossly underpaid by team owner Charles Comisky, eight members of the Chicago White Sox, led by first baseman Chick Gandil, conspired to lose the World Series to the underdog Cincinnati Reds—if they could find a gambler willing to pay them to lose. Gandil approached Abe Attell, a former featherweight boxing champion who had fought under the name "the little Hebrew" and, in retirement, was Arnold Rothstein's bodyguard. Gandil told Attell that for $100,000, he could guarantee that his teammates would lose to Cincinnati. Attell in turn told Rothstein that he could fix the Series for the right price, but by most accounts Rothstein rejected the proposition, sensing that Attell was trying to horn in on his own sphere. The idea seemed a good one, though, so Rothstein apparently arranged through another intermediary to pay the White Sox players $80,000 to lose. They did, and Rothstein made a significant sum betting against Chicago.

In 1921, the eight players were convicted of fraud and banned from baseball. Abe Attell was convicted of trying to fix the Series. Rothstein, who never met the players and could honestly say that he had never approved Attell's scheme, testified in his own behalf and was acquitted.

In 1928, a fellow gambler shot Rothstein. True to the underworld code, he died several days later without revealing his assailant's name. Historian Rockaway reports, "Out of respect for the older Rothstein, Arnold received an Orthodox Jewish funeral with a renowned Orthodox rabbi, Leo Jung, delivering the eulogy."

Sponsored by Constance and Harvey Kreuger

3

Syd Koff's Olympic Protest

The scandals surrounding the 2002 Salt Lake City Olympics remind us that the Games have often been enmeshed in controversy. The first time the United States team was caught up in Olympic politics was in the period before the 1936 "Nazi" Olympics. American Jewish athletes were at the center of the political maelstrom.

In 1932, the International Olympic Committee chose Berlin as the 1936 Olympic site. In 1933, Adolf Hitler was elected chancellor of the Reich. The Nazi Party's anti-Semitic violence and legal decrees, particularly those banning Jews from participating with "Aryans" in sports, spurred the American Jewish Congress and the Non-Sectarian Anti-Nazi League to call for an American boycott of the Berlin Games. They argued that, since the international Olympic rules decreed that no athlete could be denied the right to compete because of race, ethnicity or religion, the Games should be relocated to another country. The American Jewish Congress took its case to the American Olympic Committee (AOC), hoping to persuade it to boycott the Games if Germany remained the host.

The plea was ignored. Avery Brundage, president of the AOC, had received assurances that no Jewish athlete would be barred from competing for the German team and that no Jewish athlete from any other nation would be barred from the Games. Brundage persuaded his fellow AOC members to vote for American participation. The American team was going to Berlin.

As an act of protest, several American Jewish athletes refused to go to Berlin. Among them was a young woman named Syd Koff, born Sybil Tabachnikoff in 1912 on the Lower East Side of New York. In her teens, against her parents' wishes, Sybil sneaked out of the house to compete in high school and other amateur track and field events. In 1930, a member of the Millrose Athletic Club, of which the great Jesse Owens was also a member, saw Sybil practicing the broad jump on the beach at Coney Island and asked her to join the club. Syd began competing—and winning—against famed rivals Babe Didrickson, Lillian Copeland, and Stella Walsh.

In 1932, Syd Koff represented America at the first Maccabean Games in Tel Aviv. It took three weeks for the American team to arrive in the Holy Land by boat, train, donkey cart and camel. Once there, Koff competed against the world's best Jewish athletes and emerged as the 1932 Games' greatest star, leading the American team to the overall championship. She won gold medals in four events: the 50- and 100-meter dashes, the high jump and the broad jump, and finished fifth in two other field events. Syd made such an impression on the Jews of Palestine that young women on the streets of Tel Aviv began wearing berets at the same jaunty angle she favored. When she competed in her second Maccabean Games in 1935, Koff garnered two additional gold medals.

When it was time to compete in the 1936 Olympics, Koff faced a difficult decision. She qualified for the 1936 Olympic team in the broad and high jumps. By the time the American team was ready to depart, however, the Jews in Germany were clearly being persecuted and the Nazi regime seemed bent on destroying the German Jewish community. German Jews were losing legal rights, being physically brutalized, having their businesses boycotted and their synagogues destroyed. Syd and other American Jewish athletes who qualified for the 1936 Olympics had to choose between competing and proving that Jewish athletes could defeat the specious Aryan "super race," or honor the plea of Jewish organizations to boycott the Games rather than lend legitimacy to the Nazi regime.

Koff chose to join the boycotters. There is good reason to believe that if she had participated, the Brundage-chosen U.S. Olympic coaching staff, apparently under pressure to keep Jewish athletes from winning medals, might well have found some excuse not to let her compete, much as the men's track coaches refused to let Jewish sprinters Marty Glickman and Sam Stoller run as part of the men's 4 x 100 relay team (see page 146).

In 1940, despite the outbreak of World War II a year earlier, the Olympics were scheduled for Helsinki, Finland. Just weeks before, the Soviet Union ruthlessly invaded Finland in a surprise attack. The Olympics were canceled and Koff never got her chance to win an Olympic medal. She married, had children and retired from competitive track and field. However, the call of the cinders was too strong. In the 1960s, she returned to world competition in the Masters' division, in which she competed until 1972, when a broken hip stopped her. Syd Koff, deprived of her Olympic moment of glory, never lost her competitive drive. She died in New York City in 1999.

Sponsored by Judith Ross Connor and Stanley Epstein in memory of Ruth and Samuel Ross

4

Marty Glickman's Stolen Medal

Perhaps the most controversial of all modern athletic contests was the 1936 "Nazi" Olympics, held in Berlin and immortalized in filmmaker Leni Riefenstahl's documentary, *Olympiad*. Hitler tried to use the Olympic Games to demonstrate the superiority of "pure Aryans" over nations that allowed Jews, blacks and other "mongrel" races to compete on their behalf. Jesse Owens and other African-American track stars embarrassed the Führer by winning several gold medals in the men's track sprints and relays, easily defeating their German rivals.

Less remembered about the Nazi Olympics is the saga of two American Jewish sprinters, Marty Glickman and Sam Stoller. The eighteen-year-old Glickman starred in track and football at Syracuse University, while Stoller competed in track for the University of Michigan. The two young men made the U. S. Olympic squad as members of the 4x100-yard relay team. Glickman and Stoller traveled to Germany and prepared diligently for the relay race. The day before the race, however, the U.S. track team coaches replaced Glickman and Stoller with two other runners, Jesse Owens and Ralph Metcalfe.

By Glickman's account, the last-minute switch was a straightforward case of anti-Semitism. Avery Brundage, chairman of the United States Olympic Committee, supported Hitler's regime and denied that the Nazis were implementing an anti-Semitic program. Brundage and assistant Olympic track coach Dean Cromwell belonged to America First, an isolationist political movement that attracted many Nazi sympathizers. Additionally, Cromwell coached two other Olympic sprinters at the University of Southern California, Foy Draper and Frank Wyckoff, and openly favored them over Glickman and Stoller.

Glickman's suspicions about the relay team selection process began at the American Olympic team trials in New York, when he was told he had placed fifth of the seven runners competing in the sprint finals. Finish-line photography was not yet in use at that time, but films of the race seem to indicate that Glickman had actually finished third, behind Owens and Metcalfe. The judges, apparently under pressure from Cromwell, placed Glickman fifth behind Draper and Wyckoff. As a result, Glickman was not entered in the 100-yard dash, a premiere Olympic event. Instead, he traveled to Berlin as part of the 4x100-yard relay team.

As an eighteen year old, Glickman was grateful to be going to the Olympics even if he felt that he'd been robbed of his chance at a medal in the 100-yard dash. Some American Jewish organizations tried to convince the U.S. Olympic committee to boycott the Nazi Games, but Brundage prevailed and the team went. Glickman, like many American Jews, assumed that the anti-Semitism he might encounter in Berlin would be no worse than what he had faced growing up in Brooklyn. Like most Americans, Glickman had no inkling of the horrific fate awaiting German Jewry.

Once in Germany, Glickman, Stoller, Draper and Wyckoff spent two weeks practicing as the 400-yard relay team. They were confident of victory. Then, on the day of the qualifying trials, head track coach Lawson Robertson told Glickman and Stoller that Owens and Metcalfe would replace them. To his credit, Owens protested to Robertson that Glickman and Stoller deserved to run. Robertson told Owens to do what he was told. Glickman pointed out to Robertson that any combination of the seven teammates could win the race by 15 yards. Robertson replied that he suspected the Germans were hiding their best sprinters to upset the American team and he intended to enter his four best athletes in the relay. In his judgment, Owens and Metcalfe were better than Stoller and Glickman. His goal was winning, nothing more. Glickman turned to assistant coach Cromwell and said, "Coach, you know that Sam and I are the only two Jews on the track team. If we don't run there's bound to be a lot of criticism back home." Cromwell retorted, "We'll take our chances." The American team won in record time as Glickman watched from the stands.

Glickman (who remained a close friend of Owens until the latter's death) and Stoller were devastated by the decision. Stoller, age twenty-one, announced his retirement from track competition, but later reconsidered. Later that year he won an NCAA sprint championship. Glickman returned to college and became a football All-American. After a brief professional career in football and basketball, Glickman had a distinguished career as a sportscaster, best known as the voice of the New York Knicks and Rangers and the football Giants and Jets. Despite his later success, the disillusionment of the 1936 Olympics loomed large for Glickman, who died in 2001. He recalled returning to Olympic Stadium in Berlin in 1985 as part of a tribute to Jesse Owens. Glickman was surprised by his reactions. He told historian Peter Levine:

> As I walked into the stadium, I began to get so angry. I began to get so mad. It shocked the hell out of me that this thing of forty-nine years ago could still evoke this anger. . . . I was cussing . . . I was really amazed at myself, at this feeling of anger. Not about the German Nazis . . . that was a given. But the anger at Avery Brundage and Dean Cromwell for not allowing an eighteen-year-old kid to compete in the Olympic Games just because he was Jewish.

Sponsored by the Merryl H. and James S. Tisch Foundation

5

John Slade's Olympian Journey

Courtesy of John Slade

In the summer of 1948, at age forty, John Slade marched into Wembley Stadium in London in front of 120,000 spectators. A goalie for the American field hockey squad, Slade was one of the oldest athletes on the United States Olympic team. According to Slade, "It was the proudest moment of my life."

Becoming a member of the Olympic team was particularly meaningful for adopted American John Slade. Born Hans Schlesinger in Frankfurt, Germany, in 1908, Slade grew up in a family of (in his own words) "highly assimilated Jews" who had lived in Frankfurt continuously since the thirteenth century. Young Hans was given no Jewish education, but—to his parents' amazement—at age thirteen he asked to become bar mitzvah. Hans personally arranged for his own private Hebrew lessons. His bar mitzvah marked the first time his parents were inside a synagogue.

Like many young German Jews of his era, until the 1930s Hans Schlesinger led a life in which anti-Semitism played little part. Hans's father headed a very successful real estate brokerage, a position that Hans expected to inherit. A star athlete, Schlesinger was arguably the best field hockey goalie in Germany and expected to compete in the 1936 Olympics in his nation's capital, Berlin.

Hitler's rise to the German chancellorship changed all that. In 1935, the Reichstag adopted the notorious Nuremberg Laws, which stripped Germany's Jews of most of their political, economic, and social rights. These humiliating edicts effectively segregated Germany's Jews from "pure Aryan" Germans. Later that year, before an important match, the coach of the Frankfurt field hockey team told Schlesinger that he could not compete because of the restrictive new laws.

Schlesinger immediately resigned from the club. Its director begged him to stay so that the other Jewish members wouldn't quit too, but Schlesinger was adamant. Instead, he helped found an all-Jewish sports club. Slade worked as an apprentice banker in Frankfurt and Berlin, and his father's real estate business remained strong for a time. Slade recalls with bitterness that Germany's all-Aryan field hockey team won the silver medal at the 1936 Olympics, using his understudy as goalie. When he heard on a radio broadcast that a Jew could be imprisoned for kissing an Aryan, he decided that it was time to leave Germany for the United States.

The banker who had employed Schlesinger in Frankfurt referred him to Joseph Bear of the New York investment firm of Bear, Stearns. Bear gave Hans, who spoke no English, a $15 per week job as a messenger. Hans's diligence made a good impression. By 1940, he was working in risk arbitrage and could afford to bring his family to America, thereby saving them from the Holocaust. The Nazi government forced the Schlesingers to leave their real estate business and most of their personal wealth behind.

In 1942, Schlesinger, who by this time had changed his name to the more Americanized John Slade and now the head of the risk arbitrage desk at Bear, Stearns, volunteered for the United States Army. "I decided that if a guy from Oklahoma could fight against Hitler," Slade says in his still-strong German accent, "then I too must fight." He went to Joseph Bear and explained that he wanted to fight for his new country. As the sole support of his family, however, he felt he could not leave them. Bear promised that the firm would support his parents and siblings while he was gone, and Slade immediately enlisted.

As a native German speaker, Slade occasionally interrogated important captured Nazi officers, including Jurgen Stroop, the general who had ordered the Warsaw Ghetto destroyed. In 1945, a company of soldiers under Slade's command stumbled upon a Bavarian castle in which a hundred SS soldiers were hiding. He boldly strode up to the door and called on the SS men inside to surrender. They did so without a fight. Slade was awarded a medal for bravery.

At the war's end, Slade returned to his arbitrage desk at Bear, Stearns. At age forty, he decided to try out for the 1948 American Olympic field hockey team. He and another German Jewish immigrant made the team.

If history were poetic, the 1948 United States Olympic field hockey team would have defeated Germany for the gold medal and John Slade would have made a last-second save to preserve the victory. Only occasionally, however, does history have such a tidy ending. The outmanned American team lost every game and, although he continued to play, Slade suffered a head injury that required ten stitches. He couldn't have cared less. "Here I was a Jewish refugee, and I played on the American team. It meant more to me than if I had won a medal for the German team in 1936."

When the 1948 Olympics ended, Bear, Stearns asked Slade to stay in Europe and set up an overseas department for the firm. Under Slade's leadership, the overseas department opened offices all over Europe, including Germany. In the 1980s, the firm opened an office in Frankfurt, where Slade is now received as an honored native son. The Frankfurt club from which he resigned has offered a full apology.

Sponsored by Kathy and Alan Greenberg

6

Mike Jacobs and Joe Louis, Champion of the Jews

In American sports, few titles carry as much status as heavyweight champion of the world. As symbols of virility and power, boxing titles have become a source of pride for various ethnic and racial groups. In the 1920s and 1930s, American Jewish champions Benny Leonard and Barney Ross became heroes to their people. Contenders like Max Baer and Maxie Rosenbloom proudly wore Stars of David on their trunks.

Arguably, the non-Jewish boxing champion American Jewry most closely embraced was Joe Louis, an African-American who in June of 1938 knocked out Max Schmeling, Nazi Germany's best heavyweight. American Jewry claimed Louis's victory as its own, for the fight refuted Hitler's argument that German Aryans constituted a "master race." Art Buchwald, who grew up in New York City, recalled that as a child in 1938 he was sure of three things: "Franklin Roosevelt was going to save the economy . . . Joe Dimaggio was going to beat Babe Ruth's record [and] Joe Louis was going to save us from the Germans."

Louis might not have had a chance at the heavyweight title if a New York Jewish promoter, Mike Jacobs, had not been his manager. Born on the Lower East Side in the 1880s, "Uncle Mike" Jacobs had become the sport's leading promoter by the mid-1930s.

In 1942 alone, he promoted 250 boxing cards. In the course of his career, Jacobs staged sixty-one championship fights. He excelled at developing a fighter's public identity.

Jacobs recognized Louis's boxing talent but also knew that as a black man, Louis would have a difficult—if not impossible—time getting a title shot. Jack Johnson, the flamboyant, self-confident and only previous black heavyweight champion, won the crown in 1908, but his relationships with white women created a backlash that led to his conviction on a morals charge. The next black champion, if there were to be one, would have to be low-keyed and circumspect. He would have to be marketed as representing *all* Americans, not just African-Americans.

Jacobs recognized that American boxing crowds, and particularly the numerous Jewish fans, ached to see Schmeling and Primo Carnera, an Italian heavyweight and symbol of fascist might, defeated by an American fighter. In the early 1930s, Schmeling and Carnera had each briefly held the world title. In 1934, Jacobs lined up Joe Louis's first fight with Carnera. The young Louis knocked out Carnera in six rounds. In 1935, Louis knocked out Max Baer in the fourth round, setting up a showdown with Schmeling to determine who would be in line to fight the reigning champion, Jim Braddock.

Many in the Jewish public longed for Louis—or anyone else—to conquer Schmeling and embarrass Hitler, but some Jewish groups opposed giving Schmeling an American platform. Several of them pressured Mike Jacobs to cancel the Louis-Schmeling fight. Jacobs replied that Louis would defeat Schmeling, giving the lie to Nazi propaganda. More than 45,000 fans filled Yankee Stadium expecting to see the "Brown Bomber" defeat Schmeling. They left disappointed. After a lopsided battering, Louis was knocked out in the twelfth round. Hitler cabled Schmeling to congratulate him on his "splendid patriotic achievement."

Schmeling had earned the right to fight for Braddock's crown, but Jacobs and Braddock's Jewish manager, Joe Gould, decided the American public would rather not run the risk of seeing Schmeling, as one sportswriter put it, "take the title back to Germany and present it to Adolf Hitler for the German Museum." Jacobs guaranteed Braddock a whopping $500,000 payday to fight Louis instead and the match was made. Louis knocked out Braddock and became champion. As historian Peter Levine observes, the fight "launched [Louis's] reign as one of boxing's greatest champions and secured his place as a hero of an oppressed American black population. It also set the scene for one more battle with Max Schmeling that enhanced Louis's status as a hero for all Americans." One might add: especially for Jews.

Jacobs promoted the second battle between the two men, in June 1938, as a bat-tle between democracy and fascism. When Schmeling's ship docked in New York, it was met by hundreds of anti-fascist pickets. The Non-Partisan Anti-Nazi League and the American Jewish Congress urged Jacobs to cancel the fight. Jacobs offered to donate 10 percent of the gate to groups helping Jewish refugees. Louis proclaimed that he was "backing up America against Germany," and promised he would be "going to town" against Schmeling.

Louis delivered on his boast, knocking out Schmeling in the first round. Americans cheered, and African-Americans and Jews celebrated the loudest. In their eyes, Louis had vindicated American democracy. In 1946, after the world had learned how brutally far the Nazis had carried their racial theories, a story in the *American Hebrew* praised Mike Jacobs for giving Joe Louis the opportunity to strike "a terrific blow to the theory of race supremacy." While Schmeling's defeat did not save European Jewry from the Nazi killing machine, Louis's knockout punch helped American Jews believe that members of an American minority could defeat Germans. The lesson was not lost on the hundreds of thousands of American Jews who fought against Germany in World War II.

A footnote: During the war, Max Schmeling harbored and saved several German Jews from extermination. A symbol of Aryan supremacy for Hitler, Schmeling himself never accepted the Führer's racial beliefs.

Sponsored by Constance and Harvey Kreuger

7

Sid Luckman: Legendary Quarterback

No American sport currently generates more interest and attention than football. Because of its speed and excitement, physicality and strategy, football has replaced baseball as America's national pastime. One of the pioneers of modern-style football was Sid Luckman, a Brooklyn-born observant Jew and All-Pro quarterback for the Chicago Bears. Luckman combined intelligence, toughness and talent to help transform the position of quarterback into what experts claim is the most demanding role in all of American professional sports.

Luckman became interested in football in 1924, at the age of eight, when his father gave him a football as a gift. After he graduated as an All-City halfback for Erasmus Hall High School, Sid received more than a dozen athletic scholarship offers from colleges around the nation. He set his heart on attending Columbia University, where he could get a quality education and live close to his family, even though Columbia did not offer him a scholarship.

Luckman spent his freshman year proving himself academically and became Columbia's starting halfback as a sophomore. Despite a cast of weak teammates, Luckman proved the greatest all-around player in Columbia's history. In 1938, playing both offense and defense, he carried Columbia to a 20–18 upset victory over powerful Army, bringing his team back from an 18–6 half-time deficit by skillful running, kick returning, and throwing the winning touchdown pass.

Luckman was selected as an All-American in 1937 and 1938 and was later inducted into the College Football Hall of Fame. Red Freisell, a referee who officiated at several of Luckman's college games, later put his achievements in perspective:

> In each of those games, [Luckman] threw at least 30 passes, and on nearly every one of them he was knocked nearly out of his britches by some fast charging opponent. . . . Never once did I see him throw in fright or see him wince when he got his lumps. I never heard a word of protest about the beating he was taking. That brand of courage, coupled with his uncanny knack of hitting his target, put Luckman down in my book as the greatest forward passer I ever saw in the college ranks.

After his last college game, Luckman announced his retirement from football, but George Halas, owner-coach of the Chicago Bears, had other ambitions. Halas was certain that Luckman would make the ideal professional T-formation quarterback. In college, Luckman had played halfback and thus received the ball several yards behind the line of scrimmage. In the T-formation, which the pros had just developed, the quarterback, standing immediately behind the center, calls the plays, receives every snap and has the option of running, passing, or handing off the ball. In sum, he is central to the action, and his team's success depends on his resourcefulness.

Halas believed that Luckman's passing and play-calling ability would lead Chicago to preeminence in the National Football League. In fact, after a mediocre 1939 rookie season during which he learned the T-formation, Luckman blossomed in 1940 into what sports writer Ira Berkow called "the first great T-formation quarterback." Luckman led the Bears to five Western Conference championships and four World Championships in seven years. In the 1940 championship game, Luckman's Bears won the most lopsided victory in NFL history, a 73–0 thrashing of the Washington Redskins.

Luckman's best year statistically was 1943, when he led the Bears to a record of 8–1–1. On "Sid Luckman Appreciation Day" against the home team New York Giants at the Polo Grounds, Luckman led his visiting Bears to a 56–7 triumph, passing for a record seven touchdowns and 443 yards. That year, he set the league record for touchdown passes in a ten-game season with twenty-eight, including five touchdowns in Chicago's victory over the Redskins in the 1943 championship rematch between the teams.

When the 1943 season ended Luckman volunteered for the Merchant Marine. He was stationed stateside. While he could not practice with the team, Luckman was given permission to play for the Bears on game days during the season. He returned to the Bears full-time in 1946 and led them to a fifth World Championship. In 1950, Luckman retired from professional football, having thrown for 189 touchdowns in only 1,747 passes, and in championship games having completed forty-one of seventy-six passes for 670 yards and seven touchdowns—a remarkable rate of one touchdown in every eleven passes. In 1965, Luckman was elected to the Pro Football Hall of Fame.

When his playing days ended, Luckman became a successful businessman in Chicago and tutored quarterbacks in T-formation skills at Notre Dame, Pittsburgh, Holy Cross and his alma mater, Columbia. When Columbia tried to pay him for his services, Luckman returned the check with a note saying: "Please ask the college to accept this to help some worthy student as partial thanks to my former coach and college." In 1994, when Sid Luckman was seventy-eight, Erasmus Hall High School named its football field in his honor, inspiring a new generation of Brooklyn boys to believe that if you harness your courage, intelligence and talent, you can rise to greatness.

Sponsored by Joan, Peter, Clifford, Alan and Rebecca Cohn

8

Moe Berg's Multifacited Life

Moe Berg's biography proves the adage that "truth is often stranger than fiction." One of the best-educated, intellectually accomplished and patriotic athletes in the history of American sports, Berg got his start in baseball in 1906, at the age of four, playing catch with the beat policeman in front of his father's Newark, New Jersey, pharmacy. Berg became an excellent linguist while an undergraduate student at Princeton University, where he studied Latin, Greek, French, Spanish, Italian, German and Sanskrit. He began his career as a spy on a hospital roof in Japan (more about that later).

After graduating from high school at the top of his class, Moe enrolled at Princeton, an unusual accomplishment for a Jewish boy in the 1920s. He became the star shortstop of the college baseball team, graduated *magna cum laude* and was offered a teaching post in Princeton's Department of Romance Languages. Wanting to study experimental phonetics at the Sorbonne but unable to afford graduate study overseas, Berg signed a contract to play shortstop for the Brooklyn Dodgers. Demoted to the minors after the 1924 season because his hitting was below par, it was Moe who inspired a professional scout to coin the immortal baseball phrase, "Good field, no hit." One teammate said, "Moe, I don't care how many of them college degrees you got, they ain't learned you to hit that curve ball no better than the rest of us."

The Chicago White Sox summoned Berg back to the major leagues in 1926. At the same time, he attended Columbia Law School. Despite his hectic schedule, the brilliant Berg managed to finish second in his class at Columbia. That year, the White Sox asked him to play catcher, a position that took advantage of his strong arm and intelligence. Casey Stengel compared Berg's defensive skills to those of the immortal Bill Dickey. Moe hit .287 in 1929 and received votes for Most Valuable Player. In 1930, unfortunately, he seriously injured his ankle, ending his career as a full-time player. He played as a reserve for three more teams until he retired in 1939.

In 1934, Berg toured Japan with a group of major league all-stars, including Babe Ruth and Lou Gehrig. Still respected as a linguist, Moe was invited to lecture at Meiji University, where he delivered an eloquent speech in Japanese. Before the trip, the U.S. government recruited Berg as a spy. While at a Tokyo hospital ostensibly visiting an American mother who had just given birth, he snuck onto the roof and took photos of the city. Pilots reportedly later used the photos during World War II bombing raids.

As a Jew eager to fight Nazism, Berg volunteered to serve when America entered the war in 1941. He was asked to become a goodwill ambassador to Latin America. Before he left on his ambassadorial mission, Berg made a radio broadcast to the Japanese people in which, to quote historians Harold and Meir Ribalow, "In fluent Japanese, he pleaded at length, 'as a friend of the Japanese people,' for the Japanese to avoid a war 'you cannot win.'" The Ribalows report, "Berg's address was so effective that several Japanese confirmed afterwards they had wept while listening."

After his stint in Latin America, Moe returned to the United States to work for the Office of Strategic Services, forerunner to the Central Intelligence Agency. He parachuted into Yugoslavia and, after meeting Tito, suggested that the United States should back him rather than his Serbian rival. Despite the fact that he was not a scientist, Berg was next assigned to help determine how close Germany was to developing an atomic bomb. In a few weeks, Berg taught himself a great deal about nuclear physics. Traveling through Europe, Berg discovered that a factory in Norway was producing an atomic bomb component for the Nazis, and Allied planes bombed it. Berg then learned that the Nazis had an atomic research center at Duisberg, Germany, and it too was bombed.

In a famous episode, Berg disguised his identity and lured the leading German atomic physicist, Werner Heisenberg, to Switzerland to give a lecture on quantum theory. Berg prepared himself with a crash course on nuclear theory and, supposedly, had orders that if he heard Heisenberg indicate that he was working on an atom bomb, he was to assassinate him. The lecture was inconclusive, and at a dinner after the lecture Berg heard Heisenberg imply that Germany lagged behind the United States in bomb development. Heisenberg lived and President Roosevelt greeted Berg's report warmly.

Berg spent part of 1944 and 1945 in Germany, helping to capture several prominent German atomic scientists before the Russians got them. At war's end, Berg modestly declined the Medal of Merit, the highest military award given to civilians. He lived out a quiet life in Newark, where he died at age seventy.

Some of Berg's friends felt he had squandered a brilliant career in law or academics to play baseball. His brother observed that "all [baseball] ever did was make him happy." His teammate Ted Lyons said, "A lot of people tried to tell him what to do with his life and brain and he retreated from this. . . . He was different because he was different. He made up for all the bores of the world. And he did it softly, stepping on no one."

Sponsored by Miriam and Mort Steinberg

9

Barney Ross's Greatest Battles

As a boy in Chicago, Barnet Rasofsky planned to become a talmudic scholar and Hebrew teacher. In 1924, when he was fourteen years old, two men robbed the family grocery store and killed his father. Left with five children, Barnet's mother had a nervous breakdown and went to live with relatives. Barnet and his oldest brother lived with a cousin; his three youngest siblings went to an orphanage.

Barnet Rasofsky vowed to make enough money—by whatever means he could—to reunite his family. He renounced his Orthodox faith and became a petty thief, numbers runner and brawler. He took up amateur boxing, pawning his medals for the few dollars they would bring. Sometimes, he had six fights in a week. At age nineteen, he turned professional and took the name Barney Ross so that his mother, now back on her feet, wouldn't worry about him. As Barney Ross, he won world championships and election to the Boxing Hall of Fame.

After almost 200 fights as an amateur and more than twenty as a professional, Ross's big break came in 1933, when he fought "Tough Tony" Canzoneri in Chicago for the world lightweight title. Ross won by a split decision and agreed to a rematch in New York City, Canzoneri's hometown. In front of 60,000 spectators, he won a unanimous decision. Never a powerful puncher, Ross showed unflinching courage by counter-punching when hit hard and always staying on his feet, a formula that served him throughout his life.

Ross entered the ranks of the boxing greats in a brutal series of welterweight championship fights against Jimmy McLarnin, who outweighed him by several pounds. McLarnin was a harder puncher with a reputation for beating Jewish boxers. In their first and bloodiest battle, Ross defeated McLarnin by a split decision. Ross offered McLarnin a rematch five months later, and McLarnin avenged the defeat in a vicious battle, the only fight in which Ross suffered a knockdown. When they met for the third time, Ross took the rematch in a fight that showed his clear superiority as a boxer.

Ross's most courageous prizefight was his last, in 1938, against Henry Armstrong, the only man at that time to hold the featherweight, lightweight and welterweight crowns. Only twenty-eight years old by the time he faced Armstrong, Ross had already fought almost 300 times. He started strong, but tired after the fourth round. Armstrong pummeled him at will. After the tenth round, the referee asked Ross if he wanted to stop, but the champion refused. After the twelfth, the referee approached Ross's managers, asking them to throw in the towel, but Ross told them, "You do that and I'll never talk to you again. I want to go out like a champion." Through rounds thirteen, fourteen, and fifteen, Armstrong pounded away at Ross, who would not go down. Voices in the crowd pleaded with the referee to stop the fight, but he respected Ross's wish to end his career without ever having failed to go the distance. In the last minute of the fight, Ross rallied and stood toe to toe with Armstrong, exchanging blows. The crowd was on its feet, many with tears in the their eyes, cheering for Ross, knowing they had seen the heart of a true champion.

Ross retired after the fight and opened a restaurant. When the Japanese attacked Pearl Harbor, although at thirty-two he was beyond draft age, Ross volunteered for the Marines. Assigned as a boxing instructor, Ross asked for combat duty and was sent to Guadalcanal, scene of some of the bloodiest fighting in the Pacific. One night, a superior Japanese force attacked Ross and three comrades. All three were wounded. Ross gathered them in a shell crater and defended them by firing over 400 rifle rounds. When he ran out of ammunition, he threw twenty-two grenades at enemy machine gun positions. Ross said two hours of prayers, many in Hebrew, hoping to make it through the night. Finally, at dawn, with two of his three comrades dead, out of ammunition and himself wounded in the leg and foot, the 140-pound Ross picked up his 230-pound surviving comrade and carried him to safety. Ross, whose helmet had more than thirty shrapnel dents, was awarded the Silver Star for heroism.

At the military hospital, medics gave the wounded Ross all the morphine he requested. Released from the hospital, he toured defense plants to raise morale among workers but couldn't shake his need for morphine. When his habit began costing him $500 per week and his wife left him, Ross finally checked into a drug treatment facility. While few gave him much chance of succeeding, Ross went "cold turkey" and, after much agony, emerged 120 days later having kicked the habit. While he lived in constant pain from his wounds, Ross spent the remainder of his life speaking out against drug abuse. Hollywood later turned Ross's autobiographical account of his addiction into a movie, *Monkey on My Back*.

In his autobiography, Ross recounted that a rabbi once told him that, since he was a Jew in the public eye, he would have to lead an exemplary life. Barney Ross did not let the rabbi—or his people—down. Of all the things Ross achieved in his life and all the obstacles he overcame, the one that meant the most to him was having earned enough money in the first Canzoneri fight to reunite his mother at home with her three youngest children who had been placed in an orphanage.

Sponsored by the Wyner/Stokes Foundation

10

Hank Greenberg:
Baseball's First Jewish Superstar

For decades, baseball was America's national pastime and symbol of the values of competition and fair play. Nonetheless, the professional game reflected the nation's prejudices. Jews, African-Americans and other "outsiders" were not easily welcomed into the sport. In 1949, Jackie Robinson's broke the major league color barrier. A decade earlier, Hank Greenberg crossed a different line: he became baseball's first Jewish superstar.

Born into an Orthodox Bronx household in 1911, Greenberg stood 6-foot 3 by the time he reached high school and was an All-City athlete in soccer and basketball. His favorite sport, however, was baseball. Somewhat awkward in the field, Greenberg chose to play first base. In 1929, the New York Yankees offered him a contract but he turned it down because the immortal iron man Lou Gehrig was the incumbent Yankee first baseman. Instead, he signed with the Detroit Tigers.

Greenberg spent three years in the minor leagues, working hard each day to improve his fielding and hitting. After being named the Most Valuable Player in the Texas League, he was promoted to the Tigers in 1933, batted .301 and drove in 87 runs.

In 1934, led by Greenberg's .339 batting average, the Tigers jumped from fifth place in the American League into the battle for the pennant. Never before had a Jewish player assumed such a significant role for a major league team, and as a result, Greenberg—and Jewish baseball fans all over the country—faced a unique dilemma. On September 10, which was Rosh

Hashanah, the Tigers, who led the league by four games in the standings, would be playing the Boston Red Sox. Fans and rabbis debated whether Greenberg, who by his accomplishments was winning acceptance for Jews among non-Jewish Americans, should play on the High Holy Days. Greenberg came up with his own compromise: he played on Rosh Hashanah and hit two home runs that won the game, 2–1. Ten days later, he spent Yom Kippur in a synagogue. That day, the Tigers lost. Greenberg's observance inspired Edgar Guest to write a poem that read in part:

> Come Yom Kippur—holy fast day wide-world over to the Jew—
> And Hank Greenberg to his teaching and the old tradition true
> Spent the day among his people and he didn't come to play.
> Said Murphy to Mulrooney, "We shall lose the game today!
> We shall miss him in the infield and shall miss him at the bat,
> But he's true to his religion—and I honor him for that!"

Greenberg came back the next day and hit a home run that clinched the pennant for the Tigers, but they lost the World Series to the Cardinals in seven games. A year later, the Tigers won the World Series and Greenberg was the first Jew voted Most Valuable Player in either major league.

The 1938 season brought more drama for Greenberg when he challenged Babe Ruth's record of sixty home runs in a season. With five games remaining, Greenberg had hit fifty-eight. As the world watched Greenberg in those last five games, several pitchers walked him rather than give him a good pitch to hit. While Greenberg himself gave the charge no credence, and noted that he struck out several times, many observers believed that he got so few good pitches to hit because major league baseball did not want a Jew breaking Ruth's record.

In May of 1940, the Army interrupted Greenberg's baseball career. One of baseball's highest-paid stars, his salary dropped from $11,000 to $21 per month. In August, Congress decided that men over twenty-eight years old need not serve and Greenberg was honorably discharged. He planned to return to the Tigers the next season, but on December 7, 1941, the Japanese bombed Pearl Harbor. Greenberg was the first major leaguer voluntarily to enlist in the Army. While he could have accepted a stateside job as an athletic instructor, he chose to serve in the Army Air Corps in the China-Burma-India Theater, where he earned a distinguished record.

When the war ended in 1945, Greenberg, age thirty-four, returned to the Tiger lineup in mid-summer and hit a home run in his first game back. Greenberg led the Tigers to another World Series victory that year, personally clinching the American League pennant with a grand-slam home run on the final day of the season. Greenberg played two more seasons and then retired.

After retirement, Greenberg compiled another series of "firsts": he became the first Jewish owner/general manager in baseball, assembling the 1954 Cleveland Indians team that won a record 111 games. In 1959, Greenberg and Bill Veeck purchased the Chicago White Sox. That year, the White Sox won the pennant for the first time in forty years. In 1961, Greenberg sold his baseball interests and launched a successful career on Wall Street. In 1954, he became the first Jewish player elected to baseball's Hall of Fame.
Sponsored by George Blumenthal in honor of Steve Greenberg

11

Tiby Eisen:
In a League of Her Own

One of the most versatile and talented Jewish professional athletes in America was Gertrude "Tiby" Eisen. Born in Los Angeles in 1922, Tiby Eisen was a star of the All-American Girls Professional Baseball League, the only professional women's league in baseball history. The women's hardball league, which lasted from 1943 to 1954, was restored to memory by the 1992 Hollywood hit movie, *A League of Their Own*. One of at least four Jewish women in the AAGPBL, Eisen was its only Jewish superstar and a pioneer in American women's sports.

The young Eisen was an outstanding athlete in her native Los Angeles and started playing semi-pro softball at age fourteen. In 1940, at age eighteen, Eisen's all-around ability led her to try her hand at women's professional football. California investors had started a short-lived women's professional football league (an undertaking that still awaits its Hollywood chronicler), and Eisen played fullback for one of the two Los Angeles teams. When the city council passed an ordinance that banned women from playing football within the confines of Los Angeles, the teams traveled to Guadalajara, Mexico, where, according to Eisen, they "filled the stadium."

Before she joined the All-American Baseball League, Eisen applied for a job at the Bank of America in Los Angeles, which sponsored a women's softball team. The salary for women at the bank was, Eisen recalled, about $60 per month. "You'd work for the bank, then play for the team. I had my interview, but never heard from them," she reported. "My girlfriend, who played on the team, told me they didn't hire me because I was Jewish—but she didn't tell me that until twenty years later because she didn't want to hurt my feelings."

When the All-American Girls Professional Baseball League was founded in 1943, Eisen won a spot on the Milwaukee team, which moved the next year to Grand Rapids, Michigan. Eisen's best season was in 1946, when she led the AAGPBL in triples, stole 128 bases, and made the all-star team.

Eisen's family was ambivalent about the career choice this "nice Jewish girl" had made, although she ultimately won their respect. "We played a big charity game in Chicago for a Jewish hospital," Eisen recalled in an interview with historian David Spaner. "My name and picture were in every Jewish newspaper. My uncle, who had said, 'You shouldn't be playing baseball—you'll get a bad reputation, a bad name,' was in the stands . . . bursting with pride that I was there."

During her professional baseball career, Eisen could recall only one instance in which her religion was raised as an issue:

When I was playing for Fort Wayne, I was in the outfield and thought there were three outs. There were only two, but I was coming in from the outfield. The manager Bill Wambsganss [the first man in major league history to complete an unassisted triple play] was waving, "Go back, go back." And he turned to one of the players sitting on the bench and said, "I never heard of a Jew that couldn't count."

When Eisen retired from professional baseball in 1952, she became a star for the Orange Lionettes softball team and led them to a world championship. In 1993, she helped establish the women's exhibit at the Baseball Hall of Fame in Cooperstown, New York. Eisen told David Spaner, "We're trying to record this so we have our place in history. It's important to keep our baseball league in the limelight. It gets pushed into the background . . . [just as] women have been pushed into the background forever. If they knew more about our league, perhaps in the future some women will say, 'Hey, maybe we can do it again.'"

A footnote: In the movie *A League of Their Own*, Madonna plays the character of baseball player Faye Dancer. In 1947, the real-life Faye Dancer was traded for another player, none other than Tiby Eisen.

Sponsored by Barbara G. and Maurice L. Zilber in honor of Sidney Zilber's 75th birthday and Norman Zilber's 70th birthday

1

Judah Touro:
American Jewish Philanthropist

According to Judah Touro's tombstone, he is inscribed in "the Book of Philanthropy, to be remembered forever." No epitaph could be more deserving. Touro's name is indelibly associated with the history of American Jewish philanthropy, a communal trait of which American Jews can be justly proud.

Touro grew up in Newport, Rhode Island, the second son of Dutch-born Isaac Touro, *hazzan* of Yesuat Israel, Newport's Sephardic synagogue. The Revolutionary War destroyed Newport's prosperity and marked Judah Touro's childhood with poverty and deprivation. A Tory, Judah's father remained with his family in Newport after the British captured the city. The

Touros became dependent upon the charity of the British occupying forces, which eventually helped the family relocate to Jamaica, West Indies, where Isaac died in 1783. His widow took her children to Boston to live with her brother, Moses Michael Hays (see page 22). Her death in 1787 left Judah Touro an orphan at the age of twelve.

Moses Michael Hays raised the Touro children. He taught Judah and his brother Abraham to observe Jewish rituals and apprenticed them in his international commercial ventures. In 1801, Judah Touro unexpectedly left Boston for New Orleans. No one is certain why he left in such haste, but the gossip of the time had it that his uncle refused to allow Judah to marry his first cousin, Catherine Hays. In any event, he never married.

When the United States acquired New Orleans in 1803, its economy boomed and Touro established himself as a merchant, shipper and leader in the city's social life. During the War of 1812, he fought as a volunteer under the command of General Andrew Jackson. In the great battle of January 1, 1815, Touro was severely wounded and near death, but over the next year a close friend nursed him back to health. The trauma seems to have had psychological as well as physical effects: previously social, Touro withdrew almost entirely from civic life and devoted himself to his businesses.

Despite his financial success, Judah Touro always remembered his youthful poverty and lived modestly. He invested in real estate but never mortgaged his properties to finance other ventures. He is quoted as observing that he had "saved a fortune by strict economy, while others had spent one by their liberal expenditures."

In his fifties and sixties, Touro directed most of his charity to non-Jewish causes. He donated the last $10,000 needed to complete the Bunker Hill Monument in Boston, which for nearly twenty years had languished as an unfinished stump for want of funding. He made a major gift to the public library in his native Newport, and in New Orleans he contributed to constructing a number of churches and the Catholic cathedral.

In his early seventies, Touro met two outstanding Jewish leaders and his life was significantly changed. Around 1847, he developed a friendship with Gershom Kursheedt of New Orleans and began a correspondence with Rabbi Isaac Leeser of Philadelphia (see page 92). These men con-

vinced Touro that it was important to be Jewish in more than words. He joined eagerly in founding congregation Nefuzoth Yehuda in New Orleans, which followed the Sephardic rituals of his youth. He subsequently built its synagogue, provided the land for its cemetery and a building for its religious school, and annually made up for any deficits incurred. He also founded the city's Jewish hospital, the Touro Infirmary.

In the last year of his life, Touro wrote a will that set the standard for American Jewish philanthropy. After modest bequests to friends and family members, he donated the bulk of his fortune to strengthen Jewish life in America. He left $100,000 to the two congregations and various Jewish benevolent associations in New Orleans. Another $150,000 went to Jewish congregations and charitable institutions in eighteen other cities around the United States, providing support for virtually every non-Reform synagogue then existing in America. He directed that $50,000 be disbursed to relieve poverty and provide freedom of worship to Jews in Palestine. He also left bequests to non-Jewish institutions such as the Massachusetts General Hospital, which his brother Abraham had helped found.

At his request, Touro was buried with his family in the Jewish cemetery in Newport. One of his legacies made it possible to reopen and restore the long-abandoned synagogue where his father had served as *hazzan* and which now bears the family name. The *Jewish Encyclopedia* observed of Touro that, in his day, "No American Jew had ever given so much to so many agencies and causes; nor had any non-Jew done so much in such varied ways."

Sponsored by Toni and Stuart B. Young in memory of Helen and Samuel Field

2

The Kings of Copper

The Hendricks family of New York helped lay the foundations for the Industrial Revolution in America. Their pioneering production of copper was vital to the growth of the American economy and the nation's military might. When the company closed in 1938, Hendricks Brothers was the oldest continuous privately held Jewish family business in the United States.

Uriah Hendricks, the patriarch of the family, was born in Amsterdam, Holland, in 1737 and emigrated from London to New York City in 1755. In New York, he opened a dry goods store and became an active member, and eventually *parnas*, or president, of Shearith Israel, the Spanish and Portuguese Synagogue. In 1764, Hendricks established a metals business, importing copper and brass from England, which dis-

couraged manufacture of these commodities in its colonies. On his death, Uriah's only son, Harmon, took over the importing company and the family's role in Shearith Israel, where he too served as parnas from 1824 to 1827.

Recognizing that the United States could never attain true independence so long as it depended on overseas production of such essentials as copper, Harmon Hendricks helped transform the new republic from an importer to a manufacturer of copper. In 1812, during the second war with England, Hendricks and his brother-in-law Solomon Isaacs built one of the nation's first successful copper rolling mills in Soho, New Jersey. Historian Maxwell Whiteman observed that Hendricks became "his own metallurgist at a time when the secrets of the science of refining metals were jealously guarded by the English." Because of his skill, Hendricks made possible the use of copper rather than iron in the manufacture of steam boilers, a development that allowed boilers to be heated to higher temperatures without cracking.

One of Hendricks's most important copper customers and closest friends was Paul Revere, the famous patriot and metalsmith who lived in Boston. The American Jewish Historical Society's archives contain letters between the two men. Another good customer was the fledgling United States Navy. The Hendricks firm produced the copper used to sheath the bottoms of three naval vessels in New York harbor. At the same time, Revere was cladding a fourth ship, the *Constitution,* now ironically known as Old Ironsides, with copper that was probably supplied by Hendricks. These ships, their lower hulls protected against barnacles by their copper sheathing, helped the United States fight the British to a standstill in the War of 1812. Hendricks made another contribution to the war effort by subscribing the then-considerable sum of $40,000 to government-issued war bonds.

Robert Fulton, who is credited with inventing the steamship, was another frequent Hendricks customer. In the spring of 1807, Hendricks supplied the copper used to build the boiler for the *Clermont,* the first inland steam-driven packet boat in the world. The movement of goods and passengers by Fulton's steamships and their successors dominated interstate travel and commerce until the invention of the railroad.

When Harmon Hendricks died in 1838, he had helped transform American industry. His advocacy of the use of copper in shipbuilding made America a naval power. His three sons and four grandsons succeeded him in the business. The last member of the family to operate the business was Harmon Washington Hendricks, who died in 1928. Hendricks Brothers closed its last copper mill in 1938.

Just as Harmon Hendricks was able to build a business that could be handed down to his descendants, so he was able to continue the tradition of religious commitment bequeathed to him by his father, Uriah. Each of Harmon's children found a spouse among the families at Shearith Israel. Son Henry joined his father-in-law, Tobias I. Tobias, as an officer of one of the earliest American Jewish charities, the Society for the Education of Poor Children and Relief of Indigent Persons of the Jewish Persuasion, which was founded in 1827. In 1833, Henry joined his brother-in-law, Benjamin Nathan, as a founder of the Hebrew Benevolent Society, which was modeled on a similar organization established in Philadelphia by Rebecca Gratz. In 1852, Henry Hendricks and eight others founded Jews' Hospital, now Mount Sinai Hospital, in New York City, the oldest Jewish-affiliated medical institution in the United States.

Isaac Leeser, editor of the *Occident,* the leading American Jewish newspaper of the pre–Civil War era, was often critical of the aloof and uncharitable attitudes of the Sephardic "grandees." To quote Maxwell Whiteman, Leeser "singled out the liberality of the Hendricks family as an exception. . . . Modesty and reserve continued to govern the family attitude in matters of philanthropy, and the practice of keeping such activity from the public eye, begun by Harmon Hendricks, was maintained by his descendants." In the same low-key and generous manner, Hendricks descendants continue to be active in Shearith Israel and other areas of Jewish communal life today.

Sponsored by Carol and Earle I. Mack in memory of Hyman Bert Mack

3

Humble Roots of American Retailing

We associate the settling of the American frontier with pioneers in covered wagons and cowboys fighting Indians. We less frequently identify it with the peddlers and merchants who sustained the early settlers, shared their hardships and improved the quality of their lives. Starting in the 1840s, Jews from German-speaking lands seeking opportunity in America chose the difficult life of a peddler. They trudged America from rural New England to Gold Rush California.

In his *Reminiscences*, Isaac Mayer Wise, the founder of Hebrew Union College in Cincinnati, unsympathetically recalled that by 1846 there were several different classes of German-Jewish peddlers already established in America:

> (1) The basket peddler—he is altogether dumb and homeless; (2) the trunk-carrier who stammers some little English, and hopes for better times; (3) the pack-carrier, who carries from one hundred to one hundred and fifty pounds upon his back, and indulges the thought that he will become a businessman some day. In addition to these, there is the aristocracy, which may be divided into three classes: (1) the wagon-baron, who peddles through the country with a one or two horse team; (2) the jewelry-count, who carries a stock of watches and jewelry in a small trunk, and is considered a rich man even now; (3) the store-prince, who has a shop and sells goods in it.

Wise observed of these peddlers, "At first one is the slave to the basket or the pack; then the lackey of the horse, in order to become, finally, the servant of the shop." Despite its constraints, for most peddlers owning a store seemed far better than trudging the roads.

Abraham Kohn's experiences in rural New England were typical of the travails facing back-packing Jewish peddlers. Beyond the risk of theft, loss, accident or illness, peddlers fought the weather. In winter 1842, trudging near Lunenburg, Massachusetts, the recently arrived Kohn noted in his diary, "We were forced to stop on Wednesday because of the heavy snow." He continues:

> We sought to spend the night with a cooper, a Mr. Spaulding, but his wife did not wish to take us in. She was afraid of strangers, she might not sleep well; we should go on our way. And outside raged the worst blizzard I have ever seen. Oh, God, I thought, is this the land of liberty and hospitality and tolerance? Why have I been led here?

The incident ended happily. "After repeatedly pointing out that to turn us forth in a blizzard would be sinful, we were allowed to stay. She became friendlier, indeed, after a few hours, and at night she even joined us in singing."

The peddler's life posed challenges for Jews wishing to maintain their religion. In March of 1843, Kohn reports:

> I came to Worthington, [Massachusetts] where I met a peddler named Marx . . . married and an immigrant. . . . Wretched business! This unfortunate man has been driving himself in this miserable trade for three years to furnish a bare living for himself and his family. O God, our Father, consider Thy little band of the house of Israel. Behold how they are compelled to profane Thy holy Torah in pursuit of their daily bread. In three years this poor fellow could observe the Sabbath less than ten times. . . . This is religious liberty in America.

Eventually, Abraham Kohn settled in Chicago, where he became a retail store-owner and a pillar of the city's Jewish community.

Not all German Jewish peddlers recalled their years on the road unfavorably. Isaac Bernheim, who arrived in the United States just after the Civil War and had a successful business career in Louisville, Kentucky, fondly described his years carrying a pack:

> The new avocation afforded me many opportunities to familiarize myself with the language and customs of the people and with the country itself as perhaps no other pursuit could. It developed me physically, and what was worth still more to me, it gave me a spirit of independence and self-reliance which stood me in good stead afterward. . . . I trudged along the peaceful Pennsylvania highways dreaming of future triumphs.

Jewish merchants brightened the lives of their clientele. Meyer Guggenheim, who later made a great fortune in copper and silver mining, proudly recalled that he had started his career with a pack on his back, going from farm to farm trying to talk the mistress of the house into purchasing shoe laces, needles, spices or ribbons. His biographer observed:

> If the housewife was in a receptive mood and had a little spare cash, Meyer was greeted not without respect. As he slung his pack to the floor, the children crowded about to peer into its awesome, delightful depths and reinforce his halting English with cries of joy. . . . In time housewives began to expect the monthly visit from the cheerful, friendly young Jewish peddler.

Several important American Jewish families—the Gratzes of Kentucky, the Strauses of Georgia and New York, the Bambergers and Blooms of Louisville, the Felses of Philadelphia—got their start as peddlers. When new methods of manufacturing, transporting and marketing goods, rendered peddling obsolete, they opened retail shops and, eventually, department stores such as Macy's, Filene's, Thalheimer's, and Gimbel's. These former peddlers revolutionized the way Americans purchased consumer goods. The great American consumer culture arose from these modest beginnings.

Sponsored in memory of Roy Rogoff by his family

4

Levi Strauss:
A Durable Legacy

The discovery of gold in California in 1848 changed the face of America. One product created in those heady times evolved into an enduring part of American popular culture: Levi's jeans. The durable denim pants were brought to market by Levi Strauss, a Jewish dry goods merchant living in San Francisco. Strauss succeeded by meeting the needs of miners in California's gold fields. Today, Levi's jeans have evolved into a world-recognized fashion statement.

When the magic words "Gold in California" leaked out, hundreds of thousands of Americans, Mexicans, Europeans and Asians risked their lives to go there. The small northern California town of San Francisco became the hub through which 300,000 fortune hunters passed in the course of five years. The city grew almost overnight to rival New York in wealth and commerce.

Some of the many prospectors who panned for gold in northern California's rivers or dug mines struck it rich, but the great majority of the 'Forty-Niners, as they were known, came up empty-handed. A much larger number of fortunes were made providing goods and services to the miners and other migrants. Levi Strauss was one of the fortunate entrepreneurs.

While Strauss was not the "inventor" of the garment known worldwide today as blue jeans, he was responsible for its suc-

cess. In 1847, at the age of eighteen, Loeb (known as Levi) Strauss, the youngest of the seven children of a Bavarian Jewish couple, emigrated to New York, where his older brothers had established a branch of the family's dry goods business. After peddling the company's wares in the rural areas of Kentucky for three years, in January 1853 Levi Strauss became an American citizen. He subsequently joined his two older brothers and sister Fanny in San Francisco to establish a branch of the business there. After opening his own shop on Sacramento Street in downtown San Francisco, he invited Fanny's husband, David Stern, to help him run the business. By 1866, bolstered by a reputation for honesty and fair prices, Strauss opened larger headquarters on Battery Street in which he installed gaslight chandeliers, a freight elevator, and other modern conveniences.

By his mid-thirties, Levi Strauss was a leader of the Jewish community, supporting San Francisco's Temple Emanu-el and helping to fund a gold medal awarded each year to the congregation's best Sabbath School student. He was also a contributor to the Pacific Hebrew Orphan Asylum and Home, the Hebrew Board of Relief, the University of California, and various other civic and cultural institutions.

Strauss's big break came in 1872,

when he was approached by Jacob Davis, a Nevada tailor who had developed a new process for securing the seams of denim pants by riveting them at the pockets and the base of the button fly. Davis could not afford the $81 needed to apply for a patent for his riveting process, so he asked Strauss to pay the fee in return for a share in the patent. Strauss brought Davis to San Francisco to oversee the pants manufacturing. The riveted jeans quickly developed a reputation for durability and quality, and Levi Strauss and Company soon after employed several hundred sewing workers. In 1890, Strauss incorporated the business with his sister's four sons and placed them in charge of day-to-day operations. Unmarried, Levi Strauss turned his company into a family business by sharing it with his nephews, who helped develop Levi Strauss and Company into a worldwide force in retail clothing. In an age of public ownership and Wall Street capitalization, the firm remains a family business owned and managed by Strauss descendants. The family has maintained Levi Straus's personal commitment to Jewish and general philanthropy.

Even as his company grew in size, Levi Strauss insisted that his employees, whatever their position in the company, call him Levi rather than Mr. Strauss. When he died peacefully at home at age seventy-three, the city of San Francisco declared a holiday so that its business leaders could attend his funeral at Temple Emanu-el. After the service, Straus's employees accompanied the casket to the railway station, where it was put on a train for burial in the Jewish cemetery in Colma, a town south of San Francisco.

Levi Strauss, a man of integrity who built a legendary business by providing a durable, high quality product backed by his own name and his family's reputation, has left an enduring mark on American and world fashion.

Sponsored by Jill and Sherman S. Starr

6

Don Solomono, Jewish Indian Chief

From the earliest contact between North American Indians and white European settlers, the Europeans held the upper hand. Almost unremittingly, the Europeans imposed the idea of private ownership of land on the Native Americans, obtaining it from them by purchase, stealth and war. Virtually every Indian tribe in North America found its contacts with white settlers painful, if not fatal, and few Indians trusted or respected, much less loved, the white men and women they knew.

One exception to this generalization was Solomon Bibo, a white trader who won the trust and affection of the Acoma Pueblo Indians of New Mexico. In 1888, "Don Solomono," as he was known to the Acomas, became governor of the Acoma Pueblo, the equivalent of chief of the tribe. Remarkably, the Acomas asked the United States to recognize Bibo as their leader. Even more remarkably, Bibo was a Jew.

Solomon Bibo was born in Prussia in 1853, the sixth of eleven children. In 1866, two of his brothers ventured to America and settled in New Mexico, which in 1848 had become part of the United States after being first a Spanish colony and then part of Mexico. Initially, the older Bibo brothers worked for the Spiegelberg family, pioneer Jewish merchants in New Mexico, but moved on to the tiny village of Ceboletta,

where they set up a trading post to exchange goods with the Navajos. In 1869, at the age of sixteen, Solomon Bibo left Germany for America. After spending some months on the East coast learning English, he joined his brothers in Ceboletta.

All three Bibo brothers developed reputations for fairness in their dealings with the local Indian tribes, who used to bring the Bibos the farm produce they grew. In turn, the Bibos, under contract to the U.S. government, supplied the army posts in the area with produce. The Bibos paid the Indians a fair price for their produce and encouraged them to improve their farming techniques. They also became deeply involved in mediating the many disputes over land ownership that arose between the Indians and the Mexican residents of the area, who for centuries had coveted the Indians' lands. They also tried to intercede with local white Americans (Anglos) who tried to purchase Indian lands at below-market prices. The Bibos were considered pro-Indian and were not embraced by either the Mexicans or their fellow Anglos.

None of the Bibos endeared himself more to the Indians than Solomon, whom the Acomas held in high esteem. In 1882, he arrived at the Acoma pueblo and set up a trading post. He learned Queresan, the Acoma language, and helped the tribe fight legal battles to restore its traditional lands. By treaty in 1877, the Acomas had been granted 94,000 acres of land by the U.S. government, far less than the Indians thought the historical evidence entitled them to. The Acomas were determined to lose no more than had already slipped through their hands.

To accomplish this end, in 1884 the tribe decided to offer Bibo a thirty-year lease to all their land, in exchange for which he would pay them $12,000, protect their cattle, keep squatters away, and mine the coal under the Acoma lands, for which he would pay the tribe a royalty of ten cents per ton for each ton extracted. Pedro Sanchez, the U.S. Indian agent from Santa Fe, learned of the deal and, jealous of the success of this *"rico Israelito"* (rich Jew), tried to get the federal government to void the lease.

The Bibo family fought back. Simon Bibo petitioned the Board of Indian Commissioners in Washington to the effect that Solomon's "intentions with the Indians are of the best nature and beneficial to them—because the men, women and children love him as they would a father and he is in the same manner attached to them." In 1888, convinced at last that Bibo had acted honorably, the Indian agent for New Mexico wrote, "To the people of the pueblo of Acoma, having confidence in the ability, integrity and fidelity of Solomon Bibo . . . I hereby appoint [him] governor of said pueblo."

In 1885, Solomon married an Acoma woman, Juana Valle, granddaughter of his predecessor as governor of the Acoma Pueblo. Juana was originally a Catholic but observed the Jewish faith and raised her children as Jews. In 1898, wanting their children to receive a Jewish education, Solomon and Juana relocated to San Francisco, where he invested in real estate and opened a fancy food shop. Their oldest son marked his bar mitzvah at San Francisco's Ohabei Shalome, and the younger attended religious school at Temple Emanu-el. Solomon Bibo died in 1934, Juana in 1941. Solomon Bibo, governor of the Acomas, America's only known Jewish Indian chief, is buried with his Indian princess in the Jewish cemetery in Colma, California.

Sponsored by Constance and Harvey Kreuger

7

Alfred Huger Moses, Industrial Visionary

From the first Sephardic settlers in North America who engaged in shipping and overseas trade, to German Jewish retailing geniuses like the Straus and Rosenwald families, America's Jewish entrepreneurs have been associated with trade and commerce. Some, however, have dreamed of founding great industrial cities.

One such dreamer was Alfred Huger Moses (1840–1918), the oldest son of Levy and Adeline Moses, and one of the nine children born to them in Charleston, South Carolina. In the eighteenth and early nineteenth centuries, Charleston had been a major center of American Jewish life and many of its leading retailers and merchants were Jewish. However, Charleston's slave-owning planter aristocracy looked down on those "in trade." A non-Jewish commentator wrote in 1818, "I should think my own father an accomplished knave if he had at any time made money in the dry-goods line in King Street [Charleston's commercial thoroughfare]. They are all Jews and worse than Jews—Yankees, for a Yankee can Jew a Jew directly."

Alfred Moses had higher ambitions than to remain in an atmosphere unfavorable to Jews and commercial enterprise. In 1860, at age twenty, after graduating from the College of Charleston, Alfred moved to Montgomery, Alabama, a city that balanced its traditional cotton economy with commerce and manufacturing. Moses apprenticed in a local law office. When the Civil War erupted in April, 1861 he became the clerk of the Confederate District Court in Montgomery and a member of the Alabama Rebels, a volunteer militia company.

During the war, Alfred's brothers Mordecai and Henry joined him in Montgomery. When hostilities ended, the three brothers entered the city's heavily depressed real estate market. By the 1870s, the brothers had developed one of Montgomery's leading real estate investment firms. In 1875, Mordecai Moses was the first Jew elected mayor of Montgomery and later served as president of the Montgomery Gas and Electric Light Company. In 1887, the brothers financed the Moses Building, Montgomery's first highrise.

By 1880, the railroad junction town of Birmingham experienced a boom when coal and iron ore were discovered in the northern reaches of Alabama. Birmingham rapidly grew into a great steel-manufacturing city. Alfred Moses envisioned building a city that would surpass it.

In 1883, Moses toured some mines near Florence, Alabama. Viewing the rolling hills across the Tennessee River from Florence, he thought he had found the ideal spot for a new city, which he named Sheffield after the great steel-producing city in England. Moses and a partner purchased the site and more than 30,000 adjacent acres of mineral lands. They incorporated a company, then laid out streets and invited railroads to lay tracks connecting Sheffield to Birmingham, Mobile and Chicago. Moses promised to construct a water system and a railroad link to Florence. An investor announced plans to build a blast furnace that would produce at least 100 tons of pig iron per day.

In three days in early 1884, Moses sold 75 acres in the proposed town for $350,000, earning a profit of more than a quarter of a million dollars. A few days after the land sale, a number of New York banks failed, including two that were financing the rail link to Sheffield. Construction on the line stopped; panicked owners dumped their newly acquired land in Sheffield and the iron foundry investor backed out. Sheffield property became worthless and Alfred Moses's dream seemed a failure.

Yet Moses had the emotional and financial strength to endure, and by the end of 1884 he started building houses and grading streets. By 1885, railroad construction resumed and, in 1886, the first blast furnace was operating. In February of 1887, the Alabama and Tennessee Iron and Coal Company decided to make Sheffield the center of its operations and erected three more furnaces. Moses's endurance had borne fruit. Stock in the Moses-controlled Sheffield Land, Iron and Coal Company rose rapidly.

By 1891, however, the enterprise failed permanently, along with the Moses family bank in Montgomery. Alfred Moses had miscalculated the willingness of railroads to link Sheffield with major cities and had overestimated the region's iron ore supply. When the market price for steel dropped below $12 per ton, less than the cost for Sheffield's foundries to produce and deliver it, the town's furnaces were banked and most of its residents departed. Moses and his family moved to St. Louis and lived there for another thirty years in greatly reduced circumstances, his dreams destroyed by the boom and bust cycle of the Gilded Age.

However, all was not lost for the Moses children. Alfred's daughter Adeline met Carl M. Loeb, a twenty-year-old Jewish metals dealer employed by a German firm to work in the St. Louis office of its subsidiary, the American Metal Company. Adeline and Carl married, and Carl went on to found the great investment banking firm of Loeb, Rhoads.

Sheffield's blast furnaces were reopened in 1901 but went bankrupt again in 1907. U.S. Steel eventually bought the furnaces, but closed them for good on the eve of the depression in 1929. Today, Sheffield is a small industrial city no longer producing iron or steel. Alfred Moses and his wife are buried in Montgomery, Alabama, where he had his greatest success, rather than in Sheffield, a city he envisioned and built, but then lost.

Sponsored by Ambassador John L. Loeb, Jr.

9

Nathan Straus and the White Peril

The American most responsible for ensuring a safe milk supply in the nation's cities was not a physician, scientist or politician, but a department store magnate. In 1923, Nathan Straus's battle against unsanitary milk, which he termed the "white peril," won him the accolade of "most useful citizen in New York."

Born in Bavaria in 1848, Nathan Straus came to Georgia with his mother, brothers and sister in 1854. After the Civil War the Strauses moved to New York City, where Nathan and his older brother Isidore became the sole owners and managing directors of the R. H. Macy department store. In 1914, deeply affected by the loss of Isidore and his wife, both of whom perished on the

Titanic, Nathan retired from business to devote himself full-time to public service and philanthropy.

Nathan's career in public service had begun earlier, in 1889, when he was appointed New York City's parks commissioner. In 1894, he received the Democratic Party's nomination for mayor of New York, an honor he declined. Three years later he was named president of the New York City Board of Health.

During the 1890s, Straus became especially concerned with the plight of New York's tenement dwellers. During the terrible depression winters of 1892 and 1893, he operated a chain of centers to distribute food and coal to the poor and he built shelters for the homeless. However, his main concern was the high mortality of infants and children, which, he became convinced, was caused chiefly by their consumption of unsanitary raw milk.

Straus was sensitized to child mortality by the deaths of two of his three children. Straus claimed that it was the sudden death of his own cow that first drew his attention to the relationship between raw milk and child mortality. After an autopsy revealed that the animal had tuberculosis, Straus worried that it might have passed the disease along to his family. Doctors, scientists and social reformers had long denounced the poor quality of the milk available in the nation's cities, especially during the summer, and they blamed bad milk for the deaths of hundreds of thousands of American children. Straus saw a need to act.

Convinced that the discoveries of Louis Pasteur offered the best hope for a remedy to the milk problem, Straus built his own plant to sterilize milk bottles and pasteurize milk to kill bacteria. In 1893, at his own expense Straus opened the first of eighteen milk distribution depots throughout the city, which sold his sterilized milk for only a few cents and made free milk available to those unable to afford even that.

Straus believed that ensuring safe milk should be a government responsibility. He tirelessly lectured civic groups and bombarded political leaders around the United States with missives describing the menace of raw milk. He carried the campaign abroad by building pasteurization plants in Europe and the Middle East to demonstrate the technique to foreign governments.

Farmers and commercial milk distributors unwilling to undertake the expense of pasteurization opposed Straus's campaign, which he waged together with his wife Lina. Some scientists, suspicious of "newfangled" ideas, and politicians reluctant to see government conduct social experiments also resisted Straus's campaign. His views took hold as statistics showed that infant mortality rates in the areas around his milk depots had dropped precipitously. In Manhattan and the Bronx alone, Straus was credited with saving the lives of thousands of children. Considering the mortality rates in other cities that adopted his methods, the effects reached millions of children. By the early twentieth century, cities and states began requiring milk pasteurization and in the 1920s Congress enacted national milk health regulations. In 1920, Straus donated his pasteurization plant to the city of New York and turned the milk depots over to public agencies.

The milk fight won, Nathan and Lina devoted the last decade of their lives to Zionist activities and promoting Jewish life in America. They helped underwrite the first nursing missions sent to the Holy Land by Hadassah and funded pasteurization plants, hospitals, and other facilities in Jerusalem and Tel Aviv. The Strauses ultimately gave nearly two-thirds of their wealth to improve living conditions for Arabs and Jews in Palestine. Nathan also helped found the American Jewish Congress and in 1917 launched the Jewish War Relief Fund with the largest single financial contribution.

In 1923, Nathan Straus won an opinion poll asking New Yorkers to name the individual who had done the most to promote the city's public welfare during the preceding quarter-century. Said one admirer, Straus was "a star in the milky way of philanthropy, a man whose heart is bubbling over with the sterilized milk of human kindness."

Sponsored by Robert Arnow

10

Fraces Wisebart Jacobs
Builds a Hospital: 1899

The arrival of masses of Eastern European Jewish immigrants in America, starting in the 1880s, corresponded with a rapid increase in the number of tuberculosis cases in the United States. Physicians at the time knew of only one treatment for the "white plague," as the disease was termed: clean air and sunshine. With its mountain air and crisp climate, Denver, Colorado, became a preferred destination for infected Jewish immigrants from places like New York's Lower East Side and Chicago's Maxwell Street.

Frances Wisebart Jacobs led the effort to make Denver a center for the organized treatment of tuberculosis in the United States. The daughter of immigrants from Bavaria, Frances Wisebart was born in Harrodsburg, Kentucky, in 1843. At age twenty, she married Abraham Jacobs and the couple moved to Colorado. In 1872, Jacobs launched her first foray into organized Jewish charitable relief, forming the Denver Hebrew Ladies' Relief Society, which assisted Denver's small population of needy Jews.

According to historian Marjorie Hornbein, Jacobs "realized that the problems of poverty, sickness, malnutrition and unsanitary living conditions were not limited to the Jewish community." In 1874, she helped organize the Denver Ladies' Relief Society and, in 1887, she joined with the

city's Congregational minister and the Catholic archdiocese to form the Charity Organization Society, forerunner of Denver's United Way. Her efforts would later earn her the name "Denver's mother of charities."

Jacobs left her most enduring mark in the field of tuberculosis treatment. According to Hornbein, hundreds of tuberculosis victims from the industrial Northeast, both Jewish and non-Jewish, who found their way to Denver in search of a cure discovered that "no facilities existed to give them treatment or even shelter." Even worse, "Most of the Denver community ignored those who roamed the city coughing or hemorrhaging." Not Jacobs. Unafraid to touch the ill, she would help them when they fell on the street, get them to a physician, and pay for their treatment. However, as there was no place for the tubercular to stay during treatment, many were transported to the local jail.

Jacobs insisted that the Denver community face the reality that the city was attracting needy tuberculosis victims. According to a Denver journalist at the time, "Everyone put down his pencil to hear her tell of the crucial need for a hospital. Although she could move any hardboiled editor, the response was always the same— 'What you say is true, but this is the Queen city of the Plains, and we can't blacken the name of the city'" by making it a TB refuge.

Jacobs found an ally in the newly appointed rabbi of Denver's Temple Emanuel, William S. Friedman. In 1889, Rabbi Friedman argued from his pulpit in favor of Jacobs's plan to build a Jewish-sponsored tuberculosis hospital. In April of 1890, Denver's Jewish Hospital Association was incorporated and, in October, the cornerstone of a new hospital was laid. A month later, Frances Jacobs contracted pneumonia while visiting among the city's poor. In early November, she died at the age of forty-nine. The hospital's trustees voted to build the hospital in her name. Construction was completed in 1893.

A precipitous drop in silver prices that year caused a depression in the western mining states. The Frances Jacobs Hospital stood empty for lack of funds. In 1895, Louis Anfenger of Denver, the district president of B'nai B'rith, asked the national organization to adopt the Denver tuberculosis hospital as a project. According to Hornbein, "In 1899 the B'nai B'rith decided that the hospital in Denver was the responsibility of all American Jews and that the [Denver] lodge would supervise it." On December 10, 1899, six years after Frances Jacobs's death, the hospital opened its doors.

While a project of B'nai B'rith and the Denver Jewish community, the renamed National Jewish Hospital was nondenominational. Its first patient was a Swedish woman from Minnesota. To reflect its openness to the impoverished of every background, the hospital adopted the motto, "None may enter who can pay, and none can pay who enter."

Another aspect of the hospital's philosophy was more controversial. The trustees limited admission to those who had incipient (early stage), rather than advanced, cases of TB. However, a large number of Orthodox Jews with advanced cases traveled to Denver from eastern slums in search of a cure. The National Hospital would not admit them. Moreover, having been organized primarily by German Reform Jews, it lacked a kosher kitchen. The Orthodox would not eat there even if admitted.

After a debate in which some members of the German Jewish elite argued that Denver must not be swamped with "dying consumptives," Dr. Charles Spivak, representing the East European faction, organized the Jewish Consumptives' Relief Society, which built a new hospital for those in advanced stages of the disease. The new hospital served kosher food.

Today, tuberculosis is no longer epidemic—in part because of research done at the National Jewish Hospital. The "National" remains, after several evolutionary transformations, one of America's great research hospitals for respiratory diseases.

In Colorado's state capitol, there are sixteen stained-glass windows depicting important state pioneers. The only woman represented is Francis Wisebart Jacobs.

In memory of Charles Schayer

11

Minnie Low and Scientific Tzedakah

Chicago social worker Minnie Low has been called the Jane Addams of the Jews. Comparison with the founder of that city's renowned Hull House—perhaps the best-known settlement house serving immigrants in early twentieth-century America—while flattering to Low, disguises the differences between the two women.

Unlike the more privileged Addams, Low was born in New York to poor immigrant Jewish parents who moved to Chicago when she was ten years old. Addams attended college and medical school and could afford to serve unpaid in her various leadership roles. By contrast, because of illness, Low dropped out of public high school and never completed her formal education. She remained single and supported herself through a paid career in social work. Addams's involvement with the poor stemmed from a patrician sense of *noblesse oblige* and a Christian sense that her personal salvation lay in the doing of good deeds. Low was motivated by a sense of solidarity with her fellow Jews, particularly those who emigrated from Russia. Both women were pioneers in American social work, but it is Low's ideas, and not Addams's, that currently dominate social welfare thinking.

Born in 1867, Minnie Low's calling to Jewish social service initially came in 1893, in the depths of a great national eco-nomic depression. That year, Low helped found the Maxwell Street Settlement House in the heart of Chicago's immigrant Jewish ghetto. Low and Addams became friends at that time; in fact, the meetings that led to the establishment of the Maxwell Street Settlement were held at Hull House.

The dominant mode of settlement house work, established by Jane Addams, focused mainly on giving the immigrants recreational, cultural and social opportunities—exposure to music, art, crafts and English language—rather than marketable skills. By contrast, Low believed that charity should be less cultural and more "scientific." She wanted philanthropy to foster the economic independence and moral character of its recipients. To borrow a popular metaphor, rather than feeding the poor a fish dinner, Low's scientifically targeted philanthropy tried to provide them with fishing rods and fishing lessons so they could learn to feed themselves.

Low put her ideas to work in 1897, when the recently formed National Council of Jewish Women appointed her director of its Seventh Ward Bureau in Chicago, later renamed the Bureau of Personal Service. The bureau helped the city's Jewish immigrants secure housing, medical care, legal assistance and credit. Its employees, on Low's instructions, did not simply dispense alms to their clients, but helped them take responsibility for finding their own jobs. She encouraged Chicago's middle-class Jewish women to become "friendly visitors" in the homes of the poor and provide them with mentoring and encouragement. Her agency created a workroom that employed Jewish immigrants and paid them in coal and secondhand shoes and clothing.

Low believed strongly in the American Jewish communal practice of providing interest-free loans, rather than charity, to those in need. In 1897, she tested her beliefs by creating the Woman's Loan Association. Starting with a treasury of $87, by 1918 the organization was distributing $33,000 per year in interest-free loans, primarily to Jewish immigrants who used the money to establish or sustain small businesses. Historian Shelly Tenenbaum quotes an essay Low wrote in 1905:

> Loan a small amount to a man struggling for existence . . . [give] him some time to repay the loan in installments [and he will do so] without flinching, and without shirking his responsibility. . . . What greater proof do we require that undaunted courage, ambition, honor and manliness are virtues of the poor?

Low made several innovative contributions to the Chicago social welfare system. With Judge Julian Mack, Jane Addams and others, she helped organize the Juvenile Court of Chicago (1899), the first separate juvenile justice system in America. She also established the Juvenile Protective Association, an organization devoted to delinquency prevention. Low was active in Chicago's Central Bureau of Jewish Charities, the Home for Jewish Friendless and the Jewish Finding Home Society, an adoption bureau for children without families. Low was also active in attempts to suppress the white slave trade, a serious threat to poor Jewish girls. Recognizing her tireless efforts on behalf of the less fortunate, in 1914 her colleagues elected her president of the National Conference of Jewish Charities. She used the position to fight for better pay for women in Jewish communal service.

Low's name is little remembered today, but her belief that Jewish charity should provide the poor with employable skills rather than encourage their dependency on handouts makes her an intellectual forerunner of today's leading welfare reform theorists. Her notion of scientific tzedakah foreshadows the current emphasis on moving recipients off welfare rolls and onto payrolls and made her a thinker well ahead of her time.

Sponsored by M. Bernard Aidinoff

12

Celia Greenstone:
The Angel of Ellis Island

In 1907, at just twenty years of age, Celia Greenstone was hired by the New York Section of the National Council of Jewish Women (NCJW) to serve as assistant immigrant arrival agent at Ellis Island. Between 1892 and 1924, more than 15,000,000 immigrants—most of them from Eastern and Southern Europe, and many of them Jews—passed through Ellis Island. The New York Section of NCJW was concerned that thousands of single Jewish women might be "misled into immoral lives, and other girls [will be] subjected to great dangers because of the lack of some directing and protecting agency at Ellis Island." The New York Section appointed pioneer social worker Bessie Meirowitz as their Ellis island agent and when her work load got too heavy, Celia Greenstone was hired to serve as her assistant.

At age thirteen, while still living in Bialystok in Russian Poland, Celia had been left in charge of the family's cigarette facto-ry while her father went off on business. She learned to deal with suppliers, customers and corrupt officials. At the same time, the idealistic Greenstone avidly read Karl Marx, joined a utopian socialist-Zionist movement and even unionized her father's cigarette factory workers. She marched in socialist demonstrations that were brutally suppressed by the police. In 1905, when Celia was eighteen, the family business failed and pogroms swept Bialystok. The Greenstones elected to emigrate to America.

Vowing to teach herself English quickly, Celia Greenstone spent hours each day at the Astor Library in New York, voraciously reading books in English, Hebrew, German, Russian and Yiddish, which brought her to the attention of the head of the Hebrew Department. He asked Greenstone to serve as his volunteer assistant. According to her great-grandson, Jesse Peterson, after a few months Greenstone asked the librarian for money to defray the cost of her lunch and travel, and he berated her for being ungrateful. Greenstone protested her exploitation to the head librarian, who promised to arrange a job for her. A few months later, he helped find Greenstone a position as translator for Jacob Schiff, the famous Jewish banker and philanthropist. Impressed by Greenstone's facility with languages, Schiff's wife brought her to the attention of the New York Section of NCJW, which hired her to assist at Ellis Island.

Greenstone worked six long days a week for months on end, ushering single women, mothers, and children through the intake process on Ellis Island. Greenstone was particularly moved by the plight of those women who, rejected by the health inspectors, were scheduled for deportation back to *shtetls* where poverty and pogroms threatened their survival. Greenstone intervened on behalf of several frightened young girls labeled "retarded" by the inspectors simply because they could not understand questions posed to them in English. She helped girls traveling alone to locate their families or to obtain work and respectable lodgings after they left Ellis Island. Greenstone also tended those detained on the island while being treated for temporary health problems or awaiting deportation. Importantly, she arranged for kosher food to be delivered to inmates of the island hospital and established Shabbat and holiday services.

In 1912, NCJW promoted Greenstone to head agent on Ellis Island. Her responsibilities now included conducting weekly follow-up meetings at the Educational Alliance in Manhattan with women she had helped through Ellis Island to assure that they were learning English, receiving support and searching for work.

Greenstone also made a weekly visit to the Bedford Reformatory for girls to visit the Jewish inmates.

World War I dramatically cut into European immigration to America. Whereas 878,000 immigrants landed at Ellis Island in 1914, only 28,000 arrived in 1918. When the war ended, a series of restrictive laws that excluded most of the Jewish immigrants who wanted to enter the United States. The need for Greenstone's services at Ellis Island had come to an end. After marrying and having two children, she resumed her work with immigrants at Hamilton House, the Henry Street Settlement and the Grand Street settlement on the Lower East Side. In 1986, Celia Greenstone was posthumously elected to the New York Settlement House Hall of Fame.

In 1962, at her seventy-fifth birthday party, Greenstone looked back on her years helping Ellis Island's Jewish immigrants become American citizens:

> I remember clearly visiting an immigrant in his new home one day. In the kitchen I see three cots, in which three men sleep. I learned that those cots were never empty. While three men slept, three men worked . . . when those who were working came home, those who had been sleeping left for their own jobs. And in other rooms it was the same. And in every [immigrant] home the basic story was the same. Human beings lived only to work. Rest, recreation, culture and togetherness of families, everything was sacrificed to the need to work, to survive.
>
> To rescue human dignity from this nightmare—that was the single thought my co-workers and I had. To show the immigrants that in all the hard sorrows of their lives, they did not stand alone, and that they did not have to succumb. To show them that if one person misused or betrayed them, another would not.

Sponsored by Philip Lax

13

Hebrew Free Loans: Lending a Helping Hand

In 1909, a group of Seattle Jewish women formed a whist and sewing club with dues of 25 cents per month. When they had accumulated $64, they offered to purchase a gift for their local synagogue. The rabbi refused it, knowing that the women had raised the money by playing cards. Undaunted, they used the money to start the Hebrew Ladies' Free Loan Society of Seattle. Their thoughtfulness helped some of Seattle's Jewish entrepreneurs get started in business.

Hebrew free loan societies and *aktsiyes*, or credit cooperatives, helped fuel Jewish immigrant economic success during the first third of the twentieth century. Free loan societies charged no interest on their loans, whereas *aktsiyes* charged a small amount. The need for Jewish loan societies was a product of the times.

Before the 1930s, only a handful of banks loaned money to individuals or small businesses, especially those started by immigrants. By one account, more than 85 percent of all Americans were excluded from access to commercial credit. More than any other immigrant group at the time, American Jews of Eastern European background worked in or owned small businesses—one-room retail shops, small workshops, or peddlers' pushcarts and wagons. Without access to the loans provided by the free loan societies and *aktsiyes*, many of the businesses

founded by and employing immigrant Jews would not have been created. Minnie Low, founder in 1897 of the Chicago Women's Loan Association, observed, "In the Chicago Ghetto, along the Jefferson Street market, as well as throughout the entire district, there are comparatively few of the peddlers, vendors and keepers of small stands and shops who have not been given a start in life or helped over rugged places by loans from local organizations" (see page 186).

Historian Shelley Tenenbaum notes that the societies were "based on the biblical and Talmudic concept of providing the Jewish poor with interest-free loans." Maimonides considered the interest-free loan one of the higher forms of tzedakah because it respects the dignity of the borrower, provides him with a means of self-sufficiency, and does not saddle him with large debt. At the peak, there were more than 500 Jewish free loan societies operating in the United States. In 1920 alone, the New York Hebrew Free Loan Society distributed more than $1 million in loans to Jewish-owned small businesses.

The societies restricted themselves to meeting the capital needs of small business enterprises rather than other charitable requirements. As a Rhode Island newspaper reported, the Providence Hebrew Free Loan Society provided "means whereby the Jew can start in business for himself, or can meet the obligations of his business till it becomes established on a paying basis. This does not mean that a member of the race who is pressed for money for other purposes, because of illness or other emergency, is left without possibility of aid from his own people. There are other [Jewish philanthropic] associations which will help him."

Unlike the free loan societies, *aktsiyes* worked on the same basis as credit unions: individual members deposited money in savings accounts and were paid interest. An *aktsiye* loaned a portion of the deposits to members who wanted to start enterprises. The first credit union in New York State was founded in 1911 by the Jewish Agricultural and Industrial Aid Society, which began as an informal *aktsiye*. In 1918, there were ten Jewish credit unions in New York City alone. By 1927, Boston had 139 credit unions, three-quarters with explicitly Jewish names or a majority of whose directors were Jewish.

Edward A. Filene, a Boston Jewish department store owner and philanthropist, encouraged low-interest loans because, in his own words, he wanted to "fight the age old prejudice that all Jews were usurers." The rabbi of Boston's Temple Israel thought the free loan societies and *aktsiyes* were valuable because they proved that "there are Jews who are ready to serve, to help, to give, to lend, not for what they can get out of it but for the good they can thus do."

Unlike formal credit unions, *aktsiyes* were not licensed or regulated. When state governments began bringing them under regulatory control in the 1920s, the institutions could no longer limit their lending to Jews. In the 1930s, banks made further inroads into the customer base served by Jewish free loans. Inspired by the fact that Jewish credit cooperatives had default rates of less than 1 percent despite the depression, commercial banks set up personal loan departments to provide individuals and small businesses with larger loans than the free loan societies could risk. By the late 1940s, bank personal credit departments had become common. With some exceptions, Jews were able to obtain access to this credit on the same basis as other borrowers.

By the 1960s, the surviving Hebrew free loan societies found new and creative ways to distribute their funds, such as interest-free loans to Jewish college students. All of the surviving societies now lend to Jews and non-Jews alike. Some have found new life in providing loans to Russian Jewish immigrants. While Jewish-owned small businesses no longer have difficulty obtaining commercial credit, the surviving free loan societies continue to perform the mitzvah for which they were created.

Sponsored by the Boyerker Society in memory of Paul Feldberg

15

The Iceberg, the Radio and David Sarnoff

As the *Titanic* sank on the night of April 14, 1912, the great ship's wireless telegraph officers remained at their posts until the very end, sending out distress signals. The liner *Carpathia*, 58 miles away, heard the frantic radio signals, reversed course and steamed to the rescue. In America, twenty-one-year-old David Sarnoff stayed at his wireless telegraph listening post atop the Wanamaker department store in New York for seventy-two uninterrupted hours, relaying to newspapers and frantic family members news of the sinking. His diligence made his career—and assured the future of radio communication.

Born in 1891 in a shtetl near Minsk, David was five when his father left for America. David went to study for the rabbinate with his grand-uncle, who lived 500 miles away. At age nine, he rejoined his mother and two brothers for the journey to New York's Lower East Side. Young David sold newspapers and held jobs before and after school and on weekends, and earned extra money singing in a synagogue. When he was fifteen, his father died, leaving him as the family's main support. He left school to work as a messenger at the Commercial Cable Company, where he taught himself Morse code and learned about the new wireless form of communication called radio. Sarnoff's boss at Commercial Cable fired him for requesting time off for High Holy Day services, but he promptly found work with the infant Marconi Wireless and Telegraph Company, where his diligence attracted the attention of Guglielmo Marconi, the firm's founder and inventor of commercial shortwave radio.

Wireless communication was then regarded as a novelty. Some ships had radios and sent signals in Morse code, mainly to relay messages for the convenience of wealthy passengers. A retailer, John Wanamaker, installed wireless communication stations in his New York and Philadelphia department stores, hoping that customers drawn to watch the messages come in would remain to shop. In 1912, Wanamaker hired Sarnoff to operate the wireless station at the New York store.

Arriving at work on April 14, Sarnoff picked up faint coded messages from the *Carpathia* reporting the loss of the *Titanic*. For three days and nights, Sarnoff remained glued to his earphones, listening for the names of the rescued and relaying them to newspaper reporters and frantic family members. Years later, Sarnoff recalled:

> I felt my responsibility keenly and, weary though I was, could not have slept. . . . Much of the time, I sat there with nothing coming in. It seemed that the whole anxious world was attached by my earphones during the seventy-two hours I crouched tensely in the station. I sat for hours—listening. Now we began to get the names of some of those who were known to have gone down. This was worse than the other list had been—heartbreaking in its finality, a death-knell to hope. I passed the information on to a sorrowing world, and when messages ceased to come in, fell down like a log at my place and slept the clock around.

In the aftermath of the *Titanic* disaster, new laws made wireless communications mandatory on all ocean-going vessels and the Marconi Company prospered. In 1919, the newly formed Radio Corporation of America (RCA) acquired the American Marconi Company; Sarnoff came along as commercial manager. He rose steadily to chairman of the RCA board of directors.

As early as 1915, Sarnoff prophesied that he could make radio "a household utility in the same sense as a piano or phonograph." He explained, "The idea is to bring music into the home by wireless." He created the National Broadcasting Corporation, which pioneered home broadcasting of music and news. In later years, Sarnoff encouraged the development of television and, despite the skepticism of experts, color television. When he spoke on the nation's first live television broadcast in 1939, Sarnoff said (again with prescience), "It is with a feeling of humbleness that I come to the moment of announcing the birth in this country of a new art so important in its implications that it is bound to affect all society." From the 1940s to the 1970s, RCA manufactured more than half of the world's television sets.

Sarnoff never forgot his humble roots. He served until his death in 1971 as a trustee of the Educational Alliance, the Jewish settlement house on the Lower East Side that had given him his first schooling in America, and the Jewish Theological Seminary of America. The Weizmann Institute of Science named Sarnoff its first honorary fellow in 1952. Looking back at the visionary role he had played in modern communications, Sarnoff recalled that he got his start because of a tragedy: "The *Titanic* disaster brought radio to the front, and also me."

Sponsored by Ralph and Shirley Shapiro in memory of Paul and Toby Shapiro

195

16

Regina Margareten:
Matriarch of the Kosher Food Industry

Every Passover, we are reminded that American Jewry has developed its own traditional means for celebrating the holiday, including the use of highly recognizable commercial staples on countless American Seder tables: sweet red Manischewitz wines, kosher Barton's candies, Rokeach gefilte fish and Horowitz-Margareten matzohs. The enduring success of these brand- name product can be attributed, at least in part, to the driving force of their family founders. Regina Horowitz Margareten's matzoh is a case in point.

Born in Hungary in 1863, Regina came to America as the twenty-year-old bride of Ignatz Margareten. Regina's parents, Jacob and Mirel Horowitz, accompanied the newlyweds. The two families went into business together, opening a grocery store on Willett Street on New York's Lower East Side. Remaining true to their Orthodoxy, the families baked their own matzoh for their first Passover in America. The following year, they purchased fifty barrels of flour, rented a bakery, and produced extra matzoh for sale in their store. According to historian Shulamith Z. Berger, during that first year of baking matzot commercially, Regina Margareten "lit the fires, worked the dough and found customers." Within a few years, the matzot were so popular that baking it became the family's sole business.

In 1885, two years after the family arrived in America, Regina's father died. She, her mother, her four brothers and her husband, Ignatz, continued to run the firm, now named Horowitz Brothers & Margareten Company. According to historian Berger, Regina Margareten worked through the night at the company's Manhattan bakery and, for weeks at a time, saw the light of day only on the Sabbath. Her mother died in 1919 and her husband in 1923, at which time Regina Margareten formally joined the company's board of directors and took the title of treasurer. As *de facto* head, she grew the business steadily. In 1931, the company used 45,000 barrels of flour and grossed the then-considerable sum of $1 million.

According to the *New York Times*, Regina Margareten became the "matriarch of the kosher food industry." She would arrive at the plant on New York's Lower East Side each day at 8:30 a.m., taste the matzoh and have samples sent to her office throughout the day—a one-woman quality control department. She was instrumental in the company's 1945 decision to relocate from the Lower East Side to a larger plant in Long Island City that would provide room for future growth. Her influence also pushed the firm to diversify its product line to include noodles and other kosher food products.

Regina Margareten was a model of tzedakah (*charity*). Throughout the years of the Great Depression, she made certain that any beggar who came to the Horowitz Brothers & Margareten factory left with something to eat. She supported more than 100 charitable organizations and took an active role in many of them. Among her favorites was an organization that supplied indigent boys at a Talmud Torah with new clothes at Passover and another that provided for needy women during pregnancy and childbirth.

Margareten had a sense of adventure. During the 1920s and 1930s she traveled annually to visit relatives in Hungary. Family lore has it that one year in the early 1920s she flew the London to Paris leg of the journey in an open-cockpit airplane. On another visit, she helped a relative purchase a coal mine in Edeleny, Hungary, so that family members in the area would have jobs. When World War II began, she had her son Jacob file affidavits promising to employ European relatives at the company so they could get visas and escape to America.

Regina Margareten was the company's spokesperson to the community. At Passover during the 1940s and 1950s, she annually broadcast a Yiddish radio greeting to the American Jewish community, which she would then repeat in English "for the sake of the children who may be listening in." In 1952, at age eighty-nine, Margareten's talk served as a valedictory to what life in America had meant to her. She thanked the United States for the "freedom, prosperity and happiness we have here." These bounties, she reminded her audience, had made it possible for American Jewry to help other Jewish communities around the world and to build the new State of Israel. For these blessings, she was grateful to America, and urged every American Jew to be mindful of their good fortune.

As late as two weeks before her death in 1959 at the age of ninety-six, Regina Margareten traveled daily to the factory in Long Island City, tasted the matzoh and checked on the price of flour. Her life was defined by three values: excellence in business, charity toward her fellow Jews and loyalty to family. She succeeded at all three.

In honor of Ronald C. Curhan

17

Lane Bryant Malsin: Fashion Revolutionary

In 1895, a sixteen-year-old immigrant named Lena Himmelstein arrived in New York, having traveled alone from her native Lithuania. Without family, she supported herself as a seamstress, working for a dollar a week. A gifted dressmaker, Lena quickly became skilled at her craft and within a year was earning the extraordinary wage of $15 per week. Before she was twenty, Lena married a Jewish immigrant jeweler from Russia named David Bryant. Soon after their son, Raphael, was born, David Bryant died suddenly. The widowed Lena Bryant, thrown back on her own devices, supported Raphael and herself by returning to dressmaking at home in their cramped apartment.

By 1904, Bryant's business was so successful that she moved to a shop that had living quarters in the rear. A bank officer misspelled her name on a business account application and Lena's first name became Lane. Thus began the pioneering women's clothing enterprise known as Lane Bryant.

Lane Bryant was an innovator, well ahead of her times as a designer and an entrepreneur. According to historian Louise Klaber, at the turn of the century proper ladies who happened to be pregnant were rarely if ever seen in public. When one of Bryant's pregnant customers asked her to design something "presentable but comfortable" to wear on the street, Bryant created a dress with an elasticized waistband and an accordion-pleated skirt. In doing so, she produced the first known commercial maternity dress. The garment liberated the increasing number of middle-class women who wanted to break with Victorian tradition. It also helped poorer pregnant women who had no choice but to go to work. The maternity dress soon became the best-selling item in Bryant's shop.

In 1909, Bryant married Albert Malsin, who became her business partner. Lane Bryant Malsin continued as chief designer and Albert Malsin concentrated on the firm's business operations. By 1911, Lane Bryant's shop was grossing $50,000 per year. Its growth potential was limited, however, because none of New York's newspapers would accept advertising for maternity clothes. Tradition still dictated that such topics were not discussed in the press. It took the Malsins until 1911 to persuade the *New York Herald* to accept an ad. When the paper did, Lane Bryant's entire stock was sold out the next day. The company's success was now assured.

To cope with newspaper discrimination against maternity clothes advertisements, the Malsins decided to create the first mail-order catalog for maternity wear. By 1917, mail-order sales revenues for Lane Bryant, Inc. exceeded a million dollars. By

1950, the company's mail-order sales made it the sixth-largest mail-order retailer in the United States.

Having succeeded in maternity wear and catalog sales, Lane Bryant Malsin's next great innovation was ready-made clothing for the stout-figured woman. Before World War I, no mass manufacturer of women's clothing addressed this market. After measuring some 4,500 women in her store and analyzing statistics gathered on some 200,000 others, Lane Bryant Malsin determined that there were three general types of stout women, and she designed clothes to fit each type. By 1923, the firm grossed $5 million, with sales of full-figured clothing outstripping sales of maternity wear. In 1915, Lane Bryant opened its first branch retail store, in Chicago, and by 1969 the chain had grown to more than 100 stores with combined sales of $200 million.

Lane Bryant Malsin pioneered in customer relations and corporate philanthropy. At her suggestion, Lane Bryant, Inc. worked with the Red Cross to replace any Lane Bryant customer's wardrobe that was destroyed in a disaster. In 1947, for example, after a major explosion and fire in Texas City, Texas, the company reoutfitted fifty-eight mail-order customers whose homes were destroyed. After World War II, Lane Bryant stores became clothing donation centers to benefit displaced persons in Europe.

Lane Bryant, Inc. also pioneered in employee benefits at a time when few companies, particularly in the retail sector, offered meaningful employee support beyond wages. By 1950, the more than 3,500 Lane Bryant employees participated in profit sharing, pension, disability, group life insurance plans and fully reimbursed physician's visits and hospitalizations. When the company went public, 25 percent of the stock was reserved for employee subscription.

On a personal level, Lane Bryant Malsin was active in Jewish communal charity. She supported the Hebrew Immigrant Aid Society, the New York Federation of Jewish Philanthropies, and a number of other causes. When she died in 1951, her sons succeeded her in the business. In 1969, Lane Bryant, Inc. was purchased by another innovator in women's retail clothing: the Limited, whose founder, Leslie Wexner, has also been deeply involved in American Jewish philanthropy. Lane Bryant Malsin would probably be pleased to know that her company and name are linked with someone whose values fit so well with her own.

Sponsored by Linda D. and Phil Bleich

Part IX

AMERICAN ZIONISM, THE HOLOCAUST, AND THE FOUNDING OF ISRAEL

1

John Adams Embraces a Jewish Homeland

John Adams

The correspondence of John Adams, second president of the United States, reflects the ambivalent attitude toward Jews and Judaism that typified enlightened Christians in the late eighteenth and early nineteenth centuries. Like Thomas Jefferson, Adams venerated the Jews of ancient times for laying the groundwork for Christianity and held that present-day Jews, as individuals, deserved rights and protection under the law. At the same time, again like Jefferson, he regarded Judaism as an archaic religion, and held that the Jewish people were worthy candidates for conversion to Christianity.

In an 1808 letter, Adams forthrightly criticizes the way Jews were depicted by Voltaire, the French Enlightenment philosopher:

> How is it possible [that he] should represent the Hebrews in such a contemptible light? They are the most glorious nation that ever inhabited this Earth. The Romans and their Empire were but a Bauble in comparison of the Jews. They have given religion to three quarters of the Globe and have influenced the affairs of Mankind more, and more happily, than any other Nation ancient or modern.

Aware of Adams's views, American Jewish newspaper editor, politician, diplomat, and playwright Mordecai Manuel Noah (1785–1851) initiated a correspondence with the former president. In 1818, Noah delivered a speech consecrating the new building erected by Congregation Shearith Israel, in New York. Noah's "Discourse," a copy of which resides in the archives of the American Jewish Historical Society, focused on the universal history of Jewish persecution at the hands of non-democratic governments and their nations, and declared that the Jewish people would only live free of oppression when they were reestablished in their own home and could govern themselves. Eager to engage Adams in a discussion of this idea, Noah sent him a copy of the "Discourse."

The former president responded encouragingly, although he was evasive about Jewish self-governance. After stating his personal wish that "your Nation may be admitted to all Privileges of Citizens in every Country of the World," Adams continued:

> This Country has done much. I wish it may do more, and annul every narrow idea in Religion, Government and Commerce. . . . It has pleased the Providence of the "first Cause," the Universal Cause [i.e., God], that Abraham should give Religion, not only to the Hebrews but to Christians and Mahomitans, the greatest Part of the Modern civilized World."

For Adams, Jews had earned their rights by virtue of their historic contributions and their citizenship, but he did not endorse Noah's call for a Jewish homeland.

Remarkably, a year later, a letter from Adams to Noah included a statement that clearly favored Jewish resettlement of Palestine. In 1819, Noah sent Adams a copy of his recently published *Travels in England, France, Spain and the Barbary States*. Acknowledging the gift, Adams praised it as "a magazine of ancient and modern learn-ing of judicious observations & ingenious reflections" and expressed regret that Noah had not toured "Syria, Judea and Jerusalem." Had Noah done so, Adams said, he would have attended "more to [his] remarks than to those of any traveller I have yet read," adding, "Farther I could find it in my heart to wish that you had been at the head of a hundred thousand Israelites . . . & marching with them into Judea & making a conquest of that country & restoring your nation to the dominion of it. For I really wish the Jews again in Judea an independent nation."

What was the source of Adams's sudden Zionist sympathy? What moved him to make this extraordinary statement? A clue can be found in the next sentence:

> I believe [that] . . . once restored to an independent government & no longer persecuted they [the Jews] would soon wear away some of the asperities and peculiarities of their character & possibly in time become liberal Unitarian christians for your Jehovah is our Jehovah & your God of Abraham Isaac and Jacob is our God.

The French social commentator Alexis de Tocqueville observed, "The Americans combine notions of Christianity and of liberty so intimately in their minds, that it is impossible to conceive the one without the other." Adams was clearly confident that freedom would lead the Jewish people to enlightenment, and that enlightenment would lead them to Christianity. For Adams, Jewish self-governance in the Holy Land was a step toward their elevation. Today, our understanding of democratic freedom includes respect for diversity and support for the retention of one's religious faith. Adams's views would be far from the mainstream.

Sponsored by Gail and Ephraim Propp

2

Moses Elias Levy and a Jewish Zion in Florida

In 1821, Moses Elias Levy purchased 53,000 acres of land in northeastern Florida. Levy believed that Florida could be a new Zion, a home for the persecuted Jews of Europe. Today, in a very different way and with an American rather than European Jewish clientele, Levy's vision has become a reality. South Florida is now home to the third-largest concentration of Jews in the United States.

Born in Morocco in 1781, Moses Elias Levy was the son of a government official. After the sultan's death in 1790, anti-Semitic violence drove the Levy family to Gibraltar. There, at the age of fifteen, while praying in a synagogue, Levy had a revelation. He later described the moment as "surpassing the idea of hellfire." According to historian Chris Monaco, "During this episode . . . Moses Levy 'swore never to doubt the Bible.'" While many nineteenth-century American Jews took a lax approach to religious observance, Levy remained staunchly traditional, keeping the Sabbath and observing kashrut throughout his life.

In 1800, the death of Levy's father and a yellow fever epidemic forced Moses, his mother and his infant sister to leave Gibraltar for the Danish Virgin Islands, where they joined a thriving Jewish community. Three years later, at age twenty-two, he became partners in a lumber business with Philip Benjamin, whose son Judah, much later, served as a United States senator and then as a member of the Confederate cabinet (see page 52). Levy subsequently moved to Puerto Rico, where he became a munitions contractor. After separating from his wife, he moved to Cuba, where he built a fortune in shipping.

While in Cuba, Levy decided to use his wealth to purchase a tract of land near Micopany in Florida, soon thereafter ceded by Spain to the United States. Levy built houses and dug wells in hopes of attracting European Jews living under oppressive conditions. Jews in the Diaspora needed a homeland, he reasoned, because "no amelioration can be expected at the hands of nations for us. . . . The race of Jews has miraculously been continued unmixed with the people of the nations through which they have been scattered. . . . Every Jew who contributes to the . . . amalgamation of the House of Israel is an enemy to his nation, his religion and, consequently, to the world at large."

Levy named his colony Pilgrimage Plantation. Between 1820 and 1824, he sought financial support for his plan in New York, Philadelphia, and Norfolk. Few Jews emigrated from Europe to the wilds of Levy's experimental plantation, however. Perhaps the fact that Florida was inhabited by hostile Indians, snakes and alligators discouraged them. Perhaps they did not want to leave Europe for a strange land.

In 1825, Levy went to London, hoping to persuade Jewish philanthropists there to support Pilgrimage Plantation. His pleas fell mostly on deaf ears. Through his willingness to address leading English Christians, however, he had an impact on the campaign to reestablish full Jewish rights in England. In 1826, a number of upper-class Christian Londoners took a genuine interest, on liberal grounds, in restoring full political equality to England's Jews, whose rights had been suspended 500 years earlier. Levy addressed reform-minded Christian groups on several occasions and impressed them with his learning. The sophisticated yet pious Levy helped dispel the notion that all Jews were peddlers living in poverty in London's East End.

Levy also confronted the evangelical London Society for the Promotion of Christianity among the Jews, challenging their attempts to "save" the Jewish people through conversion. His contacts with evangelicals gave him access to the British anti-slavery movement. Levy had lived with slavery in the Caribbean and Florida. A group of British evangelical abolitionists known as the Clapham Sect listened to him with rapt attention when he lectured on slavery. Because Levy observed the Sabbath, spoke fluent Hebrew and knew the Bible, the Claphamites treated him as a lineal descendant of the ancient Hebrews whose religion, they believed, was the wellspring of Christianity.

British abolitionists urged immediate emancipation to save the souls of both slave and slaveowner. Levy argued that, for emancipation to succeed, banks and businesses would have to be created first to invest in non-slave agriculture and the children of slaves would have to be taught efficient agricultural techniques. Levy thought that a generation of gradual preparation for emancipation was necessary. Despite these reservations, he was one of the few Southerners to propose any form of emancipation—even if he was in the relative safety of London when he made his views public.

Ironically, little that Levy stood for survived his own lifetime. In 1835, Pilgrimage Plantation was burned during the Second Seminole War. Levy's son, David Levy Yulee, later became a United States Senator from Florida, the first Jew to serve in that body. Unlike his father, however, the younger Levy was pro-slavery and rejected his Jewish identity, eventually converting to Christianity. Nevertheless, Moses Elias Levy proved a visionary in predicting that Florida would one day make an excellent home for Diaspora Jews.

Sponsored by Samson Bitensky

3

Noah's Second Landing at Ararat

Grand Island sits in the Niagara River between Buffalo, New York, and Canada. On a pedestal at Grand Island Town Hall sits a cornerstone engraved with the Sh'ma prayer in Hebrew and the following inscription:

> ARARAT
> A City of Refuge for the Jews
> Founded by Mordecai Manuel Noah in the month of Tizri 5586
> Sept. 1825 and in the 50th Year of American Independence

What was this place, Ararat, and who was Mordecai Manuel Noah?

Born in Philadelphia in 1785 to German-Jewish and Sephardic parents, Noah pursued simultaneous careers in journalism and politics. At age twenty-six, he

petitioned Secretary of State Robert Smith to grant him a consular position with a not-so-subtle reminder that the appointment of a Jew to the diplomatic corps would favorably impress Jewish voters and "prove to foreign powers that our government is not regulated in the appointment of their officers by religious distinction." Noah was subsequently appointed consul in Riga Latvia and then in Tunis. Later, he was elected sheriff of New York City, appointed surveyor of the city's port and made a judge of its Court of General Sessions. As editor of six different New York newspapers over the years, he was assured a public platform. That he used it to advocate for Jewish rights all over the world.

In the Ararat project, service to world Jewry and personal advancement merged. Noah declared in 1818:

Never were prospects for the restoration of the Jewish nation to their ancient rights and dominion more brilliant than they are at present. There are seven million of Jews . . . throughout the world . . . possessing more wealth, activity, influence, and talents, than any body of people of their number on earth. . . . they will march in triumphant numbers, and possess themselves once more of [Palestine], and take their rank among the governments of the earth.

In 1820, he began private negotiations to purchase Grand Island, then completely undeveloped, as a temporary "New Jerusalem" where oppressed European Jews could live safely until they repossessed the Holy Land.

Grand Island stood where the Erie Canal, then under construction, would enter the Niagara River. Noah hoped to attract French and German Jewish merchants and bankers as investors and Eastern European Jews to farm the land. After five years, he raised funds to purchase a portion of the island.

Had Noah simply resold land on Grand Island to his co-religionists, he would have differed little from other land speculators of the time. However, he had more grandiose ambitions than mere profit, as the inaugural ceremonies at Ararat revealed.

To accommodate the large crowd, Noah rented a Buffalo church. Cannoneers fired a salute and Seneca Chief Red Jacket arrived by boat (Noah believed the Indians were one of the Lost Tribes of Israel). Historian Jonathan Sarna describes Noah's dramatic entrance: "Resplendent in a Richard III costume, complete with a gold medallion neck chain—all lent by the Park Theater—Noah assumed his role as [self-proclaimed] 'Judge of Israel.'" After an ecumenical service led by a Protestant minister, Noah issued his "Proclamation to the Jews"

establishing Ararat as a city of Jewish refuge, proclaimed "the Jewish Nation 'under the auspices and protection of the constitution and laws of the United States of America' and appointed himself 'Judge of Israel.'" Noah called for every Jew in the world to be taxed "three sheckels of silver" to support the Jewish Nation and for the Paris Jewish Consistory to elect a Judge of Israel every four years—after Noah had finished his self-appointed term.

Noah's presumption caused a firestorm of protest and ridicule, not least from fellow Jews. Isaac Harby, a Jewish newspaper editor in Charleston, accused him of arrogating the role of the Messiah. As Harby pointed out, the authentic Messiah would someday "lead [the Jewish people] to New Jerusalem and not to New York." The secular press labeled Noah an opportunistic land speculator.

Ararat failed to attract settlers. In a society with an open frontier, no American Jew felt the need to live as Noah's colonist. Since he could not afford recruiters abroad, the colony had little chance of attracting European Jewry. Worse, the grand rabbi of Paris ridiculed the plan. Before the end of 1825, Noah was advising his friends not to invest in Ararat; in 1833, he sold his share of unpopulated Grand Island to a timber investor.

All that remains of Noah's Zionist dream today is Ararat's cornerstone. Despite the fiasco, Noah continued as an influential spokesman for American Jewry and much of his vision has come to fruition. Noah's assertions that a Jewish polity must be reestablished in the Holy Land and that America must play a special part in the restoration foreshadowed the role of American Jewry in the twentieth-century development of Jewish statehood.
In honor of Rabbi Abraham J. Karp

4

Warder Cresson: America's First Consul to Jerusalem

Warder Cresson's journey to Jerusalem, and to Judaism, followed a convoluted path. Born in Philadelphia in 1798, Cresson was raised a Quaker. He became a wealthy farmer in rural Pennsylvania, married, and had a son. He also became a lifelong seeker of religious truth. By the 1840s, Cresson had been, a Shaker, a Mormon, a Seventh-Day Adventist and a Campbellite. The latter two denominations believed that the Second Coming of Christ was imminent. Cresson became notorious in Philadelphia for "haranguing in the streets" about the rapidly approaching apocalypse.

By 1844, Cresson was convinced that God was about to gather the Jewish people in Jerusalem as a prelude to the "end of days." Cresson wrote, "God must choose some medium to manifest and act through, in order to bring about his designs and promises in this visible world. . . . This medium or recipient is the present poor, despised, outcast Jew. . . . God is about gathering them again [in Jerusalem]." Cresson decided to move to Jerusalem to witness the great event. His family stayed behind.

Before departing, Cresson volunteered to serve as the first American consul in Jerusalem, which was then a part of Syria. His congressman, Edward Joy Morris, lobbied the Sate Department to have him appointed. Soon after Cresson sailed, however, a former cabinet official warned John C. Calhoun, then secretary of state, that Cresson was mentally unstable. Calhoun dispatched a letter to Cresson, which reached him in Jerusalem, informing him that his appointment had been rescinded.

Despite this disappointment, Cresson decided to stay in Jerusalem. He had come as an evangelical Christian to witness God's ingathering of the Jewish Diaspora. His time in Jerusalem, however, drew him to become a Jew. The impoverished, deeply religious Jews he found in Jerusalem, touched Cresson's heart. He was offended by the "soul snatching" Christian missionaries who used bribes of food and clothing to lure these destitute Jews. He wrote, "The conversions which have been reported . . . [by] the Protestant Episcopal Mission were owing to the wants of the converts, not to their conviction." He expressed admiration for those who resisted the missionaries.

Historian Abraham J. Karp notes, "By 1847 Cresson already felt himself more Jew than Christian." In March 1848, Cresson converted. "I became fully satisfied," he wrote, "that I could never obtain *Strength* and *Rest* but by doing as *Ruth* did, and saying to her *Mother-in-Law*: . . .'thy *People* shall be my *people*, and thy God my God' . . . I was circumcised, entered the Holy Covenant, and became a Jew."

Cresson returned to Philadelphia to close out his affairs. "Soon after my return," Cresson wrote, "I found that there was a growing OPPOSITION and ENMITY toward the course I had taken." Cresson's wife and son started a civil "Inquisition of Lunacy" for having chosen Judaism. The jury declared Cresson a lunatic. In 1850, he appealed the verdict and received a new trial, which the press gave sensational coverage. More than 100 witnesses testified. The jury ultimately found for Cresson. An editorial in the *Philadelphia Public Ledger* hailed the verdict "as settling forever . . . the principle that a man's 'religious opinions' never can be made the test of his sanity."

During the four years Cresson spent in Philadelphia waiting for his trial to end, he worshipped at Congregation Mikveh Israel, living according to halachah and participating in Jewish communal life. At some point, he divorced. He also took a new name: Michael Boaz Israel. In 1852, Cresson/Israel sailed for Jerusalem. He brought with him a self-published plan "for the Promotion of Agricultural Pursuits [and] for the Establishment of a Soup-House for the Destitute Jews in Jerusalem." Cresson's desire for a soup house was to *prevent* any attempts being made to take *advantage* of the *necessities* of our poor brethren" that would "FORCE them into a *pretended conversion.*"

His vision of agricultural development, anticipated the principles later adopted by the Zionist movement. Cresson called for "the Restoration and Consolidation of all Israel to their own land . . . because *Unity* and *Consolidation is Strength.*" This strength, Cresson thought, would come from agriculture. To prove his plan could work, Cresson announced that he was starting a model farm in the Valley of Rephaim, outside Jerusalem, that would "introduce an improved system of English and American Farming in Palestine." He hoped that a Jewish agricultural Palestine would become "a great center to which all may come and find rest to their persecuted souls."

Cresson's planned model farm never developed for want of capital, but he continued to pray for its success. In the mid-1850s, he married Rachel Moleano and became an honored member of Jerusalem's Sephardic community. He died in 1860, and was buried on the Mount of Olives "with such honors as are paid only to a prominent rabbi." After a long journey, Warder Cresson found his home in Jerusalem as Michael Boaz Israel.
In honor of Bernard Wax

5

Chicago:
Incubator of American Zionism

Historians of the Chicago Jewish community claim that the Chicago Zion Society, founded in the mid-1890s, was the first Zionist organization in America. While historians of New York and Boston Jewry might quibble, it is clear that Chicago was one of the earliest seedbeds of organized Zionist activism in the United States. Interestingly, the Zionist cause in the Windy City was initially encouraged by a Protestant evangelical, powered by Eastern European immigrants, opposed by the local Reform rabbinate and ultimately embraced by Reform's elder statesman. The history of Zionism in Chicago encompasses many of the elements that shaped American Zionism from its very origins.

The first champion of Zionism in Chicago was William Eugene Blackstone, an evangelical Protestant layman and successful real estate entrepreneur who was convinced that the return of the Jews to Palestine was a critical forerunner to the second coming of Christ. In 1888, Blackstone and his daughter visited Palestine. The journey confirmed his belief that the Jews were "a people chosen by God to manifest His power and His love to . . . a world steeped in deepest idolatry."

In 1891, Blackstone drew up a petition calling for the creation of a national homeland in Palestine for the 2 million oppressed Jews of Russia. "According to God's distribution of nations," Blackstone's petition read, "[Palestine] is their home—an inalienable possession from which they were expelled by force. . . . Let us now restore them to the land of which they were so cruelly despoiled by our Roman ancestors." More than 400 prominent individuals signed Blackstone's appeal, including the publisher of the *Chicago Tribune* and Melville W. Fuller, chief justice of the United States Supreme Court. The petition was submitted to President Benjamin Harrison with a request that he influence the Ottoman sultan to create a Jewish homeland. Blackstone pursued this idea again in May of 1916 with a petition asking President Woodrow Wilson to advocate for a Jewish homeland when World War I ended. Among the signers were Andrew D. White, president of Cornell University, retail magnate John Wanamaker and Rabbi Judah L. Magnes, chairman of the Kehillah of New York City.

The Russian, Lithuanian and Polish Jewish immigrants who came to Chicago to escape the pogroms also engaged in Zionist activities. Settling in the tenements of the city's West Side, more than 100,000 Yiddish-speaking immigrants came to Chicago in the 1880s and 1890s, toiling in sweatshops or peddling goods from pushcarts in the Maxwell Street neighborhood.

Some were secular, radical socialists and atheists, while others retained their Orthodox practices. Particularly for the secularists, Zionism offered hope for the revitalization of Jewish nationhood, not so much from a religious but from a cultural and social justice standpoint.

Chicago's Eastern European Jewish Zionists produced such leaders as Bernard and Harris Horwich, brothers who emigrated to Chicago from Lithuania, and Leon Zolotkoff, editor of the *Chicago Courier.* These men founded the Chicago Hebrew Literary Society, whose members learned to read and speak Hebrew (as opposed to Yiddish) and debated the Jewish issues of the day. The Horwiches and Zolotkoff went on to found the Knights of Zion, which raised funds to purchase land for European Jews who wanted to settle in Palestine. Zolotkoff was later a delegate to several World Zionist Congresses.

The Knights of Zion, William Blackstone and other Zionist idealists met resistance from most of Chicago's Reform rabbis. Emil G. Hirsch of Sinai Congregation proclaimed that "We modern Jews do not wish to be restored to Palestine. . . . The country wherein we live is our Palestine. . . . We will not go back to form a nationality of our own." Hirsch asked, "What will [Jewish settlers] do in Palestine? Few of them have the physical strength requisite" to farming. He declared Zionism "a fool's errand."

Hirsch was concerned that support for a Jewish homeland in Palestine would open American Jewry to charges of disloyalty. Rabbi David Philipson, writing in the *American Israelite,* illuminated this view when he defined Judaism as a religion and not a nationality: "There is no longer a Jewish nation; there is a Jewish religious community. . . . the Jews in America are to be distinguished by naught else but their religious life." In every other way, Philipson implied, the nation's Jews were Americans, not Israelis in waiting.

One leading Chicago Reform rabbi spoke in favor of Zionism, however, and his voice carried great authority. Bernhard Felsenthal, German-speaking rabbi of Zion Congregation, was the only Reform rabbi in Chicago who supported the Hebrew Literary Society and mingled easily with the Eastern European immigrants. In 1891, Felsenthal wrote to Hirsch:

> A colonization in Palestine of the poor suffering Jews living in Russia [and elsewhere] is feasible, more so than bringing them over to America. . . . Not all Jews will return to Palestine; none will be compelled to go there. . . . I vote for colonization. . . . The Jewish colonies in Palestine—hail to them! . . . May they flourish! May they bring happiness to those who dwell in them!

History, of course, has sided with Felsenthal, the Horwiches and Blackstone. While the founding of Israel did not come soon enough to help the victims of the Russian pogroms of the 1880s and it has not brought the Messiah, a later generation of Russian Jews has found safety and freedom in the Jewish homeland envisioned by Chicago's early Zionists.

Sponsored by Joseph S. Steinberg in honor of Morton Steinberg

---

The Extraordinary Life of Henrietta Szold

Henrietta Szold with Junior Hadassah members. 1930. Courtesy of Hadassah the Women's Zionist Organization of America, Inc.

Henrietta Szold's name is forever linked with Hadassah, the Women's Zionist Organization of America, the largest women's volunteer organization in the United States and one of the world's most successful volunteer agencies. Had Szold's only contribution been her intellectual accomplishments before founding Hadassah, however, she would still hold a place in the pantheon of great American Jews.

Szold was born in Baltimore in 1860. She died in 1945, just before the end of World War II. Szold possessed a prodigious intellect and physical energy, which she combined with practical sense. The daughter of immigrants Rabbi Benjamin and Sophie (Schaar) Szold, Henrietta graduated from Baltimore's Western Female High School with the highest grades. At home, she learned Hebrew, German and sacred Jewish texts. On her graduation, Miss Adams's French and

English School for Girls hired Szold to teach French, German and algebra. She also taught a course on Judaism at her father's congregation. As a result, the overworked young woman never attended college.

In the 1880s, when Eastern European Jewish immigrants flooded into Baltimore, Szold organized a night school to teach them English and civics. She saw the Americanization of immigrants not as the "opposite . . . to Jewish living and thinking" but as a means to improve their lives. She also began a second career as an essayist and editor in the American Jewish press. In 1888, she became the youngest member— and the only woman—on the publications committee of the newly formed Jewish Publication Society. Two years later, she collaborated with Cyrus Adler in writing the article on American Jewry in the society's first publication, *Outlines of Jewish History*. Szold translated major works by renowned Jewish scholars Simon Dubnow, Nahum Slouschz and Louis Ginzburg. She created the *American Jewish Yearbook*, spurred the Jewish Publication Society to issue a new translation of the Bible and urged it to publish works in Yiddish—an extraordinary step at that time for an organization dominated by upper-class German-American Jews. She also served as secretary of the American Jewish Historical Society.

Scholarship was Szold's profession. Her deepest passion, however, was Zionism. In 1896, one month before Theodor Herzl published *Der Judenstaat*, Szold described her vision of a Jewish state in Palestine as a place to ingather Diaspora Jewry and revive Jewish culture. In 1898, the Federation of American Zionists elected Szold as the only female member of its executive committee. During World War I, she was the only woman on the Provisional Executive Committee for General Zionist Affairs, which helped hold together the Zionists in the warring nations.

In 1909, at age forty-nine, Szold visited Palestine for the first time and, as historian Michael Brown observes, "found her life's vocation: the health, education and welfare of the Yishuv [the Jewish community of pre-state Palestine]." Szold joined with six other women to found Hadassah, which recruited American Jewish women to implement and support medical improvements throughout the Holy Land. Hadassah's first project, begun in 1913, was an American-style visiting nurse system in Jerusalem. Contributions from Hadassah funded hospitals, a medical school, dental facilities, X-ray clinics, infant welfare stations, soup kitchens, and other services for Palestine's Jewish and Arab inhabitants. Szold persuaded her colleagues that practical programs open to all were critical to Jewish survival in the Holy Land. Regardless of the changes in Israeli politics and population since 1948, Hadassah still follows this philosophy.

In 1920, at age sixty, Szold settled permanently in Palestine. In 1927, she was appointed to the World Zionist Organization's three-member Palestine executive with the public health and education portfolios. She is credited with inculcating respect for formal education at a time when the Yishuv respected manual labor more highly. Szold inspired Hadassah volunteers to come to Palestine and teach domestic skills to Jewish pioneer women. She urged the American volunteers to "rouse a noble discontent" among the Yishuv women for better living conditions. Szold also established the country's first social work school, which today is part of the Hebrew University.

In the early 1930s, Szold foresaw the threat posed by Hitler and urged Hadassah to work closely with Youth Aliyah to bring German Jewish children to Palestine. In the absence of their parents, Szold arranged for their care. When war erupted in 1939, many Americans left Palestine for the safety of home but Szold stayed with the Yishuv.

While Szold remained in Palestine, she retained her cultural ties to America. At her last Passover Seder in Jerusalem in 1944, she sang African-American spirituals. As American as she remained, her days in Palestine transformed her. In 1936, Szold declared that, "philosophically considered, there is nothing but Zionism . . . to save us." She predicted that one day "Palestine, resplendent intellectually," would repay "to the Diaspora its whole investment . . . in terms of spiritual succor, stimulation and strength."

In honor of Bonnie Lipton

8

Golda Meir's American Roots

Golde Mabovitch Meyerson, better known as Golda Meir or simply Golda, was a founder of the modern State of Israel. Her name ranks in the Zionist pantheon with Theodor Herzl, Chaim Weizmann, and David Ben-Gurion. Unlike these others, however, Golda was shaped by her formative years as an American.

Born in 1898 near Kiev, Ukraine, Golda was named for her maternal great-grandmother, who always took salt instead of sugar in her tea to mark the bitterness of Jewish life in the Diaspora. Golda's memories of Ukraine were of grinding poverty, hunger, and pogroms. According to biographer Letty Cottin Pogrebin, Golda later "attributed her lifelong commitment to Jewish security to her [childhood] memories

of anti-Semitic violence and the experience of hiding from the Cossacks."

In 1903, her father, a carpenter, emigrated to America, promising to return for his family when he had enough money. Three years later, her mother, tired of waiting, took Golda and her two sisters to join him in Milwaukee. They settled in a tiny apartment in the city's poor Jewish section, and Golda's mother opened a convenience store in which all the girls worked.

Despite having learned English only six years earlier, at age fourteen Golda graduated from Milwaukee's Fourth Street Elementary School as class valedictorian. She longed to be a teacher, but her father opposed her going to high school. Showing signs of the independence that would characterize her adult life, Golda defied him and enrolled in North Division High School, taking after-school jobs to pay her expenses. When her father insisted that she quit school and find a husband, Golda ran away to Denver and moved in with her married sister. It was in Denver that Golda fell under the sway of socialism and Zionism and fell in love with Morris Meyerson, a sign painter who cherished poetry, music and history but never shared her Zionist passion. In 1913, she returned to Milwaukee, graduated from high school, enrolled in teachers college and taught as a volunteer at a Yiddish *folkshule*.

In December 1917, one month after Britain declared its support for a Jewish homeland in Palestine, Golda married Meyerson on the condition that they move to Palestine and live on a kibbutz. Eager to prove to the Jews of the Yishuv that she was not a "soft" American Jew, Golda persuaded Morris to settle in Merhavyah, one of the country's most bleak and vulnerable kibbutzim. There, despite her fear of chickens, she became a poultry expert. Soon she was representing the kibbutz at meetings of the Histadrut, the General Federation of Labor. It was at this time that she hebraicized her name to Meir.

In 1928, she was offered a job with Histadrut's Council of Women Workers, which she accepted. Golda moved to Tel Aviv against Morris's wishes. A charismatic speaker, she rapidly became a spokeswoman for Histadrut and later the World Zionist Organization and the Jewish Agency.

While Golda was now an Israeli, her early years in America shaped her career—not to mention her spoken Hebrew, which was filled with English-sounding pronunciations—and helped lay the groundwork for her rapid rise in politics.

She was particularly effective at raising funds from Americans. When Israel declared its independence in 1948, Golda rushed off to the United States to raise $25 million so that the newborn state could purchase arms to defend itself against Arab attackers. Her quick wit, charm and passion for Israel enabled her to raise $50 million—twice her goal. She would return frequently to raise money from American Jewry. As she saw it, Diaspora, and especially American, Jewry had a duty to help build the Jewish homeland.

When Golda was elected to the Knesset in 1949, David Ben-Gurion appointed her minister of labor. In 1956, he promoted her to foreign minister, the second-highest cabinet post. According to Pogrebin, Meir renounced the pomp associated with diplomacy and "entertained foreign dignitaries in her kitchen, in an apron, serving them her homemade pastry along with a stern lecture on Israel's security." Diagnosed with lymphoma, Golda retired from government service in 1966. Three years later the Labor Party persuaded her to come out of retirement to serve as prime minister.

In the early 1970s, polls revealed that Golda was the most respected woman in America, despite the fact that she was no longer an American. Nevertheless, Golda's stint as national leader ended sadly in 1973 when Israel suffered heavy losses in the Yom Kippur War. Blamed for Israel's military unpreparedness, Meir resigned in June of 1974. In the years before her death in 1978, she garnered the affection accorded an elder stateswoman. Golda Meir now ranks as one of the great female heads of state in modern history.

Sponsored by The Leo Rosner Foundation, Inc.

9

Sosua:
An American Jewish Experiment

In March 1938, President Franklin Roosevelt convened a thirty-two-nation conference at Evian-les-Bains, France, to discuss the resettlement of German and Austrian Jewish refugees to other lands. The assembled delegates endorsed the idea of resettlement but agreed that no nation would "be expected or asked to receive a greater number of emigrants than is permitted by existing legislation." Given the anti-immigration and anti-Semitic mood of the depression era, this meant that, in effect, no nation—even the United States—was expected to take more than a few thousand refugees. Only the Dominican Republic was willing to accept a significant number: between 50,000 and 100,000.

Despite the difficulties such a massive resettlement project posed, the American Jewish Joint Distribution Committee jumped at the Dominican offer. At that time, the Nazi regime was willing to let Jews emigrate if they transferred their assets to the German government. Thus, Jewish resettlement in Dominica would have to be financed entirely by private Jewish sources outside Germany—in other words, by American Jewry.

A powerful argument against spending millions to build colonies for a few thousand refugees was that the money could be better used to feed the many hundreds of thousands of Jews then starving across Europe. Nonetheless, the American Jewish Joint Distribution Committee decided that the Dominican offer was too good to turn down, both on humanitarian grounds and because the resettlement project might provide a model for relocating Europe's Jews after the war that seemed imminent. (At this time, of course, few had any idea of the mass extermination the Nazis would soon unleash on European Jewry.) The willingness to consider resettlement in Latin America also assumed that the British might not keep their promise to make Palestine a Jewish homeland.

Headed by dictator Rafael Trujillo, the Dominican government welcomed the Jews on the condition that they become agricultural workers rather than, to quote one official, "commission agents, like the previously admitted Jews." The Joint Distribution Committee created a special organization, the Dominican Republic Settlement Association (DORSA) and funded it to purchase 26,000 acres in the town of Sosua, which had been developed as a banana plantation but then abandoned by the United Fruit Company.

On January 30, 1940, DORSA signed a contract with the Trujillo regime. Historian Nicholas Ross quotes the contract:

The Republic . . . hereby guarantees to the settlers and their descendants full opportunity to continue their lives and occupations free from molestation, discrimination or persecution, with full freedom of religion . . . civil, legal and economic rights, as well as other rights inherent to human beings.

Despite this encouraging start, the Sosua experiment struggled. German U-boat attacks in the Atlantic and the need to use Allied ships for troops and supplies made it possible to relocate only fifty or so refugees in the first year. Most of the first settlers were fifty or older, typical of German Jewry at this time. Some of the refugees wished to begin life again as Dominican farmers, but an equal number saw Sosua only as a place to wait until they could get a visa to enter the United States. It soon became clear that it would cost about $3,000 to settle a family on a tract of Sosua land and equip it for farming. The land was not highly fertile and its drainage poor. The settlers needed a period of adjustment to the semi-tropical climate. Tomatoes, the first crop chosen for commercial exploitation, proved unattractive to the local Dominican populace. The colony seemed destined for disintegration.

James N. Rosenberg, head of DORSA, refused to let the experiment die. Nicholas Ross quotes him: "Half the world lives now under the shadow of war, persecution, horror and death. . . . Now an open door of hope beckons. . . . We must carry this endeavor to accomplishment. . . . We dare not falter."

DORSA imported experts from kibbutzim in Palestine to teach the settlers communal agriculture. They helped design and build a communal meat-processing plant, established a butter and cheese factory and recommended raising lemongrass, the oil of which is used in perfume. A trickle of refugee settlers continued to Sosua despite the fact that America's entry into the war made it even harder to cross the Atlantic. In October 1941, the Nazis cut off Jewish emigration from the territories they controlled in Europe. Sosua's Jewish population peaked at about 500. By this point, DORSA had invested about $1 million in the project.

In 1944, however, Sosua's fortunes turned. DORSA abandoned communal agriculture and gave the settlers private plots. The colonists focused on raising cattle and making butter and cheese. Eventually, they prospered. While some left for the United States or Israel, others stayed.

Today, there are still about twenty-five Jewish families in Sosua. Their dairy business supplies most of the butter and cheese consumed in the Dominican Republic. Next to the town's synagogue is a museum. The final caption on its exhibit reads: "Sosua, a community born of pain and nurtured in love must, in the final analysis, represent the ultimate triumph of life."

In honor of Abram V. Goodman

10

The Tragedy of the *St. Louis*

Occasionally, a name or a phrase such as "Remember the *Maine*" or "Watergate" enters the national lexicon. One such name has been burned into the collective memory of American Jewry: the *St. Louis,* a German luxury cruise ship which on May 27, 1939, steamed into Havana harbor with more than 900 German Jewish refugees from Nazi oppression, all with the letter *J* stamped in red on their passports. When the *St. Louis* arrived in Havana, its Jewish passengers were forbidden to come ashore. Despite efforts by the American and Cuban Jewish communities to persuade the Cuban government to let them land, on June 6 the vessel departed for Germany and certain death for the refugees.

Until the late 1930s, Cuba had been a haven for European Jews. Especially because Manuel Benitez Gonzales, Cuba's director general of immigration, willingly sold visas for a fee, 500 refugee European Jews a month were landing in Cuba in early 1939. Some went on to other destinations, but the Cuban Jewish population rose to 4,000 in 1938 and continued to increase sharply. With the deepening of the worldwide economic depression, the spread of Nazi propaganda and the association of Eastern European Jews with socialism, Cuban president Laredo Brú felt public pressure to reduce the number of Jewish immigrants.

Brú also felt the wrath of Benitez Gonzales's rivals in the government, who wanted their share of the visa-selling business. They got Brú to curtail Gonzales's authority and persuaded him to announce that prospective immigrants must post $500 to guarantee that they would not become a public burden. On May 5, 1939, Brú decreed Gonzales's old visas null and void; starting May 6, immigrants had to post the bond.

When the *St. Louis* sailed on May 13, only a handful of its passengers had met the requirement. The rest had Benitez's now-invalid landing permits. The Hamburg American Line did not insist that each passenger post $500 before sailing. To the shock and dismay of the passengers when the ship arrived in Havana thirteen days later, the Jewish passengers were forbidden to disembark.

The United States government took the position that the *St. Louis* affair was an internal Cuban matter; while the American consul in Havana tried to be helpful, he took no formal action. The American Jewish Joint Distribution Committee sent an agent, New York attorney Lawrence Berenson, to Havana to negotiate with Brú to admit the refugees. Berenson had lots of business experience in Cuba and he believed that Brú's intransigence was based on his desire to have the $500 bonds paid to him directly.

Thinking he was doing business as usual, Berenson offered Brú a lesser amount.

But Berenson misjudged Brú's desire to dissociate himself from the entry of Jews to Cuba. Brú called off the talks and ordered the *St. Louis*, with its 906 Jewish passengers, to sail for Germany. Unable to face this prospect, Max Loewe, a passenger who had been in a Nazi concentration camp, slashed his wrists and jumped overboard. Cuban police fished Loewe out and hospitalized him, but then refused to let his wife or children ashore to visit him.

On June 2, the *St. Louis* steamed out of Havana harbor. Once it was at sea, President Brú—facing the pressure of world opinion, which ran counter to that of Cuba's nationalists and fascists—agreed to reopen negotiations with Berenson. The captain of the *St. Louis* diverted the ship toward Miami, where it anchored 4 miles offshore. The U.S. immigration office in Miami announced that under no circumstances would the passengers be allowed to enter. The Coast Guard shadowed the ship's every movement until it returned to international waters, steaming back to Havana.

Berenson and Brú met again on June 5 and Berenson still thought he could lower the cost of the bonds. Brú abruptly lost patience, announced that time had expired on his government's offer and ordered the *St. Louis* and two other ships with Jewish refugees to depart. The *St. Louis* headed for Germany. Acting quickly, the Joint Distribution Committee deposited $500,000 in a Havana bank, more than Brú had demanded, but it was too late. The Cuban president would not relent; the ship was not to return. The White House received more than 200 letters from Americans pleading with the Roosevelt administration to intervene. On June 8, an eleven-year-old wrote to Eleanor Roosevelt:

> Mother of our Country. I am so sad the Jewish people have to suffer so. . . . Please let them land in America. . . . It hurts me so that I would give them my little bed if it was the last thing I had because I am an American let us Americans not send them back to that slater [*sic*] house. We have three rooms we do not use. [My] mother would be glad to let someone have them.

On June 10, Ambassador Joseph P. Kennedy approached the British government to take some of the refugees, and two days later it agreed. The Netherlands, France and Belgium followed suit. Despite the Cuban and American governments' refusal to provide asylum, all 906 passengers found refuge. Sadly, many of them died between 1939 and 1945 when the Nazis overran Western Europe. These were lives that could have been saved.

Sponsored by Susan Hertog in memory of Harry Gorell

11

But They Were Good to Their People: Jewish Gangsters and American Nazism

There are few excuses for the behavior of Jewish gangsters in the 1920s and 1930s. The best-known—Meyer Lansky, Bugsy Siegel, Longy Zwillman, Moe Dalitz—participated in the numbers rackets, the narcotics trade, prostitution, gambling and loan sharking. They were not nice men. During the rise of American Nazism in the 1930s and when Israel was being founded between 1945 and 1948, however, they proved staunch defenders of their people.

The roots of Jewish gangsterism lay in the ethnic neighborhoods of the Lower East Side, Brownsville in Brooklyn, Maxwell Street in Chicago and Boyle Heights in Los Angeles. Like other newly arrived groups in American history that were blocked from access to respectable professions, a few Jews used crime as a means to "make good" economically. The market for vice flourished during Prohibition and Jews exploited it by providing alcohol, gambling, paid sex, and narcotics.

Few of these men were religiously observant. They rarely attended services, although they contributed generously to synagogues. They did not keep kosher homes or send their children to day schools. However, at crucial moments, they protected other Jews in America and around the world.

The 1930s was a period of rampant anti-Semitism in the United States, particularly in the Midwest. Father Charles Coughlin, Detroit's "Radio Priest," and William Pelley of Minneapolis openly called for Jews to be driven from positions of responsibility, if not from the country itself. Organized Brown Shirts in New York and Silver Shirts in Minneapolis outraged and terrorized American Jewry. While the older and more respectable Jewish organizations pondered a political and moral response that would not alienate non-Jewish supporters, others—some of them rabbis—asked the gangsters to break up American Nazi rallies by force.

Historian Robert Rockaway notes that German-American Bund rallies in the New York City area posed a dilemma for mainstream Jewish leaders. They wanted the rallies stopped but had no legal grounds on which to do so. Judge Nathan Perlman personally contacted Meyer Lansky and asked him to disrupt the Bund rallies, provided that his henchmen stopped short of killing anyone. Enthusiastic for the assignment if disappointed by the restraints, Lansky accepted all of Perlman's terms except for one: he would take no money for the work. Lansky later observed, "I was a Jew and felt for those Jews in Europe who were suffering. They were my brothers." For months, Lansky's gang effectively broke up one Nazi rally after another. As Rockaway notes,

"Nazi arms, legs and ribs were broken and skulls were cracked, but no one died."

Lansky recalled breaking up a Brown Shirt rally in the Yorkville section of Manhattan: "The stage was decorated with a swastika and a picture of Hitler. The speakers started ranting. There were only fifteen of us, but we went into action. We . . . threw some of them out the windows. . . . Most of the Nazis panicked and ran out. We chased them and beat them up. . . .We wanted to show them that Jews would not always sit back and accept insults."

In Minneapolis, William Dudley Pelley organized a Silver Shirt Legion to rescue America from an imaginary Jewish-Communist conspiracy. In Pelley's own words, just as "Mussolini and his Black Shirts saved Italy and as Hitler and his Brown Shirts saved Germany," he would save America from Jewish Communists. Minneapolis gambling czar David Berman confronted Pelley's Silver Shirts on behalf of the Minneapolis Jewish community.

Berman learned that the Silver Shirts were mounting a rally at a nearby Elks hall. When the Nazi leader called for all the "Jew bastards" in the city to be expelled or worse, Berman and his associates burst into the room and started cracking heads. After ten minutes, they had emptied the hall. His suit covered in blood, Berman took the microphone and announced, "This is a warning. Anybody who says anything against Jews gets the same treatment. Only next time it will be worse." After Berman broke up two more rallies, there were no more public Silver Shirt meetings in Minneapolis.

Jewish gangsters also helped establish the State of Israel after the war. One famous example is a meeting in 1945 between Bugsy Siegel and Reuven Dafne, a Haganah emissary. Dafne was seeking funds and guns to help liberate Palestine from British rule. A mutual friend arranged for the two men to meet. "You mean to tell me Jews are fighting?" Siegel asked. "You mean fighting as in killing?" Dafne answered in the affirmative. Siegel replied, "I'm with you." For weeks, Dafne received suitcases from Siegel filled with $5 and $10 bills— $50,000 in all.

No one should paint gangsters as heroes. They committed acts of great evil. Historian Rockaway presents a textured version of Jewish gangster history in a book titled *But They Were Good to Their Mothers*. One might add that despite their disreputable behavior, they could sometimes be good to their people too.

In memory of Abram Kanof, MD

12

"Mother" Ruth Gruber
and the Fort Ontario Refugees

Ruth Gruber has led a remarkable life dedicated to rescuing her fellow Jews from oppression. After earning her bachelor's and master's degrees by age nineteen, she accepted a fellowship in 1931 to study in Cologne, Germany. While completing her doctorate there at twenty (the *New York Times* described her as the world's youngest Ph.D.), Gruber attended Nazi rallies, listening to Adolf Hitler vituperate against Americans and Jews. She completed her studies and returned to America, attuned from then on to the threat that totalitarianism posed to the Jewish people.

In 1932, Gruber began her career as a journalist. In 1935, the *New York Herald Tribune* asked her to write a feature series about women under communism and fascism. She traveled across Europe to the far reaches of Siberia. In 1943, Harold L. Ickes, President Franklin D. Roosevelt's secretary of the interior, read Gruber's articles about life in Siberia and asked her to study Alaska as a prospective home for American veterans and their families when World War II ended. Gruber's life-defining moment came in 1944, when Ickes asked her to take on another special mission: secretly escorting a group of 1,000 Jewish refugees from Italy to the United States.

Despite the grim news coming out of Europe throughout the late 1930s and early 1940s, the United States Congress steadfastly refused to lift the quota on Jewish immigration from Eastern Europe to the United States. Finally acting by executive authority, President Roosevelt invited a group of 1,000 Jewish refugees living in limbo in Naples to "visit" the United States. The refugees, as "guests" of the president, were to be lodged at Fort Ontario, a decommissioned Army base near Oswego in northernmost New York. Ickes asked Gruber to travel to Italy secretly to escort the refugees.

Ickes gave Gruber the rank of "simulated general." He explained, "If you're shot down and the Nazis capture you as a civilian, they can kill you as a spy. But as a general, according to the Geneva Convention, they have to give you food and shelter and keep you alive." In Italy, Gruber boarded the Army troop transport *Henry Gibbins* along with 1,000 wounded American soldiers and the refugees. Nazi seaplanes and U-boats hunted the *Gibbins* but it completed the voyage safely.

Aboard ship, Gruber recorded the refugees' case histories. She told them, "You are the first witnesses coming to America. Through you, America will learn the truth of Hitler's crimes." She took notes as the refugees told their stories, but she often had to stop because her tears blurred the ink in her notebook. The grateful refugees began

224

calling Gruber "Mother Ruth" and looked to her for protection. As historian Barbara Seaman observed, "She knew from then on, her life would be inextricably bound up with rescuing Jews in danger."

On arriving safely in New York, the refugees were immediately transferred to Fort Ontario. As guests of the president without any rights conferred by the possession of travel visas, the refugees were locked behind a barbed-wire-topped, chain-link fence. Government officials argued about whether the refugees should be allowed to stay at the fort or, at some point, be deported back to Europe. Gruber lobbied Congress and FDR on behalf of keeping them at Fort Ontario until the end of the war.

Gruber finally prevailed. In 1945, after Germany's surrender, the refugees were allowed to apply for American residency. Some became citizens and went on to have extraordinary careers as radiologists, physicists, composers, teachers, physiciansand writers. One, Dr. Alex Margulies, who came as a teenager from Yugoslavia, helped develop the CAT-scan and the MRI. Another, Rolph Manfred, helped develop the Polaris and Minuteman missiles. Later, Manfred dedicated his life to teaching engineers in developing countries about the peaceful uses of atomic energy.

Although her mission at Fort Ontario was over, Gruber's role as Jewish rescuer was just beginning. In 1946, she resigned from her post as assistant to Ickes to return to journalism. The New York Post asked her to cover the newly created Anglo-American Committee of Inquiry on Palestine. When Harry Truman, Roosevelt's successor, learned that Jewish displaced persons were being held in camps in the American Zone of Germany under conditions that resembled the infamous Nazi concentration camps (see page 230), he ordered improvements implemented and pressed Great Britain to open the doors of Palestine to 100,000 European Jewish refugees. Stalling, Prime Minister Bevin suggested that the United States and Britain appoint the Joint Committee to meet with the refugees in Europe, as well as leaders in the Arab world and Palestine, before deciding whether Jewish immigration to Palestine was feasible. Truman assented, and Gruber accompanied the committee to the squalid DP camps in Europe, North Africa and the Middle East. What she found, and what she did about it, is the subject of the next chapter.

Sponsored by Charlotte K. Frank in memory of Rose and Abraham Kizner

13

Ruth Gruber's Exodus

In 1946, President Harry S. Truman learned that the Jewish survivors in the refugee camps of the American Zone of Germany were living under appalling conditions. As one historian observed, the camps "differed from the Nazi camps only in that the inmates were not deliberately exterminated."

Truman pressed the British to accept 100,000 Jewish refugees into Palestine. The British responded by proposing to create a Joint Committee of Inquiry to visit the displaced person (DP) camps in Germany and then go to North Africa and Palestine to assess the feasibility of resettling the Jewish DPs there.

Having finished her resettlement work with the Jewish refugees at Fort Ontario, New York, Ruth Gruber packed up her camera,

notebooks and typewriter and followed the Joint Committee as a correspondent for the *New York Post*. When the committee arrived in the DP camps, Gruber reported in her dispatches, the survivors greeted its members with signs like "We want to go. We must go. We will go to Palestine." When asked why he wanted to go to Palestine, a sixteen-year-old orphan who had survived Bergen-Belsen replied, "Why? Everybody has a home. The British. The Americans. The French. The Russians. Only we Jews have no home. Don't ask us. Ask the world."

The committee members spent four months in Europe, Palestine and the Arab countries and another month in Switzerland digesting their experiences. At the end of their deliberations, the twelve members—

six Britons and six Americans—unanimously agreed that Britain should allow 100,000 Jewish immigrants to settle in Palestine. The celebrations that followed in the camps were soon stilled, however, when the British foreign minister, Ernest Bevin, rejected this finding.

Eventually, the United Nations took up the issue. The UN appointed a Special Committee on Palestine (UNSCOP). Like its predecessor, UNSCOP visited the camps in Germany and then went on to the Arab states and Palestine. Gruber accompanied UNSCOP as a correspondent for the *New York Herald.* While in Jerusalem, she learned that a former American pleasure boat, renamed the *Exodus 1947,* had attempted to bring 4,500 Jewish refugees to Palestine—including 600 children, mostly orphans—but had been intercepted by five British destroyers and a cruiser. Gruber left immediately for Haifa and witnessed the *Exodus* entering the harbor, looking, as Gruber wrote, "like a matchbox splintered by a nutcracker."

During the "battle," the British had rammed the *Exodus* and stormed it with guns, tear gas and truncheons. The crew, mostly Jews from America and Palestine, had fought back with potatoes, sticks and cans of kosher meat. The *Exodus*'s second officer, Bill Bernstein of San Francisco, was clubbed to death trying to prevent a British soldier from entering the wheelhouse. Two orphans were killed, one shot in the face after he threw an orange at a soldier.

When she learned that the prisoners from the *Exodus* were being transferred to Cyprus, Gruber flew there overnight. While waiting for the *Exodus* detainees, she photographed Jewish prisoners from earlier landing attempts living behind barbed wire in steaming hot tents with almost no water or sanitary facilities. "You had to smell Cyprus to believe it," she cabled the *Herald.*

The British changed their plans and sent the *Exodus* prisoners to Port de Bouc in southern France, where they had initially embarked. Gruber rushed there from Cyprus. When the prison ships arrived, the prisoners refused to disembark. After eighteen days in which the refugees endured the blistering heat, the British decided to send the Jews back to Germany. The world press was outraged. While hundreds of journalists descended on Port de Bouc, only Gruber was allowed by the British to accompany the DPs back to Germany.

Aboard the prison ship *Runnymeade Park,* Gruber photographed the refugees defiantly raising a British flag that they overpainted with a swastika. Her photo became *Life Magazine*'s "Picture of the Week." Crushed together on the sweltering ship making their way back to Germany, the refugees sang "Hatikvah," the Hebrew anthem of hope. Gruber's book about the DP's endurance would later provide Leon Uris with material for his book and screenplay *Exodus,* which helped turn American public opinion in favor of Israel.

In 1951, Gruber married, gave birth to two children, and suspended her journalistic travels. She wrote for *Hadassah Magazine* and raised funds for UJA. In the 1970s, she visited Israel, where she wrote a biography, *Raquela,* that won a National Jewish Book Award. In 1985, at age seventy-four, Gruber traveled to Ethiopia, where she observed the aliyah of that nation's Jews to Israel.

Gruber's journey to Ethiopia completed a cycle that had begun with her voyage to Italy in 1944 to bring 1,000 Jewish refugees to Fort Ontario. In 2001, a television network dramatized her life in a two-part broadcast. Today, Ruth Gruber lives in New York City; she stands as a symbol of hope for Jews in danger anywhere in the world.

14

Abraham Klausner
and the Survivors' Haggadah

In April of 1946, with the taste of oppression and death still fresh in their mouths, a group of 200 Jewish displaced persons, survivors of the Shoah from all over Europe, gathered at the Deutsches Theatre Restaurant in Munich, Germany, to celebrate the first Passover after the Allied victory. For two nights, Rabbi Abraham J. Klausner, a Jewish chaplain of the U.S. Third Army, the occupying force in Bavaria, presided over these Seders, the first public Seders held in Germany since the 1930s.

For most displaced persons (DPs) living in Europe after World War II, the nightmare of the Holocaust did not end with the German surrender. Allied military policy dictated that all DPs in occupied Germany were to be treated equally. Thus Jews who had survived the forced marches from the labor and death camps of Eastern Europe were housed in the same camps, fed the same rations and used the same latrines as captured Nazi soldiers and homeless civilians who had participated in pogroms. Jewish organizations such as the Joint Distribution Committee provided extra food and medical treatment for the Jewish DPs, but nonetheless conditions remained deplorable.

American military policy required that Jews from nations other than Germany were to be repatriated to their countries of origin. Many DPs were shipped off to Poland, Russia, Hungary, and elsewhere, where they received a hostile reception from their former neighbors, some of them Nazi collaborators who now held the property the Jews had been forced to abandon. Rather than risk death, the repatriated Jews had no choice but to return to a DP camp. Most preferred the American zone in Bavaria, around Munich.

In the midst of this movement, upheaval, and disappointment, the first Passover since liberation arrived. Like his fellow American Jewish military chaplains working with the *shearit ha-pletah* (the "saved remnant"), Rabbi Klausner had spent the preceding winter properly burying the Jewish dead, mobilizing physical and spiritual support for the living and trying to reunite separated family members. Klausner believed that the Jewish DPs would recover most quickly if they became self-governing and could work to restore their bodies and their dignity. He helped them to organize a newspaper, *Unser Weg*, and compile a list of survivors to help reunite families.

In the weeks before Passover, Yosef Dov Sheinson, a Kovno writer, Zionist, and survivor of four years in the camps, prepared a "supplement" to the traditional Haggadah that spoke to the survivors' experience and articulated their dream of leaving Europe for Palestine. Sheinson's handmade Haggadah, organized around the dual theme "We were slaves to Pharaoh" and "We were slaves to Hitler," was composed with Hebrew type recovered from closed German-Jewish printing houses. Sheinson included seven stunning woodcuts of the death camps made by Miklos Adler, a Hungarian artist who was also a survivor.

Paper was scarce in Germany, but a Zionist operative and Kovno survivor named Shlomo Shafir arranged with Bruckmann, K.G., a German company that had been a wartime printing supplier for the Nazis, to print Sheinson's work. Shafir paid Bruckmann by trading cigarettes and UNRRA-supplied food. A copy of Sheinson's Haggadah was then brought to Rabbi Klausner with the suggestion that it be used at the Seders Klausner would be leading for the DPs in Munich and for Jewish military and relief personnel in the area. Klausner penned a brief introduction praising General Lucian Truscott, successor to the anti-Semitic George S. Patton as military commander of Occupied Germany, and arranged for the tricolor "A" insignia of the U.S. Third Army to be emblazoned on the Haggadah's cover so that it could be printed as a U.S. government document. Perhaps 400 were published, but only a handful of originals survive in research libraries today.

The resourceful Klausner used Army procedures to requisition food for the Seders—including the first matzohs baked in Germany since the 1930s. Leftovers from the meals went to the restaurateur, his payment for hosting the Seders. With Klausner presiding, the celebrants retold the story of the Exodus from Egypt and the deliverance of the Jews to the Promised Land. Clearly, the minds of the DP celebrants were on another exodus that they hoped to make—out of the "Egypt" of post-Shoah Europe to the promised land of Eretz Yisrael.

In 2000, the American Jewish Historical Society republished, in a limited, numbered, a facsimile edition of the *Survivors' Haggadah* created by Yosef Dov Sheinson with woodcuts by Miklos Adler, as printed by the Third Army. The edition contains a remarkable essay by Professor Saul Touster of Brandeis University on the DP experience and a detailed history of how the Haggadah was made. Contributions by sponsors ensured that 100 of the facsimile Haggadot were sent gratis to Holocaust research centers and museums worldwide. The Haggadot are a tribute to the survivors' undying spirit.

In honor of Saul Touster

15

A Particular Responsibility:
The U.S. Army Talmud

The suffering of Europe's displaced Jews did not end with the Allied victory in 1945. Homeless, stateless, unwelcome in their native lands, hundreds of thousands of Jews from all over Europe—they called themselves *shearit ha-pletah*, Hebrew for "the saved remnant"—were living in displaced persons (DP) camps operated by the Allies, most of which were located in Germany.

The camps were uniformly spare and unappealing. Some, in fact, had been Nazi concentration camps, continued in operation as DP camps by the Americans and other occupying armies. At first, the Jewish DPs had to live in the same camps with captured German soldiers or Polish, Lithuanian and other collaborators who had persecuted and even murdered Jews during the Nazi occupation of Eastern Europe. Despite the starvation many Jewish DPs had suffered, the U.S. Army did not provide them with extra rations. Traumatized, the Jewish DPs at first did little to protest their treatment.

American Jewish organizations like ORT and the Joint Distribution Committee lobbied to improve the living conditions of the Jewish DPs. At their urging, President Harry S. Truman appointed the Harrison Commission to investigate the treatment of Jewish DPs. The commission reported:

As matters now stand, we appear to be treating the Jews as the Nazis treated them except that we do not exterminate them. They are in concentration camps in large numbers under our military guard instead of S.S. troops. One is led to wonder whether the German people, seeing this, are not supposing that we are following or at least condoning Nazi policy.

Truman ordered General Dwight D. Eisenhower, commander of U.S. forces in Europe, to "get these people out of camps and into decent housing until they can be repatriated or evacuated." Truman concluded, "I know you will agree with me that we have a particular responsibility toward these victims of persecution and tyranny who are in our zone. . . . We have no better opportunity to demonstrate this than by the manner in which we ourselves actually treat the survivors remaining in Germany."

Most of the DPs could not be repatriated to their former homes because their property had been confiscated or destroyed and their neighbors had participated in, or at least condoned, the obliteration of local Jewish life. United States immigration policy was based on a quota system, which meant that only a token number could emigrate to America. Great Britain permitted only a handful of Jews to emigrate to

Palestine. Not until Israel was founded in 1948 would the Jewish displaced of Europe have a welcoming homeland.

Recognizing that the Jewish survivors might be living in the camps for a very long time, American Jewish organizations and the United Nations helped the DPs to revive and restore a communal life of sorts. Reinvigorating Judaism was an essential element in this, for along with humans, the Nazis had burned Jewish books, synagogues and schools. By 1945, not one complete set of the Talmud could be found in Europe.

Judaism draws on two bodies of tradition. The first, known as the Written Law, comprises the Torah, or Five Books of Moses. The second, known as the Oral Law, consists of a vast body of orally transmitted material that was compiled in the Mishnah in Palestine around 200 C.E., and an even larger body of discussions of the Mishnah that was compiled in the Gemara in Babylonia around 500 C.E. Mishnah and Gemara together are known as the Talmud, and in traditional Judaism this gigantic work of 63 tractates, or volumes, the ultimate source of law and custom and an essential object of study by the pious. Throughout history, going back to the Middle Ages and culminating in the Nazi book-burnings, enemies of the Jews sought to destroy Judaism by destroying the Talmud.

Restoring Jewish life in Europe meant making the Talmud available once again. In 1946, a delegation of DP rabbis led by Samuel Jakob Rose, a Dachau survivor, approached General Joseph McNarney, commander of the American Zone of Germany, asking that the Army publish a Talmud. McNarney understood the symbol-ic significance of their request. Despite severe shortages of paper, he authorized the project. With guidance from U.S. Army chaplains Philip Bernstein and Herbert Friedman, the work began.

As no complete set of the Talmud could be found in Germany, two sets were brought from New York and engravings were made from them. The Army requisitioned the Carl Winter Printing Plant in Heidelberg, which during the war had printed Nazi propaganda. After two years of work, approximately 500 sets appeared in 1948, the only time in history that a national government published an edition of the Talmud. The preface contains the work's only words of English:

> This edition of the Talmud is dedicated to the United States Army. The Army played a major role in the rescue of the Jewish people from total annihilation, and their defeat of Hitler bore the major burden of sustaining the DP's of the Jewish faith. This special edition of the Talmud, published in the very land where, but a short time ago, everything Jewish and of Jewish inspiration was anathema, will remain a symbol of the indestructibility of the Torah. The Jewish DP's will never forget the generous impulses and the unprecedented humanitarianism of the American forces, to whom they owe so much.

In 2001, the American Jewish Historical Society and the Tidewater Jewish Foundation of Norfolk, Virginia, prepared a traveling exhibition that tells the story of the U.S. Army and the *Survivors' Talmud*. The exhibit will be shown in United States military bases around the world.

Sponsored by Linda D. and Phil Bleich

16

Ben Hecht:
A Flag Is Born

On September 4, 1946, renowned actors Paul Muni and Celia Adler and a young, then-unknown actor named Marlon Brando premiered a new Broadway production, *A Flag Is Born*. Written by Hollywood's most successful screenwriter, Ben Hecht, directed by Luther Adler and with music by Kurt Weill, the blatantly propagandistic play helped mobilize American opinion in favor of a Jewish homeland in Palestine.

In 1946, Zionism was an unlikely subject for a Broadway hit. Just as unlikely, however, was the play's producer: not one of the great American Jewish impresarios like Billy Rose or the Schuberts, but the American League for a Free Palestine (ALFP). Headed by a brilliant and energetic Palestinian Jew, Hillel Kook—known in America as Peter Bergson (see page 80)—ALFP raised funds to purchase arms for the Irgun, a Jewish underground military force fighting to drive the British from Palestine. Both the British and mainstream Zionist groups labeled the Irgun as terrorists. What, then, were men who blew up British prisons and smuggled Jews into Palestine doing as producers on the Great White Way?

The Bergson Group, as it was known, came to the United States from Palestine in 1939 to raise funds for an independent Jewish legion that would fight alongside the Allies. In 1943, after the Holocaust became undeniable, the Bergsonites lobbied governments to rescue European Jewry. In 1944, they switched to forcing the British to allow unlimited Jewish emigration to Palestine.

A public relations genius, Bergson convinced the Hearst newspaper chain, political figures Eleanor Roosevelt and Herbert Hoover, writers Dorothy Parker, Thomas Mann and Langston Hughes, performers Stella Adler and Groucho Marx and composer Moss Hart, among others, to endorse his cause. Most importantly, Bergson recruited Ben Hecht, an Academy Award–winning screenwriter and novelist at the height of his career. Previously apolitical, Hecht was frustrated by the failure of American Jewry and the United States government to act decisively on behalf of European Jewry. He helped the Bergsonites raise funds and consciousness.

Earlier, in 1943, Hecht had joined forces with Kurt Weill and producer Billy Rose to create *We Will Never Die*, a pageant depicting Jewish history from the time of Abraham to the present. The production concluded with the assertion that Hitler could not exterminate the Jewish people. When it opened at Madison Square Garden on September 3, 1943, New York governor Thomas E. Dewey declared a day of mourning for the millions of Jews killed by the

Nazis. Lauded by most critics, the pageant toured the United States to audiences of hundreds of thousands.

At war's end, Hecht proposed a new production, *A Flag Is Born*, which would advocate a Jewish homeland. He convinced the stars, director Luther Adler and his friend Weill to work without pay. The rest of the cast worked at union minimum. Noted war journalist Quentin Reynolds narrated, and he too donated his fee to the Irgun.

A Flag Is Born was unabashed melodrama and, like any effective melodrama, it moved its audience deeply. Reynolds began with a retrospective, "Of all the things that happened in that time—our time—the slaughter of the Jews of Europe was the only thing that counted forever in the annals of man. The proud oration of heroes and conquerors will be a footnote in history beside the great silence that watched the slaughter." The play had a single set, a graveyard, and three characters: elderly Treblinka survivors Tevye and Zelda, who drag their tired and broken bodies searching for a path to Palestine, and Brando's David, an angry young concentration camp survivor.

In the opening scenes, Zelda recalls that it is Friday night and she lights Sabbath candles on top of a broken tombstone. As Tevye says the traditional prayers, he falls into a reverie, dreaming of his hometown synagogue before its destruction, of King Saul at the battle of Gilead and of King David. Tevye then makes a plea in his dreams to a "Council of the Mighty"

(according to historian Edna Nachshon, a reference to the Security Council of the newly formed United Nations), which goes unheard.

Tevye awakens to find that Zelda has died. He recites the Kaddish, welcomes the angel of death who has come for him and bids David farewell. Abandoned and alone, David contemplates suicide, but three Jewish soldiers approach and promise to take him to Palestine. As David leaves the graveyard of Europe for his new homeland, he incants Hecht's burning, perhaps overly harsh, indictment of Anglo-American Jewry:

> Where were you—Jews . . .when the killing was going on? When the six million were burned and buried alive in lime, where were you? Where was your voice crying out against the slaughter? We didn't hear any voice. There was no voice. . . . You Jews of America! You Jews of England! Where was your cry of rage . . .? Nowhere! Because you were ashamed to cry as Jews! A curse on your silence. . . . And now, now you speak a little. Your hearts squeak—and you have a dollar for the Jews of Europe. Thank you. Thank you.

A Flag Is Born played in six North American cities and raised more than $400,000 for the American League for a Free Palestine, the largest amount of money it was ever able to collect. Two years later, a flag *was* born, the flag of the State of Israel. Hecht's vision had become a reality.

In honor of Henry Feingold

17

Arthur Szyk:
His Brush Was His Sword

During World War II, readers of *Life, Time, Esquire*, and other American magazines enjoyed the vivid anti-Nazi cartoons of Arthur Szyk (1894–1951), a Polish-born Jewish artist and illustrator. Szyk's witty and dramatic style packed a fiery political punch.

One of his wartime cartoons was so liberal that it proved too hot for any publisher to handle. Veering away from his usual Axis targets, Szyk depicted two GIs, one white and one black, escorting German prisoners. The white soldier asks his comrade, "And what would you do with Hitler?" The black soldier replies: "I would have made him a Negro and dropped him somewhere in the US!" Not one American magazine or newspaper printed it.

During World War I, Szyk was captured by the Germans but received lenient treatment because his captors admired his artistic talents. After the war, Szyk traveled to Ukraine, where he witnessed pogroms that devastated Jewish communities. Deeply moved, he returned throughout his career to the theme of justice for the world's Jews.

In 1934, Szyk created a series of thirty-eight paintings depicting the American Revolution that were exhibited at the Paris World's Fair. They caught the eye of visiting Polish officials, who purchased them as a gift for President Franklin D. Roosevelt.

Szyk's most famous work was his illuminated *Haggadah* (1939), found to this day on Seder tables throughout the world Although hailed by the *Times* of London as "among the most beautiful books that the hand of man has produced," intimidated European publishers refused to print it, fearing that the graphic allusions to the Nazis might provoke German wrath. Finally, Szyk found an English publisher who agreed to publish the work if Szyk whittled down the anti-Nazi content to only two depictions of Hitler as the "wicked son."

When the Nazis overran Poland in September 1939, Szyk was in London. He immediately began contributing illustrations to the Allied propaganda campaign. A colleague described his political art as "powerful as a bomb, clear in conception, definite and deadly in its execution." The British dispatched Szyk to the United States in 1940, hoping his work would sway American public opinion to join the struggle against Hitler.

Living in Connecticut, Szyk became the editorial cartoonist for the *New York Post* and contributed a steady stream of anti-Nazi cartoons and illustrations to major magazines. He also designed military badges and "Buy War Bonds" billboards. Szyk thought of himself as "Roosevelt's soldier with a pen." He wrote, "I consider myself as being on duty in my cartoons." While he would have preferred to continue doing illuminated manuscripts and other forms of art, he observed, "We are not entitled to do the things we like today." Eleanor Roosevelt once remarked, "This is a personal war of Szyk against Hitler, and I do not think that Mr. Szyk will lose this war!"

Szyk's devotion to the Allied war effort was matched by his growing concern about the Jews trapped in Nazi-occupied Europe. In 1941, he joined forces with the Bergson Group, a band of activists who lobbied the Roosevelt administration to rescue endangered Jews. After the war, the Bergsonites rallied American public support for the Jewish underground revolt against the British in Palestine. Szyk's dramatic illustrations were featured in full-page advertisements in American newspapers.

Ben Hecht, who wrote the text for many of the Bergson group's newspaper ads, called Szyk "our one-man art department."

Arthur Szyk . . . worked for eight years without a pause. Nobody paid him anything and nobody thought of thanking him. . . . Szyk's art lent a nobility to the Irgun cause. His Hebrews under fire, under torture, exterminated in lime pits and bonfires . . . remained a people to be loved and admired. Their faces fleeing from massacre now, were tense and still beautiful. There was never slovenly despair or hysterical agony in Szyk's dying Jews, but only courage and beauty. If there was ever an artist who believed that an hour of valor was better than a lifetime of furtiveness and cringe, it was Szyk.

Szyk died in 1951 at the age of fifty-seven. His life was indeed that "hour of valor" to which Ben Hecht alluded. Szyk was an artist whose brush was truly his sword.

In honor of Marc Lee Raphael and Jeffrey Gurock

235

18

Dewey D. Stone, a Few Humble Coins and the Making of Israel

The creation of Israel in May of 1948 and its survival afterwards was aided greatly by the Truman administration's willingness to recognize and support the Jewish state. In the few weeks before independence, however, President Truman's promised commitment to recognize Israel began to waver. Without the efforts of American Jewish leaders such as Dewey D. Stone and Frank Goldberg—and the unlikely contribution of Eddie Jacobson—it is not clear whether Truman would have kept America's weight behind Israeli statehood.

On November 29, 1947, the United Nations voted to divide Palestine, with a Jewish national homeland to be founded in one of its parts. As Abba Eban observes, "No sooner had the partition resolution been adopted than attempts were made to thwart it." The surrounding Arab states threatened to make war on any Jewish political entity. The British, who had administered Palestine before partition, took a hands-off policy when the Arabs began attacking Jewish settlers.

Most significantly, the American government, which had been championing partition, began to have second thoughts. The outbreak of fighting between Jews and Arabs after the partition vote gave the State Department, which had never been enthusiastic about creating a Jewish state, an excuse to ask the United Nations to put Palestine under a temporary trusteeship. Partition and the creation of a Jewish homeland seemed about to be put on hold.

In contrast to the State Department, President Harry Truman had strongly favored partition. In 1945, soon after Truman took office, European Zionist leader Chaim Weizmann convinced him of the justice of creating a homeland for Jewish Holocaust survivors. Much to Truman's resentment, many American Zionists were strident critics of his administration, however, and in the early months of 1948, while evaluating his options, he refused to meet with *any* Zionist leaders—even with Weizmann, a man he admired. The administration's positive attitude toward the creation of the State of Israel was no longer guaranteed.

On March 12, 1948, Dewey D. Stone of Brockton, Massachusetts, spent the day in New York City with his close friend and mentor Weizmann, who was troubled by Truman's refusal to meet him. Stone was a leading American Zionist who would become chairman of the United Jewish Appeal, United Israel Appeal and the Jewish Agency. That night, he returned to Boston to attend a B'nai B'rith dinner at which he and Frank Goldman, national president of B'nai B'rith, were being honored. Stone conveyed

236

Weizmann's distress to Goldman, who replied that, by coincidence, he had just visited Kansas City, where he had presented a B'nai B'rith award to Eddie Jacobson, Harry Truman's former partner in a clothing store. Goldman offered to call Jacobson to urge him to intervene with Truman. Stone and Goldman borrowed a handful of coins from others at the dinner, went to the hotel lobby and phoned Jacobson.

When Goldman put Stone on the phone, the New Englander quickly surmised that Jacobson knew little of the issues and, however close they might be personally, would have a hard time making a political or moral case to the president. Stone invited Jacobson to meet him in New York as soon as possible. At breakfast a few days later, Stone briefed Jacobson on the issues and then brought him to Weizmann's apartment, where, according to Eban, "like so many people of all stations and many countries before him, [Jacobson] fell immediately under Weizmann's spell. After a few hours he left Weizmann's apartment, intellectually and emotionally prepared to exercise an influence on Truman."

Jacobson hopped a train for Washington and, according to Eban, walked in unannounced on his old friend, the president of the United States. Truman was happy to see Jacobson but reluctant to be pressured on the Zionist issue. Stymied, Jacobson pointed to the bust of Andrew Jackson in the Oval Office and told Truman that Weizmann was a national leader made of the same material as Jackson, who was Truman's hero. Truman laughed, made an off-color remark, and told Jacobson to make an appointment for Weizmann to see him.

On March 18, 1948, the two leaders met in Washington. Truman promised to continue to work on behalf of the establishment of Israel. He also vowed that when the British Mandate expired on May 14, 1948, he would recognize the state immediately. Moments after midnight on May 14, as the British withdrew, Weizmann declared the establishment of Israel. True to his word, Truman immediately extended recognition on behalf of the United States. "It was evident," Eban concludes, "that Dewey Stone together with Frank Goldman and with the aid of a few humble coins had been able to make a deep impact on the central issues affecting Jewish destiny." One might add that Eddie Jacobson's plain talk to his friend Harry Truman helped prevent a change in American policy toward Israel and, possibly, in the course of modern Jewish history.

Sponsored by Theodore Herzl Teplow

19

Mickey Marcus: Israel's American General

David Daniel "Mickey" Marcus, a tough Brooklyn street kid, rose by virtue of his courage and intelligence to save Israel in 1948 and become its first general. After a distinguished career in military and public service to the United States, the forty-six-year-old Marcus wrote his name forever in the annals of Jewish history.

Born to immigrant parents in 1902, Marcus grew up in the Brownsville section of Brooklyn where, to defend himself against neighborhood toughs, he learned to box. His high school athletic and academic record earned him admission to West Point in 1920, from which he graduated with impressive grades. After completing his required service, Marcus went to law school and spent most of the 1930s as a federal attorney in New York, helping bring "Lucky" Luciano to justice. As a reward, Mayor La Guardia named Marcus commissioner of corrections for New York City.

Convinced that war was imminent, in 1940 Marcus voluntarily went back into uniform and, after the Japanese attack on Pearl Harbor, served as executive officer to the military governor of Hawaii. In 1942, he was named commandant of the Army's new Ranger school, which developed innovative tactics for jungle fighting. Sent to England on the eve of D-Day, he voluntarily parachuted into Normandy with the troops of the

101st Airborne Division. Marcus helped draw up the surrender terms for Italy and Germany and became part of the occupation government in Berlin. Admiring colleagues identified him has one of the War Department's best brains. He had a bright military future ahead of him.

In 1944, Marcus's consciousness of himself as a Jew took a dramatic turn when he was put in charge of planning how to feed the starving millions in the regions liberated by the Allied invasion of Europe. In 1945, his responsibilities involved clearing out the Nazi death camps. Here, Marcus met the survivors of Nazi atrocities and saw the piles of uncounted Jewish corpses. Marcus was subsequently named chief of the War Crimes Division with responsibility for planning the judicial procedure for the Nuremberg trials. Through these experiences, Marcus came to understand the depth of European anti-Semitism. Though never previously a Zionist, he became convinced that the only hope for European Jewry's remnant lay in a Jewish homeland in Palestine.

In 1947, Marcus returned to civilian life. A few months later, the United Nations authorized the partition of Palestine and the eventual creation of a Jewish state. Within days, David Ben-Gurion asked Marcus to recruit an American officer to serve as military adviser to Israel. Unable to recruit one of his friends, Marcus volunteered himself. The War Department consented reluctantly on the condition that Marcus not use his own name or rank and disguise his American military record.

In January 1948, one "Michael Stone" arrived in Tel Aviv to assume command of the Israeli forces and confront an apparently impossible situation. The widely separated Jewish settlements in Palestine were surrounded by a sea of hostile Arabs. Israel had seemingly indefensible borders. Its armed forces had no air power, only a few tanks and ancient artillery pieces, and almost no small arms or ammunition. The Haganah and Irgun were effective underground organizations but had no experience as a regular national army. Facing the Israelis were well-supplied Arab armies determined to drive the Jews into the sea. The pro-Arab British administration in Palestine tried to prevent the Israelis from receiving imported military supplies.

Undaunted, Marcus designed a command structure for Israel's new army and wrote manuals to train it, adapting his experience at the Ranger school to the new army's special needs. He identified Israel's weakest points as the scattered settlements in the Negev and the new quarter of Jerusalem. When Israel declared independence and the Arab armies attacked in May 1948, Israel was ready, thanks to Marcus. His hit-and-run tactics kept the Egyptian army in the Negev off balance. When the Jewish part of Jerusalem was about to fall, Marcus ordered the construction of a road to bring men and equipment to break the Arab siege just days before the United Nations negotiated a cease-fire. Israel had withstood the Arab assault with its borders virtually intact. In gratitude, Prime Minister Ben-Gurion named Mickey Marcus lieutenant general, the first general in the army of Israel in nearly two thousand years.

Tragically, Marcus did not live to see the peace. Six hours before the cease-fire began, while headquartered in the village of Abu Ghosh near Jerusalem, Marcus could not sleep. He walked beyond the guarded perimeter wrapped in his bedsheet. A Jewish sentry saw a white-robed figure approaching and, not understanding Marcus's English-language response to his challenge, fired a single fatal shot. Marcus's body was flown to the United States for burial at West Point, where his tombstone identifies him as "A Soldier for All Humanity." Hollywood would later immortalize him in the film *Cast a Giant Shadow*. Ben-Gurion put it simply: "He was the best man we had."

Sponsored by Lief Dov Rosenblatt

20

Paul Shulman
and the Sinking of the *Emir Farouk*

When the Jews of Palestine created an Israeli state in 1948, the neighboring Arab nations—with more than a million men under arms—invaded Israel with the avowed goal of "driving the Jews into the sea." American Jewry responded immediately by contributing funds to purchase arms for the fledgling Israeli armed forces, which had fewer than 75,000 soldiers and almost no heavy weapons. A thousand or so courageous Americans did more than invest their funds; they put their lives directly on the line fighting for Israel's survival. Many made indispensable contributions. West Pointer Mickey Marcus became Israel's first commanding general; Rudy Augarten was the air force's leading ace. Paul Shulman, a twenty-six-year-old Annapolis graduate, became the first commander of the Israeli navy.

David Ben-Gurion, the first prime minister of Israel, personally recruited the tall, dark-haired Shulman to serve as naval commander. A veteran of only three years service in the U.S. Navy, Shulman, although young, had the requisite training and experience. While he did not speak Hebrew, he was familiar with the struggle for a Jewish state. The son of committed Zionists, Shulman had worked closely with the Haganah, the Jewish underground army in Palestine, to purchase surplus ships to transport European Jewish refugees to Palestine in defiance of British immigration restrictions. This pre-independence work impressed the Israelis, especially Ben-Gurion.

By the third week of October 1948, the invading Syrian, Lebanese, and Jordanian armies had largely been repelled and only Egypt remained a threat. Although true peace was remote, a United Nations–sponsored truce was scheduled for October 22, 1948. That morning, Commander Shulman learned that two Egyptian warships had anchored outside Tel Aviv harbor, one of them the cruiser *Emir Farouk*, flagship of the Egyptian navy. The Egyptians were clearly trying to prevent Israel from rearming by sea during the truce. Ben-Gurion ordered Shulman to evict the intruders.

The Haganah had obtained several armed motorboats that had been used to great effect by Italian commandos during World War II as kamikaze-type weapons. The boats would be loaded with explosives and headed toward an enemy ship. At the last moment, the pilot would leap to safety while the boat continued to its target. These boats became Shulman's secret weapon.

Shulman organized an attack force from three vessels that had brought refugees to Palestine before the war and then had been hastily converted to warships. One, the

Ma'oz, carried the Italian motorboats on deck. The three vessels drew alongside the Egyptian ships and Shulman called out over a loudspeaker: "Truce period or no truce period, if you don't get the hell out of here, I'm going to shoot!" The two Egyptian vessels departed for Gaza and the Israeli ships followed closely. An hour later, Egyptian shore batteries in Gaza opened fire at the Israeli vessels, as Shulman had hoped. He radioed for permission to attack the Egyptian vessels. "No," came the response. Shulman radioed a second time, asking that his request be forwarded directly to Ben-Gurion, who replied, "Paul, if you can sink them, shoot; if you can't, don't."

Shulman decided on a night attack, positioning the *Ma'oz* between the Egyptian ships and the moon. At dark, the *Ma'oz* lowered three small boats into the water. It took nearly an hour for them to reach the Egyptian ships. The pilot of the first boat gunned his engine and headed for the *Farouk*, explosives armed. At the last moment, he leaped into the water. He heard an explosion and saw that the *Farouk* had been hit. Almost immediately, the second assault boat scored a direct hit on the huge warship, which erupted in flames and sank within minutes. As the *Farouk* slipped below the surface, the retrieval boat plucked the commandos from the sea.

The sinking of the *Farouk* was Israel's most dramatic naval victory in the War of Independence. Some 500 Egyptian sailors perished, many from that nation's upper class. However, the event received little publicity at the time: Israel wanted to draw no attention to its arguable violation of the truce; the Egyptians hoped to keep the Israeli triumph a secret. Nonetheless, news of the enormous loss reached the Egyptian public, and for nearly a year the Egyptian navy had difficulty recruiting new sailors.

In the aftermath, Egypt complained to the U.S. State Department that an American citizen had sunk its navy's flagship. The State Department asked Shulman to resign his naval reserve commission. When the war ended in 1949 and Israel's independence was established, Shulman became an Israeli citizen and founded an engineering corporation in Haifa. While only a thousand or so dedicated Americansmost of them, like Shulman, combat veterans—fought on the Israeli side, without their contributions the Israel Defense Forces might not have prevailed against such overwhelming odds.

Sponsored by Yaffa and Arie Shapiro

For Further Reading

Reference Works

American Jewish Historical Society. *American Jewish Desk Reference: The Ultimate One-volume Reference to the Jewish Experience in America.* New York: Random House, 1999.

American Jewish Historical Society. *An Index to American Jewish Historical Quarterly/ American Jewish History, Volumes 51–80 [1961–1991].* Brooklyn, NY: Carlson Publishing, Inc. for the American Jewish Historical Society, 1996.

American Jewish Historical Society. *An Index to Publications of the American Jewish Historical Society, Volumes 21–50 [1913–1961].* Brooklyn, NY: Carlson Publishing, Inc. for the American Jewish Historical Society, 1994.

American Jewish Year Book. Philadelphia: American Jewish Committee, 1899/1900–.

Gurock, Jeffrey S. *American Jewish History: A Bibliographical Guide.* New York: Anti–Defamation League of B'nai Brith, 1983.

Hyman, Paula E. and Deborah Dash Moore, eds. *Jewish Women in America: An Historical Encyclopedia.* 2 vols. New York: Routledge Press for the American Jewish Historical Society, 1997.

Kaganoff, Nathan M. *Judaica Americana.* Brooklyn, NY: Carlson Publishing, Inc. for the American Jewish Historical Society, 1995.

Marcus, Jacob Rader. *The Concise Dictionary of American Jewish Biography.* Brooklyn: Carlson Publishing, Inc., 1994.

Sarna, Jonathan D. "The American Jewish Experience." in *The Schocken Guide to Jewish Books.* New York: Schocken Books, 1992.

Singerman, Robert, comp. *Judaica Americana: A Bibliography of Publications to 1900.* New York: Greenwood Press, 1990.

Stern, Malcolm. *First American Jewish Families: 600 Genealogies, 1654–1977.* American Jewish Archives and American Jewish Historical Society, 1977.

Periodicals

American Jewish Archives. Cincinatti: Hebrew Union College-Jewish Institute of Religion, 1949–.

American Jewish Historical Quarterly. New York and Waltham, MA: American Jewish Historical Society, 1961–1977.

American Jewish History. Waltham, MA: American Jewish Historical Society and (as of 1994) Baltimore, MD: The Johns Hopkins University Press for the American Jewish Historical Society. 1978–.

Publications of the American Jewish Historical Society. New York: American Jewish Historical Society, 1892–1960.

Southern Jewish History. Atlanta, GA: Southern Jewish Historical Society, 1998–.

Monographs

Antler, Joyce. *The Journey Home: Jewish Women and the American Century.* New York: Free Press, 1997.

Baum, Charlotte, Paula Hyman and Sonya Michel. *The Jewish Woman in America.* New York: Dial Press, 1976.

Blau, Joseph L. and Salo W. Baron, eds. *The Jews of the United States, 1790–1840: A Documentary History.* New York: Columbia University Press, 1964.

Cohen, Martin A., ed. *The Jewish Experience in Latin America: Selected Studies from the Publications of the American Jewish*

Historical Society. 2 vols. Waltham, MA and New York: American Jewish Historical Society and KTAV, 1971.

Cohen, Naomi. *Encounter With Emancipation: The German Jews in the United States, 1830–1914*. Philadelphia: Jewish Publication Society, 1984.

Davidowicz, Lucy S. *On Equal Terms: Jews in America, 1881–1981*. New York: Holt, Rinehart and Winston, 1982.

Davis, Moshe and Isidore S. Meyer, eds. *The Writing of American Jewish History*. New York: American Jewish Historical Society, 1957.

Feingold, Henry, ed. *The Jewish People In America*. 5 vols. Baltimore: Johns Hopkins University Press for the American Jewish Historical Society, 1992.

Feingold, Henry. *Zion in America*. New York: Hippocrene, 1981.

Glazer, Nathan. *American Judaism*. Chicago: University of Chicago Press, 1988.

Glenn, Susan A. *Daughters of the Shtetl*. Ithaca: Cornell University Press, 1990.

Gurock, Jeffrey S. and Marc Lee Raphael, eds. *An Inventory of Promises: Essays on American Jewish History in Honor of Moses Rischin*. Brooklyn: Carlson Publishing, Inc., 1995.

Howe, Irving. *World Of Our Fathers*. New York: Schocken Books, 1989.

Karp, Abraham J. *Haven and Home: A History of the Jews in America*. New York: Schocken Books, 1985.

Karp, Abraham J, ed. *The Jewish Experience in America*. Waltham, MA: American Jewish Historical Society, 1969.

Korn, Bertram W. *American Jewry and the Civil War*. New York: Atheneum, 1970.

Marcus, Jacob Rader. *The American Jew, 1585–1990: A History*. Brooklyn: Carlson Publishing, Inc., 1995.

Marcus, Jacob Rader. *The American Jewish Woman: A Documentary History*. New York: KTAV Publishing House, 1981.

Marcus, Jacob Rader. *The Colonial American Jew, 1492–1776*. 3 vols. Detroit: Wayne State University Press, 1970.

Marcus, Jacob Rader, ed. *Memoirs of American Jews, 1775–1977*. 3 vols. Philadelphia: Jewish Publication Society, 1955.

Marcus, Jacob Rader. *United States Jewry, 1776–1985*. Detroit: Wayne State University Press, 1989.

Moore, Deborah Dash. *At Home In America*. New York: Columbia University Press, 1981.

Papo, Joseph M. *Sephardim in Twentieth-Century America: In Search of Unity*. San Jose: Pele Yoetz Books, 1987.

Raphael, Marc Lee. *Profiles in American Judaism: The Reform, Conservative, Orthodox, and Reconstructionist Traditions in Historical Perspectives*. New York: Harper and Row, 1988.

Rezneck, Samuel. *Unrecognized Patriots: The Jews in the American Revolution*. Westport, CT: Greenwood Press, 1975.

Sachar, Howard. *A History of the Jews in America*. New York: Knopf, 1992.

Sarna, Jonathan D, ed. *The American Jewish Experience*. New York: Holmes and Meier, 1986.

Sarna, Jonathan D. *Jews and the Founding of the Republic*. New York: Markus Weiner for Hebrew Union College–Jewish Institute of Religion, 1985.

Schoener, Allon. *The American Jewish Album: 1664 to the Present*. New York: Rizzoli, 1983.

Sklare, Marshall. *Observing America's Jews*. Hanover, NH: Brandeis University Press, 1993.

Weinberg, Sydney Stahl. *The World of Our Mothers*. New York: Schocken Books, 1990.